DIY Publishing

A STEP-BY-STEP GUIDE FOR PRINT AND EBOOK
FORMATTING AND DISTRIBUTION

Maggie McVay Lynch

Windtree Press
Portland, Oregon

Windtree Press
818 SW 3rd Avenue #221-2218
Portland, Oregon 97204-2405
855-649-0821
http://windtreepress.com
email: windtree@windtreepress.com

Cover Design by Christy Caughie at http://gildedheartdesign.com

Book Layout ©2013 BookDesignTemplates.com

Permission granted from Dr. Julian Smart to use Jutoh screenshots within this guide. Jutoh is a product of Anthemion Software Ltd. http://jutoh.com

Ordering Information:
Quantity sales. Special discounts are available on quantity purchases by corporations, associations, booksellers, and others. For details, contact the "Special Sales Department" at the address above.

DIY Publishing / Maggie Lynch. —1st ed.
ISBN 978-1-19400642-7-7

Contents

Dedicated to Elaura Renie
You talked me into it, and here it is.
Thank you!

Acknowledgments

No book comes together due to the sole work of one individual. This book contains what I have learned over the past four years about the changing DIY Publishing world. Some of that knowledge was gained through trial and error, but much of the knowledge was gained through other authors who have shared their own journey in self-publishing. Though I suspect there are hundreds of blogs and articles I have read and more than 20 loops I participate in, there are a few people who have consistently helped to form my experience and answered questions over the past few years. Those People are: Marie Force, Courtney Milan, Dean Wesley Smith, Kristine Kathryn Rusch, David Vandagriff (Passive Voice blog), Mike Shatzkin, David Gaughran, and Joanna Penn.

In addition, two individuals with amazing products have made a marked improvement on my self-publishing process: Joel Friedman with his Microsoft Word publishing templates and Dr. Julian Smith with his product, Jutoh. Again, both of these men have offered support as I found my way through putting up my first books.

The constant support of writer friends through RCRW has been invaluable. In particular Jessa Slade, Delilah Marvelle, Susan Lute, Cynthia Young, and Jamie Brazil have been available to lend an ear, proof a page, or test a system for me. Finally, my husband has been always available for feedback and support. He makes sure I eat and sleep even when against a difficult deadline, and loves me even when I ignore him for days on end. I am very fortunate indeed to have such a wonderful support group.

CHAPTER 1

Overview of DIY Publishing

Only in the last year has the combination of software programs and vendor sites converged to make the DIY publishing process significantly easier. With competing distributors vying to sell books online, the attention to helping the self-publishing author navigate the technology has become paramount. I now have a process that takes me approximately ten minutes per book to move from a Microsoft Word document to generating the file types required for both ebooks and print—PDF, MOBI, and EPUB—resulting in a nicely formatted product that competes with most NY traditionally published products. The focus of this book is to feature this method—one which produces a product that is not generic and has options for incorporating features unique to a specific book, genre, or series without adding significant formatting time.

Though self-publishing has been around since the advent of the printing press, in modern times it was the push of an e-reader—the Amazon Kindle—that spurred the current revolution. Amazon's Kindle turned six years old in 2013. This has not only changed the face of electronic book consumption, but also provided the opportunity for anyone with basic computer skills to publish a book at little to no cost.

Like any rapidly evolving technology, the ebook marketplace is exploding with options—options for reader devices as well as options for authors and publishers to create books that deliver stories in the way readers want them. Only one thing is certain—change.

Software developers, marketers, and a variety of service providers are springing into action to meet the needs of thousands of indie publishers and small presses. The new software options range from: interior and exterior templates, to ebook conversions for different devices, to tracking sales from all vendors. The good news is the programs are getting easier to use. For the parts of the process authors find too onerous, there is always someone to help for a fee.

In addition to the technical side of self-publishing, authors can elect to pay someone for any part of the publishing process: from editing to cover design, and from public relations to hiring a virtual assistant to post to social media for you.

In the new publishing marketplace, the rules change even faster than the software. What worked for marketing and book discovery a year ago, no longer works as well today. In 2009 and 2010, many writers who made their ebook FREE for some period of time found themselves on a bestseller list. In 2011 and 2012, it was the protracted 99 cent sale for a month to get enough downloads to hit a list. In 2013, that is no longer the case. Retailers changed their algorithms so that book rankings now reflect sales over a 30 day period for example, instead of focusing on short term velocity.

Pundits who wrote how to game the system were out of touch within a year as popular vendors changed their algorithms and made different decisions on the best way to feature the millions of books they have to sell, while generating the most profit. It is up to the self-published author to understand how to position her book effectively in every venue as quickly as possible, so she can move on to write the next book.

In the past, marketing dollars were put into a big splash designed to create velocity—the ability to sell tens of thousands of copies in a short period of time. If a book didn't take off within a few months, it was soon remaindered (sold at a discount) or returned to the publisher. Authors who didn't earn out their advance often found the rest of their series cancelled or they simply did not get a follow on contract to complete the series.

Discoverability today is more about the slower word-of-mouth that builds over months and even years. With the availability of digital books and print-on-demand books, publishers can now keep a book available for years without losing money. It's a new world with new rules. But, as always, it still takes a good book, hard work, commitment, and patience.

What this book contains

When I talk to other authors, one of the reasons they fear going DIY is the technical hurdle of formatting. The primary focus of this book is on the step-by-step instructions of how to get your completed manuscript professionally formatted for both print and ebook distribution, and then uploaded to sell at the various distribution sites (Amazon, Kobo, Barnes & Noble, Apple, Sony, Ingram, Baker & Taylor, and others). Over the past three years, I have tried a number of methods to create a professionally formatted book—ranging from hand-coding HTML, CSS, and

XML to uploading a Microsoft Word document to various conversion programs. My goal was to find a method that produced a nice-looking product for print, and an ebook product that worked well in all platforms. Because each e-reader has unique specifications, this meant no error codes would stop the ebook from being uploaded to a distributor. I wanted the entire formatting process to take less than 30 minutes per book. Finally, I was not willing to spend more than $50 on software to help me do this. In other words, I wanted a process that was consistent, easy to implement, and inexpensive.

Even though I have a technical background, I don't want to spend a lot of time doing technical things. I want to spend the majority of my time writing the next book. I have a very busy annual schedule which includes four to six book releases, four to five public speaking engagements, several book signings, and time reserved for family and church activities. So, my final criterion was that the method had to be accessible to the average non-technology savvy writer.

The DIY Decision Process

First, the writer must determine how much of the DIY process she is willing and able to take on. For example, I am willing to do my own formatting because I now have it down to only 10 minutes per book. Once learned, the procedure requires little creativity and can be done consistently every time. It is fulfilling to know that I can format the book to my specifications and upload it to any distributor I wish to engage. Controlling that final package is like wrapping a special gift for a friend.

On the other hand, I have decided I will not do my own cover design. I understand the technology of Photoshop and In Design, and I use them when necessary. However, creating visual media does not inspire my creativity. My imagination is best stimulated by the beauty of prose and story and the structure of characters and meaning through words.

Like most readers, when I see a great cover I'm drawn to it. However, without the talent or motivation to create visual media it would take me hours instead of minutes—hours that I would rather spend writing the next book. So, I pay someone else to do my cover designs. I also know a number of authors who are trained graphic designers. These authors enjoy creating their own covers. Some of them use the cover creation process as an inspiration for their writing. In their case, spending the time on cover design is warranted. Every decision an author makes is a time versus money decision. Each individual must determine what that balance is for her.

The step-by-step DIY Publishing Process Summary

1. Selecting (or designing) a template for print.
2. Applying that template to your finished manuscript.
3. Including appropriate front matter and back matter.
4. Saving the manuscript as a PDF for print.
5. Importing the finished manuscript into Jutoh for conversion to the various ebook platforms and devices.
6. Adding links for ebooks and making decisions around placement of front matter and additional back matter.
7. Incorporating good cover design elements for print and ebook.
8. Writing the book blurb and author bio, and how to use them effectively in marketing.
9. Setting up distribution accounts in the major distributor sites (e.g., Amazon, CreateSpace, B&N, Kobo, Apple, etc.), and

evaluating   middleman   distributors   (Smashwords, Draft2Digital, XinXii).

10. Using ISBNs—the pros and cons of purchasing your own versus accepting each distributors inventory record assignments or proprietary ISBNs.

11. Uploading your finished ebook and print files to each distributor.

12. Setting list prices, and determining when and how to use sales to increase discoverability.

13. Making changes to books once they are with distributors. When should you just leave it alone?

14. Increasing book discoverability, managing sales expectations, and becoming part of the zeitgeist of publishing today.

Setting realistic expectations for sales—a cautionary tale

Many first time authors have the mistaken belief that once their novel or non-fiction book is published readers will flock to buy it. This is a natural expectation because authors spend months, or even years, creating their book. Frequently, authors have received positive feedback on the book. Sometimes the book has finaled in or won writing competitions. All of these are nice, but do not guarantee sales.

Literary and publishing news articles extol the virtues of those few authors who made it big with their first book: Hugh Howey, Amanda Hocking, John Locke and a few others. This leads to new authors entering the self-publishing arena with high expectations of sales.

When the expected high sales don't appear within the first two to three months, the new author becomes despondent. She adds up the sales and realizes all the copies were likely sold to family and friends. In other words, sales did not go beyond her immediate network. I often hear from authors at this point who had set high expectations not only for themselves, but for those in that network. This leads to several uncomfortable conversations similar to the fictionalized scenario below.

"How is your book doing?"

She pastes a smile on her face. "Fine. Not as well as I hoped, but it's doing fine."

"That's great. When do we see it made into a movie?"

She struggles not to choke on her strained chuckle. "It won't be made into a movie. I'm not popular enough for that."

"Oh." The friend backs up a step. "When will the next book be out? Have you started it yet?"

"I'm not quite sure when it will be out. It's moving along."

It isn't exactly a lie. She knows what the next book is about…mostly. She has the characters in her head. Just because she hasn't actually started writing doesn't mean she's lying. Right? She'll start it after she finishes with all this promotion. She's certain that one more ad, or getting a few more *likes* on her Facebook page will make a difference. How can she write when she has to do all this selling?

In the mean time desperation grows. That is when some writers begin investing in advertising, blog tours, nagging friends and other authors for Facebook likes and Amazon reviews. When that fails, the author plans special events that relate to her book. Instead of writing that next book, every writing hour is spent in desperate promotion, or with a nice tub of ice cream and chocolate cake to soothe the depression.

I know one author who spent over a thousand dollars to set up a cooking demonstration in hopes that it would draw people to purchase her unique mystery novel that had a sous chef as the protagonist. It did help her sell approximately eleven print books that day, among the forty people who attended the demonstration. Her profit for the day was approximately $40. However, her expenses were over a thousand dollars to rent the room for several hours, and to purchase all the ingredients needed for the cooking demonstration. In other words, the return on investment was not good.

Unfortunately, this is not an unusual occurrence. I have seen authors expend an entire year, or more, trying to sell their first book. When I would ask the author about the next book, the response would usually be: "I'm not going to start the next book until the sales on this one are better. I don't want to waste my time if my books aren't going to make money." This author is counting on that first book to make money and build their audience so that the second book's sales cycle will be easier.

These same authors spend money on advertising in major magazines and websites, do blog tours, plan special events, and spend all their writing time on social media trying to gain more Twitter friends or Pinterest followers, or any number of other types of fans. By the end of the year they still have only one book written, and find that perhaps they made another $100 for all this effort and expense.

Please do not become one of these authors. This new world of publishing is based on your long game, not your short game. It is one of building word-of-mouth and creating a readership for your next book and your next. It is not unusual to take three or four years to build a substantial readership and backlist to create the engine you need for making money consistently.

Certainly, some small amount of promotion is needed. However, you cannot promote yourself onto bestseller lists. As an unknown person, without a platform—meaning you are not a celebrity or an expert in the field and already have a following— the odds are stacked against you making it big on your first book or your third or your eighth. This has always been the case. It is not new to self-publishing. Ask the hundreds of mid-list authors in traditional publishing how long it took to make enough money to sustain themselves.

Whether traditionally published or self-published, every new book provides another opportunity for readers to find you and for the word-of-mouth to grow. If readers like one of your books they go back and look at what else you have written and buy those too. In series, some readers won't buy the books until the entire series is done. With every new book you publish, the totality of sales is higher. With only one book, or even two, you are leaving your career to the one thing you have no control over—luck.

If promotion doesn't work, what does?

I correspond with a lot of authors who had been published by large New York publishing companies in the past and have now turned to self-publishing. Some have been self-publishing for only a year, others for three or four years. The majority of those authors indicate that it is somewhere between their fifth and eighth published book where they begin to see significant money. That is especially true if the author is writing in a single genre; and may happen even faster when the author completes a series.

The best thing you can do with your limited time is to write and publish another book, and another, and another.

If your book doesn't sell, it could be due to a lot of things: the quality of the writing, the quality of the editing, the price, the cover, the category, the metadata, the time of year it was released. Or it could be none of these.

Just as with traditional publishing, some very good books don't get discovered or don't sell well. Every editor in New York has books she acquired that she was certain would sell well and didn't. No one knows why. It just happens. On the other hand, every editor also has at least one book that got away. The one she did not acquire because she thought it was too generic, not well written, or the genre was dead. A few of those books became bestsellers. In the same way a self-published book occasionally becomes a bestseller and surprises everyone, including the author.

What makes a book sell well that everyone turned down? Why did J.K. Rowling's first *Harry Potter* novel get turned down by so many publishers? Why does a book that every editor loves not sell well? Most people say the answer is luck and timing. Two things you can't control.

In self-publishing, the things you can control *prior* to making your book available are the writing, editing, price, cover, metadata, and release schedule of additional books. I will talk about all of these throughout this book. Once a book is published and the public can buy it, the best thing an author can do is to move on and give it time to find its readers. Control what you can, but don't try to buy luck.

My *Sweetwater Canyon* series—contemporary romance that borders on women's fiction—is one example of the time it takes to find a readership. In 2011 I published the first book in the series, *Undertones.* I already had two other romance novels in my backlist.

Their sales were paltry in spite of ads, book tours, and social media promotion. Each was a stand-alone novel. *Undertones* had won several writing awards prior to publication. In spite of wide distribution, I failed to get many reviews. Though the few reviews I did get were good, there simply were not enough for anyone to take notice. When the second book in the series, *Healing Notes*, came out in 2012, I again did a blog tour and this time half the ads I did before. The second book garnered more reviews, but still not a lot. The reviews were all good. Interestingly, I began to see more sales, even though I was not doing as much social networking or advertising.

I noticed that when people did purchase the second book they went back and purchased the first in the series as well. On top of that, some of them also purchased one or both of the previous two titles. My sales from year-to-year tripled. This year, the final two titles in the series are coming out, *Heart Strings* and *Two Voices*. (I've stepped up my writing pace) Based on what happened with the second book I anticipate sales to be significant for these. However, note that by the time these are released, I will have published a total of six romance titles. I'm still not making significant money—to me significant is above $30,000 per year—but sales are growing.

Over the past two years there have been a number of studies undertaken (RWA, Bowker, and Smashwords are some of the most recent studies) to uncover the most lucrative devices to propel a book into higher sales. Everyone wants to know the secret, including major publishing companies. Making it free? Using Amazon KDP Select? Getting more Facebook likes or Twitter followers? Creating a great book trailer to post on YouTube? Getting pull quotes from your friend, who happens to be a NYT bestselling author? Hiring a public relations firm?

It turns out all of these options have little correlation to sales, and only one (free books downloaded by thousands of readers) had any correlation to discoverability. The *only* method that has shown any direct correlation to actual book sales is writing and publishing more books—particularly more books within a series or at least in the same genre. New York Publishers have known this for decades. That is why they have always advised authors to stick to one genre. That is why they like to sign series contracts. In the past three years, that is also why they will often hold a series back from publication until you have the entire trilogy, or the first three books in the series completed. Then it can be released back-to-back, one a month. This has proven lucrative and gains readers faster.

This is not to say you can only write in one genre, or that you should only write series. However, each decision you make about what to write, how many books to write each year, how many books to release, and how many pen names you use has a potential impact on sales. Each time you release another title it increases your chances for more readers to discover your books. Every time you release a new title, and someone likes that book, the reader will tell her friends and go back and look for all the other books you have written. Each time that new reader finds books in the genres and styles she likes, it keeps you on her radar for more books. She might even sign up for your newsletter to make sure she always knows what you write next.

If you wrote a book last year, and have spent all your time on promotion, what happens when that reader goes to find another book from you? The answer is NOTHING happens. And when/if you finally get around to writing that next book a year or two away, that reader has forgotten you and needs to wade through the plethora of available books to find you again.

How many titles do you need to make it big? There is no hard and fast rule. I've heard numbers such as eight books or twelve books, but there is no guarantee. I've watched some savvy authors not put up any books until they have three or more. This guarantees an instant backlist. Other authors will put up books one at a time, but only a few months apart. These authors often do not expend any energy on promotion until they have three or more books available. They do not follow the next big idea for how to increase sales. Doing only print? Doing only ebooks? Bundling them together? What about a new social media platform? Tumblr? Instagram? Group blogs? Single blogs? You can drive yourself crazy with this stuff.

Okay, I'm depressed now. Any good news?

Yes! The good news is you don't have to be a New York Times or USA Today bestseller to make decent money. If you have enough books, and each one is selling a little bit every month, it adds up to good money. If you can capitalize on reusing the same work—selling print and ebook and audiobook, perhaps a short story too—then the returns are even greater.

I ran a recent forecast spreadsheet for a ten year period with what I considered were very conservative numbers. I looked at an author producing three novels per year at an average word count of 65,000 words. I ran the spreadsheet first with ebook only sales. Then added print sales to the ebook sales, and finally audiobook sales to the ebook sales. It is very encouraging.

Ebook Only. In this scenario, the assumptions are the author is publishing three new ebooks every year for ten years. The spreadsheet assumed the author was selling one ebook per month in the first year. In each subsequent year, the author is selling one ebook per month for each title. The retail price per book is $4.99, and the commission is figured at 65%. This takes into account all the different venues that are lower than Amazon's current 70% payment.

I can already hear someone saying: "But one of my books doesn't sell an ebook every month." Yes, that does happen, but then a different book will sell two or three books that month. The one book per month, per title, is a starting point, and certainly nowhere near bestseller status.

At the end of ten years, this author will have published 30 titles and made a cumulative income of $133,920. At the ten-year mark, if the author is still only averaging one sale per month for each of those 30 titles her annual income in year ten is $36,781.

Now that is a decent income, and among those thirty titles the author has many more chances for one or more to break out and make even more money. Be aware that under this scenario, the author needed to sell 28 titles before crossing my $30,000 per year threshold.

Ebooks and Print Books. Now let's capitalize on those same three books per month by not limiting the author to ebook sales only. In the second scenario, the author is selling one ebook per month and one print book per month. This assumes a print book retail price of $15. But after costs to the author, the sales commission averages $3 per book. At the end of ten years, the author has a cumulative income of $257,806 without writing any additional words. And she is is making $70,801 as her annual income in year ten. That should be enough to convince you to always have a print book and an ebook for sale. With this scenario the author crosses over the $30,000 per year mark at 23 books in inventory. That is part way through year seven.

Ebooks, Print Books, and Audio Books. This is maximizing income opportunities with the same number of words. The author is still writing only three books per year. But now she is selling those three books in three different ways. With the same assumptions, each book is selling only one ebook, one print book, and one audio book per month. Now, at ten years the total cumulative income is $367,933. At the ten-year mark, the annual income is $101,419. The author crosses over the $30,000 threshold part way through year six at about the 19th book.

This is the long game. This is patience. This is choosing production over promotion. Want to make money faster? Up your production and resell the same words in different formats.

I end here with a great quote from Diana Love, a New York Times bestselling author with both traditionally published books and self-published books. She was responding to an article by Barbara Vey for Publisher's Weekly, about what happens after the first book is published.

(http://blogs.publishersweekly.com/blogs/beyondherbook/?p=8360)

"...rule #1 is "write, write, and write some more." If content is king in developing a publishing strategy then a connected series is queen, and quality is the foundation for that empire. One repeated mantra is that Self Publishing is a marathon, not a sprint. Putting out one novella to "test" the SP market is like tossing a baited hook in one corner of a massive lake and assuming you're going to land on the mother lode of fish the first time.

CHAPTER 2

Using a Template

One of the biggest hurdles in formatting a print book is providing a professional interior layout. Setting margins, gutters, trim size, fonts, headers, footers, pagination, etc. can be a huge pain and quite time consuming. Large publishing companies employ people to design the interior of a book. If you are a well-known author, with big sales numbers, you may get someone assigned to make your book unique. Everyone else gets the company template for your genre. The template for a non-fiction book is different than the template for a fiction book. The template for a young adult fantasy novel may be different than the template for a sexy contemporary romance novel.

You could also choose to employ someone to do the interior design of your book. The average rate for this is around $300 and some services charge as much as $1,000 depending on the type of book you have. Note, that these fees are for designing book interiors for print. If anyone charges these prices for designing an ebook interior, run as fast as you can from that con man.

Personally, this is $300 or more I don't want to spend on my DIY books.

At small presses, and particularly ebook first presses, there tends to be only one template. Many of the small presses use the free template from CreateSpace. In every case, however, you can be assured that the publisher uses a template. It makes the entire text-to-print and ebook formatting process much easier and quicker.

If traditional publishing companies use a template in order to cut down on the time spent designing the interior, then self-publishers should do the same. After all, their interest is in saving time in order to write the next book as soon as possible.

There are three ways to acquire a template for your book: 1) download a free one; 2) design it yourself; or 3) purchase one (cost of $39 and up depending on use and licensing). I have chosen to buy my templates. Because I write in multiple genres, including non-fiction, I already know that I would have to design several templates. The design process can be time consuming. In addition, I admit to not having a lot of knowledge regarding fonts and how they work together to present a pleasing and cohesive look.

If left to my own devices, I would probably have an entire book with Times New Roman and perhaps Calibri for bolded titles. In other words, my default settings would be boring and not very pleasing to the eye. And it would take time away from my writing.

Anyone can download a free interior template from a website. Here are three that I know.

- CreateSpace
  https://www.createspace.com/Products/Book/InteriorPDF.jsp

- 48 Hour Books http://www.48hrbooks.com/Free-Book-Templates/
- Lulu http://www.lulu.com/publish/books/#bookSpecs

For ebooks, you can use the same free templates. Not all the template features will transfer to ebooks because different devices display a different range of font choices. However, most of the important formatted items like chapter heads and emphasis styles like italics and bold are transferred.

I personally prefer the templates from noted and award-winning book designer Joel Friedman. This book's interior is a purchased template called *Leadership*. It is designed for non-fiction books, and thus contains options for footnotes, tables and indexes that you would not normally see in a fiction book. You can see the range of both fiction and non-fiction templates offered at his site Book Design Templates.

http://www.bookdesigntemplates.com/

Friedlander's template site provides many different licensing structures, as well as different sizing capabilities for your print book. It also provides free user guides which outline the process of downloading the template, loading it in Microsoft Word, and then saving it for print. When deciding to go this route, whether with Joel Friedman or some other template design site, be sure to purchase the appropriate license for your needs.

For this book, I purchased a single book license, the most inexpensive option. That is because I don't anticipate writing multiple non-fiction, technical education books. The majority of my writing is in fiction. However, if I change my mind later and decide I do want to reuse this template for another book, I can go back to Friedlander's site and pay for an upgrade to a multi-use license.

If a series of books is planned, it is best to purchase a multiple book license from the beginning. This reinforces the same look and feel of interior design throughout each book in the series. In addition, you can begin your writing within the template and save the time for conversion later. A multiple book license is more expensive. However, amortized over the number of books in a series, it is the most reasonable priced option. In addition, the multiple book license allows the author to do any other books, under the same name, with that interior design. Some authors may choose to use a single interior design for all books in a particular genre, or use the same interior as a signature design for a particular pen name.

I will walk you through using one of these purchased templates later in this chapter. First, let's look at the free options.

Designing Your Own Template

To design your own templates, you need to be familiar with setting up styles in your word processing software. Minimally, you will want to set up the following styles:

- Title
- Chapter
- Body Text
- Emphasis Text (such as a quote or special text needed in your document)
- Bold Text (also called Strong Text)
- Header and Footer

Depending on the book and what text alternatives are needed, you may also need to set up additional styles for:

- Body Normal

- Body Left
- Secondary Headings
- Subtitles
- Quotes (Block)
- Quotes (Centered)
- References
- Numbered Lists
- Bulleted Lists
- Borders

Some authors forgo learning how to set up styles, instead electing to apply styling ad hoc--as they type. Not using styles creates two problems: 1) consistency; and 2) transferability to ebook formatting.

Using styles allows for consistency in look and feel throughout the manuscript. If you select ad hoc styling you must keep track of everything you've done. For example, will you remember on page 283 that when you did a quote on page 94 you chose to indent ½ inch on both sides, provided a shaded box, decreased the font by one point, and made it italics? Will you remember that you made a decision to have all telepathy represented in your novel with italics and a different font than the italics you use for emphasis? Having styles assures you are consistent throughout the book.

Ebook conversion is the second reason to use styles. If you do not then, when you are ready to convert your gorgeously formatted book into the various ebook formats, your hard work of ad hoc styling will become regular text and you will have to redo it all again prior to the conversion process. That is wasted time. In addition, your document will need to be manually separated into chapters, front matter, and back matter because you did not use styles to help the conversion program recognize where and how to make section breaks.

Yes, you will get the bold and italics that you selected in your ad hoc styling decisions, but everything else will likely be lost in the display on one or more ereader devices. Creating styles allows that code to be read and understood by other programs and to be incorporated, wherever possible, in every ereader device.

If the before mentioned extensive lists of styles didn't scare you, and you are convinced that you want to set all your styles manually, I'll provide a few screenshots and descriptions of how to do this in the next section.

How to set styles manually

Even if you are going to use a purchased template or a free template downloaded from one of the sites mentioned earlier, you still need to understand how to set styles manually. Even with a pre-formatted template, many authors find that there is something they wish to change; or a style they wish to add that is specific to the type of book. For example, in my young adult fantasy novel, I had ancient scrolls that provided rules and direction for the characters. I wanted to use a special font whenever those scrolls were presented. Though I had purchased the Flourish template from Friedlander's site, I still wanted to add another style specifically for those instances. Also, many authors may choose to change the font sizing of a style to enhance the book length.

If you do not use Microsoft Word or Open Office, you will need to determine how setting styles works in your word processing program. Most modern word processing programs include a way to manage styles. What I will describe below is from

Word 2010. The screenshots are from the 2010 version for Apple computers and the 2010 version for Microsoft Windows-based machines. If you are using an earlier version, like 2007, it hasn't changed very much. However, some functionality may appear in a different place in the menu. If you are on a very early version, like Word 2003, it will look quite different. However, most of the functionality still exists somewhere. I have also provided screenshots for Open Office Version 4.

Whenever you begin a new document in your word processor, a template is engaged with particular styles provided by the software company. In Microsoft Word that template is called *Normal.* In Open Office it is called *Default.*

A **style** is a predefined combination of font style, color, size of text, paragraph settings, and line spacing that can be applied to selected text. The easiest way to start creating a new style is to begin with one that already exists. Both Microsoft Word and Open Office come with a large range of styles. If you are following along and trying this with your word processing system, it is best to begin with a page or two of typed text that represents the various style possibilities in your document.

Font and paragraph styles

Let's start with the one thing every book needs— chapter titles. Highlight the text that represents your chapter title.

> **This is a chapter title**
>
> This is body text that I want to format as normal body. The quick brown fox jumped over the whitewashed fence. The quick brown fox jumped over the whitewashed fence. The quick brown fox jumped over the whitewashed fence.

In Microsoft Word, in the **Style** group on the **Home** tab, hover over each style to see a live preview in the document. Click the **More** drop-down arrow to see additional styles. In the image below, I chose Heading 1 to use for chapter titles. The second arrow points to the drop down to create a new style.

In Microsoft Word, when you wish to create a new style, all of the parameters are entered at the same time on a form. You will want to give the style a new name. Notice, in the illustration below, I selected the name "Chapter Title." You can then change any other parameters you wish—font size, spacing before and after the selected item, text display types (normal, bold, italics) and alignment of the text (centered, left, right).

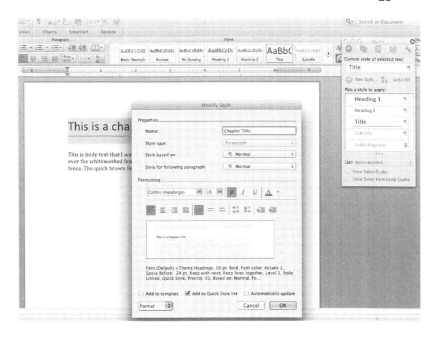

Once you have defined all the parameters needed for your new style, click the OK button. That style is now part of the multitudes of styles available to you.

Continue in this same way through the various elements of your document. Determine the style for paragraphs, both indented and not indented. If you have quotes, determine in what style they should always appear. If you use italics in different ways, you may want to set up different styles for them. For example, when your characters are speaking using telepathy do you want the italics to look different (indented or not)? Be sure to name the style something that makes sense to you, such as italics-telepathy.

Open Office contains all styles under the **styles and formatting window**. You may access this window by clicking on the drop down box next to the **default** style, or by clicking on the icon (a tack pinned into a paper) located at the left-hand end of the object bar.

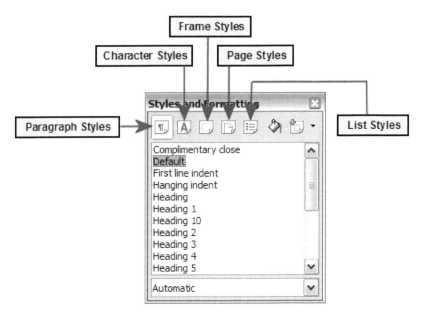

As illustrated above, a listing of all styles available in the template will be displayed. A click on the selected style will then show the applied parameters for that style. In the example below, which uses a modification of the *Flourish* template, the Chapter Number style has the font parameter of LM Roman Caps 10, and the font size is 18 points.

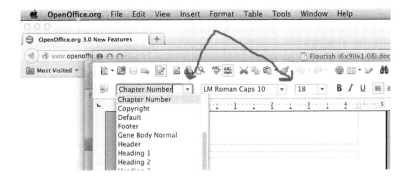

In order to change a single parameter of the style, click on the drop down arrow for the factor you wish to change. In the above example, if I wanted the Chapter Number to be larger I would click the down arrow next to the number 18 and select a different number.

You may also wish to create an entirely new style. For example, perhaps you use ancient scroll quotes in your fantasy novel. These quotes you wish to begin with a new font and italics that are not used anywhere else in the manuscript. In this case you need to create a new style.

In Open Office, click on the Styles and Formatting icon on the left of the styles bar. It will open a new styles dialog box. Again, click on the styles icon in the upper right corner of the box and it will give you the option to name a new style.

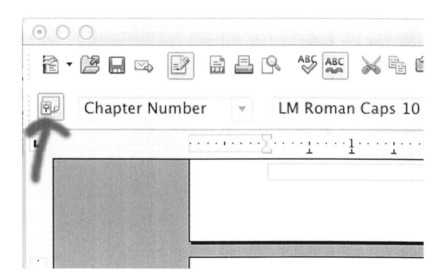

In the Create Style dialog box, type in the name of your style. Given the example of the ancient scrolls, I might name the style "Ancient Scroll" to make it easy to remember.

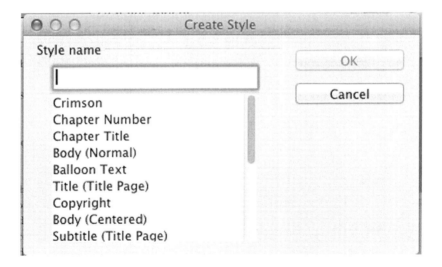

Once the style has been created, you will then have the option of selecting it and changing the font name, the font style and size just as you do with any other style item in the drop down list.

Headers and footers

The next important element of a print book is setting the headers and footers. Note: This is not required in an ebook.

Neither is page numbering. Ebook font sizes can be changed by the user, at any time, to be larger or smaller, therefore ebooks do not carry headers and page numbering. The only time this is included is in what is called *fixed format* ebooks, such as a children's book with lots of illustrations or a technical book. Fixed format is not recommended for novels, and not for most narrative non-fiction. In addition, many ereaders cannot read fixed format books. They are best displayed on computers, laptops, or tablets.

If you are reading this guide in print, you will notice that the header changes for odd and even pages.

20 • MAGGIE MCVAY LYNCH

2003, it will look quite different. However, most of the functionality still exists somewhere.

In Microsoft Word, a **style** is a predefined combination of font style, color, size of text, paragraph settings, and line spacing that can be applied to selected

On the even pages, the page number is to the left, followed by a bullet and then the page number.

DIY PUBLISHING • 23

The next most important thing, for a print book, is setting up the headers and footers. If you are reading this guide in print, you will notice that the header changes for odd and even pages. On the even pages, the page

On the odd pages, the page number is right justified, preceded by the bullet and then the title of the book.

Some authors don't like this style, and instead opt for a centered header and a centered page number in the footer. The free templates from CreateSpace, Lulu, and 48 Hr Books provide centered headers and footers.

If you do wish to have non-generic headers and footers, in Microsoft Word they are set via the document elements ribbon, or through the View menu item at the top of the page. Below is a screenshot of the options set for this book.

In this book, there is no footer. However, each chapter is a new section and that allows the header options to change from one section to another. There is no continuous pagination on the front matter (title page, dedication, table of contents). The continuous pagination begins with Chapter One. Notice, in the screenshot above, that **Different First Page** is selected. That allows for the first page of each new chapter to have no header or page number. In addition, **Different Odd & Even Pages** is selected. That option provides for the alternating right and left justified header styles mentioned above. The **Link to the Previous** selection affords continuous page numbering from one chapter to the next.

At the end of this book, where the back matter begins (author bio, buy links, sneak peek at another book), I have deselected that **Link to the Previous** option so that pagination does not continue in those sections. As you can see there are a number of options for you to consider when building a template and creating a print book interior.

In Open Office, headers and footers are defined by page styles. Select **Format** and then **Page**. Select the **Header tab**.

Be sure to click on the **Header On** option. If you want to have alternating content left and right, as is the case in this book, be sure that the box next to **Same content left/right** is NOT selected. For more in depth explanation of the variety of selections for Open Office headers and footers see

http://wiki.openoffice.org/wiki/Documentation/OOoAuthors_User_Manual/Writer_Guide/Page_numbering#Inserting_a_header

Once you have selected all the styles you need and saved them in your document, you are now ready to proceed with processing your manuscript and applying the appropriate styles. This is best done at the point of creation if you have not begun writing. If you already have a manuscript that is completed, or in the first draft, you will need to apply styles to each sections based on your new definitions.

Applying styles to an existing document

To apply formatting to a manuscript in Microsoft Word, first select the text to which you desire to apply a style. To apply a paragraph style to one paragraph, put your cursor in the paragraph. To apply a paragraph style to more than one paragraph, select the text you want to format. To apply a character style, select the text to format.

Second, click on the name of the style you wish to apply. This is found in the styles ribbon. (see illustration below)

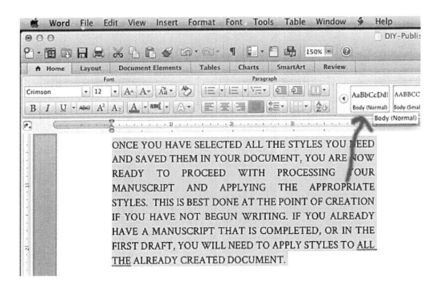

In Open Office the easiest way to apply a style to many different areas quickly is to use the **Fill Format** function. This method is useful when you need to format many scattered paragraphs, words, headers with the same style without selecting each one.

First, open the **Styles and Formatting** window and select the style you want to apply. Click the **Fill Format mode** icon (it looks like a paint bucket). The mouse pointer will change to this icon.

To apply a paragraph, page, or frame style, hover the mouse over the paragraph, page, or frame and click. To apply a character style, hold down the mouse button while selecting the characters. Clicking on a word applies the character style for that word. Repeat this step until you made all the changes for that style.

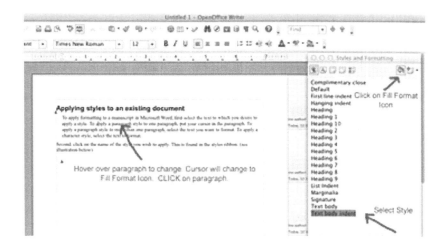

To quit Fill Format mode, click the **Fill Format mode** icon again or press the *Esc* key.

As you can see, doing all of this is time consuming. And I have only covered a couple of styles for you to select. This is why authors choose to download a free template, as previously mentioned, or purchase a template. For me, the time it takes to set styles and create a template for a specific book far outweighs the cost savings. In addition, I know that when I purchase a template I like I'm guaranteed a professional interior designer has already made the important and artistic decisions regarding which fonts work well together, the best spacing or effects for titles that a reader my enjoy, and provided options for front matter and back matter formats. Next, I'll cover what a purchased template may look like and how you can make changes to that template if you want something slightly different.

CHAPTER 3

Using a Purchased Template

This book uses a template from Joel Friedlander's bookdesigntemplate.com site called *Leadership*. Chapter headings, subheadings, quote options, the header with my name on one side and the book name on the other, odd and even paging and automatic sizing are all included in the template. Notice how different fonts are used in different sizes and places, and that subheadings include a horizontal rule. Best of all, it all works together and is pleasing to the eye.

Even with this wonderful template, I still chose to make a couple of changes. First, I increased font sizes for the "normal" text from 11 pt to 12pt. I also increased the font sizes for subheadings to draw attention to them. This decision only impacts the print version. As I said before, ebook font sizes can be changed by the user at any time and ebooks do not carry headers and page numbering.

Increasing the font size for print is a personal decision. When reading technical books I've found that many readers appreciate the text being a little larger, as well as more white space around screenshots and illustrations. The information is dense, and having more space helps learners to feel less anxious. Again, in a novel this may not be an issue.

I also knew that the length of this book would not cause me to worry about printing costs. If I had a long novel—over 100,000 words for example—I would choose to stay with the default font or even make it a little smaller in order to keep the page count down. On shorter novels or a memoir, I might elect to increase the font size to make the book feel more substantial. Print book costs are based on the total number of pages, not the format size.

Let's take a look at the options in the *Leadership* template once you bring it into Microsoft Word.

*Note: I will **not** be going through the process of purchasing the template, downloading the file, and opening it in Word. If you decide to use The Book Designer templates, their site provides a marvelous instruction sheet on how to accomplish all those steps.*

Once you have opened the template and renamed it as your book file, you can view all your style options via the **Styles** ribbon at the top of your screen. (The drop down styles in Open Office) To scroll to see more options, click on the arrows on either end of the Styles ribbon.

The default style selection is Body (Normal). The template will come with examples of the title page, copyright, dedication, front matter (perhaps a table of contents if it is a non-fiction template like this one) and back matter. You can select to use all of these sections or only a few. You may also choose to ignore the styles you won't use, or delete them if having too many styles is distracting for you.

Moving your already completed manuscript from one document into the new template

The first step is to save the template with the name of your book. In this way, the original template itself will always be available for you to come back to and reuse if you purchased a multi-book license. Friedlander's templates are provided in DOCX format. Do a **SAVE AS** and name the new file what you prefer. I typically name the file the book name and the template size (e.g., diypublishing-6x9.docx).

Tip for Open Office Users: Because all book designer templates are DOCX files they can easily be opened in Open Office. Do this through the **Import** *function. Once brought into your text area, select* **Save As ODF Text Document** *with your book file name. The extension will be ODT instead of DOCX.*

Two template functions **do not** come into Open Office effectively: headers and footers. You will need to recreate those yourself.

If you already have your book in another document, it is easiest to copy and paste sections into the new template. Let's go through each of those steps.

First, it is best to remove all styles and formatting in your other document before doing any copy and paste actions. Otherwise, those styles will carry into your template and you will need to change them following the *Apply Styles* methods described previously (pages 45-47). I've seen writers immediately panic when different styles suddenly appear in their nice clean template.

In Microsoft Word, to get rid of all the styles, text effects, and font formatting in your entire manuscript, press CTRL+A (CMD + A on Macs) to select everything in the document.

On the **Home** tab, in the **Font** group, click **Clear Formatting**. The icon looks like an eraser under the letters Ab.

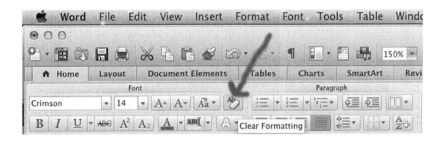

Save this cleared document as a *new* file. I usually name the new file something like title+cleared (e.g., diypublishing-cleared.docx). You want to save your document as a new file so that you can refer back to your original document for elements like italics which will be stripped with the cleared formatting.

Now copy and paste each section into the corresponding part of the template. For example, copy all of Chapter 1 into the Chapter 1 part of the template, and then all of Chapter 2 into the Chapter 2 part of the template.

Tip: For a quick copy and paste, place your cursor at the beginning of the chapter where the text begins (not the chapter title) and **click** *(right-click) your mouse. This marks the beginning of the section to be copied. Next, go to the end of your chapter. Hold down the shift key and click at the end of the last word in your chapter. This should highlight the entire section that needs to be copied. Once it is highlighted, do a* **CTRL C** *(**CMD C** on a Mac). Now your selection is on the invisible clipboard in your computer memory.*

Go to your new template. Again, place your cursor at the beginning of the chapter where the text begins (not the chapter title) and **click** *(right-click) your mouse. This marks the beginning of the section to be replaced. Next, go to the end of the template chapter. Hold down the* **shift key** *and* **click** *at the end of the last word in the template chapter. This should highlight the entire section that needs to be replaced. Once it is highlighted, do a* **CTRL V** *(CMD V on a Mac). Now the words from your previous document will have replaced all of the words in that chapter of the template.*

Repeat this same process for Chapter 2 and Chapter 3 of your manuscript. The Book Design templates typically only have three sample chapters. But don't worry, you will still be able to create as many chapters as you want. For now, stop the cut and paste process after the third chapter. Later I will talk about how to continue your manuscript Chapter 3. If you don't have all the front matter created yet, just leave the default words there for now. I will cover each of those sections in future chapters.

Now that you've practiced copying and pasting three chapters, let's go back and fix the front matter and chapter headings. A sample title is provided for each template. Highlight that title and type in your book title. Notice that the title style is highlighted in the **styles ribbon** as you work on that section. The title style in the template will automatically move words to a second line if your title is longer than the sample you are replacing.

If your template has a subtitle, and you don't have one in your book, then highlight the sample subtitle and delete it.

Tip: Book series names are often placed in the subtitle section of the title page.

Move through the front matter highlighting and changing as needed. If you haven't decided about specific content yet (e.g., the dedication), skip over it and come back to it later.

Next look at the chapter headings. Most of the book designer templates include both a chapter number and a chapter title. These are indicated by two separate styles. This means you will need to highlight them separately to make changes.

Many fiction authors use only chapter numbers (e.g., Chapter One, Chapter Two) as their chapter title. If this is the case with your manuscript, select which of the styles best fits your book and use that consistently.

1 LOOMINGS

In the example above, from the Flourish template, the assumption is that the author would use the chapter number and then a separate chapter name. You might elect to delete the chapter number 1, and then in the chapter title simply type **Chapter One**. If you have a Prologue, this is also the same process you would use, where there is no chapter number. By using the Chapter Title style, your book still retains the nice font for the title, as well as the spacing in the template which provides 80 points of line spacing before the chapter title begins and 108 points of line spacing after the chapter title, before the first paragraph for each chapter. This is a great example of providing a consistent and professional look for chapter headings.

You may be fortunate and find the perfect template for you—one that meets all your needs without any changes. However, if that is not the case, select a template that presents the overall look you want for your book. Parts of the template that don't work for you may be deleted or changed slightly, such as in the chapter titling. It is advised not to make *major* changes to the template. Changing font styles, spacing between titles and content, or spacing within the paragraphs may result in a book that looks displeasing to many readers. These templates are designed with an artist's eye for interior book design. Joel Friedlander has years of experience in book design and knows how font styles, sizes, and space all work together to present the most pleasing print book possible.

Starting a new document within a custom template

Now that I am comfortable with using templates, I always begin writing my manuscript within the template. This saves me a lot of time in the production phase of getting my book published. When the book has been edited and proofed, the editor's comments appear within the template (using Microsoft Word's Track Changes function) and are returned to me to accept or reject. For those readers who have been traditionally published, this is the similar process you would have experienced in working with galleys. Once I've made all the required changes, I don't have to worry about style, formatting, pagination, headers and footers again. I can go straight to production.

Working in a template from the moment of creation is a little different than taking an already completed document and copying it into the template. In the beginning, it may take some trial and error to find a process that works best for you. However, I believe that you will soon find it is a time saver and can also be reinforcing to your writing and creativity.

For me, seeing the automatic formatting as I write is actually motivating. It makes the book feel real from the moment of inception. The key is to not let that excitement of formatting get in the way of writing the story. Also, when it comes to initial editing, it definitely helps to print out the entire document. I find a lot more errors when looking at it on paper than I do on the screen where I've been working for months.

When starting a new manuscript within the template, the first step is to highlight the title that comes with the template and type in your own title. Go through the front matter, making your own corrections. As with the copy and paste option described previously, if a part of the front matter isn't ready then skip over it and move to sections where you are prepared to create. For example, I may know to whom I'm dedicating a book but, at the beginning of my writing process, I probably haven't decided exactly what I want to say in the dedication. Typically, I don't spend time on the wording of that dedication until the end of the book. I simply type in the persons name and move on. For the purposes of this step-by-step process, begin with the first chapter.

The easiest way to use styles during your story creation is to select the style first and then type the content. For example, let's say that the first paragraph in my fantasy book is a quote from an ancient scroll. Before typing the quote, I will go to the quote section on my style ribbon and select the style I wish to use for that quote. Once that selection is made, whatever I type will be in that quote format.

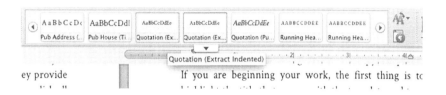

Note in the image above there are three options for quotations. If you hover over the option, a brief description appears. In some cases, as for Quotation (Extract Indented), there is also a drop down arrow for even more options in that style. Once you have completed your quote, return to the normal body of the text by clicking on **Body (Normal)** and begin typing again.

Alternatively, you can type everything in **Body (Normal)** and then come back and highlight things later to apply a specific style. Using the highlight method, click on the section that needs to change and then click on the style element that corresponds to that section.

I prefer to click the style first, because when I'm coming back for edits I'm often reading for context, or grammar, or scene structure, and my brain isn't focusing on styles. However, choose whatever works best for your style of writing, editing, and preparing your manuscript for sale. Certainly do not let the process of style selection get in the way of your writing.

What happens after Chapter Three?

As I indicated previously, the templates come with only three sample chapters. After chapter three, the next sample section is the author bio. To get additional chapters out of the template, you will need to insert a **section break** at the end of Chapter 3, and at the end of each subsequent chapter you create for your book.

Section breaks do several things for your book. First, they automatically create a new section with the formatting for a new chapter number and chapter title. Second, the appropriate header or footer information is applied to that new section in the correct format. Finally, the XML code created by a section break will become very important when you move your book from print to ebook. Section breaks help build the table of contents and all bookmarking and chapter links required in ebooks.

Let's stick with the print book for now. There are two types of section breaks to consider. The one recommended by the Book Designer guide is to use a **Section Break (odd page).** There are also options for **Section Break (even page), Section Break (Next Page)** and **Section Break (Continuous).** I will only talk about the two most common breaks—odd page and next page.

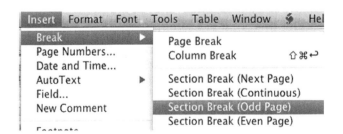

The screenshot above shows how to select a section break in Microsoft Word.

In Open Office, select **Insert** and **Break** from the main menu.

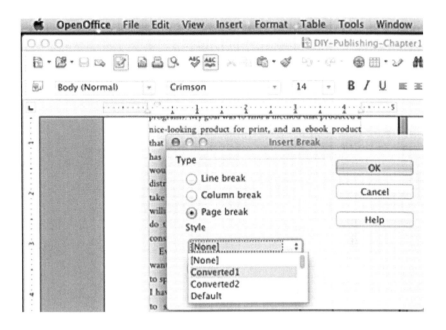

Select the Type as a **Page Break**. Then select **Default** as the style. This will be the equivalent of Section Break (Next Page) described in the Microsoft Word options below.

As I indicated previously, though Open Office converts most of the DOCX template styles when it is imported, it does not effectively convert the headers and footers. Because headers and footers are tied to section break XML data in Microsoft Word, those section break options do not translate here. If you wish to simulate the "odd page break" described below, you will need to manually add the blank page, as needed, at the end of a chapter.

In Microsoft Word, the **Section Break (Odd Page)** will always ensure that a new chapter (or section) begins on an odd page—in other words on the right hand side as you hold the book open. This means if your previous chapter ended on an even page, the next chapter will begin on the next page. You will see printed text both on the right and the left. However, if your previous chapter ended on an odd page, the section break will place a blank page between the end of that chapter and the next chapter. When you hold the book open you will see a blank page on the left and your new chapter on the right.

Personally, I love this classic way of preparing books. I like the consistency of having my chapters always begin on the right hand side. However, this is a practice that has fallen out of favor with many publishers looking to save money on production costs, and subsequently a number of indie authors don't want that blank page in their book either.

If you don't want any blank pages, instead insert a **Section Break (Next Page)**. This will ensure that a new chapter starts on a new page. However, that chapter may begin on the left or the right hand side.

Why else might you choose a specific section break? If your book is short and you want it to be longer, using the **Odd Page** section break will increase the overall page count and thus make the book appear longer. This is particularly true if you tend to write a lot of short chapters. On the other hand, if you write longer books and are concerned about the total page count from a cost perspective, using a **Next Page** section break will cut down your per book costs.

To continue past Chapter Three in the template, insert the section break of your choice. Your cursor will appear at the top of the next page. Click on the **Chapter Number style** in the style ribbon and type in the appropriate chapter number. Then click on the **Chapter Title style** and type in your chapter title name. As described previously, if you are not using both of these styles, select only the style you wish to use.

Once you create a chapter header, your cursor will automatically be placed at the appropriate spot on the page to begin typing your content for the next section. If you are doing a copy and paste, this is where your pasted text will be placed.

Remember, you can always change your mind regarding any of the decisions you have made while formatting your book. Perhaps, you loved the idea of using specialized italics for your ancient scrolls. However, once you see the style used on fourteen different pages, you may decide it was too much. You can always go back, select the scroll sections and apply a different style to those sections. That is the beauty of styles!

Tip: If you do purchase one of The Book Design templates be sure to also download the two free guides on book construction and template formatting. There is a great deal more instruction in those guides than I have space to provide within this book.

http://www.bookdesigntemplates.com/guides/

CHAPTER 4

Print Book Production

Many self-published authors make the decision to go ebook only. I'm not completely sure why this is, except out of fear that creating a print book is too difficult. Or perhaps they believe it's not worth the trouble because they can't imagine selling very many print books. With the use of a template, as described in the previous chapter, anyone can create a professional looking print book. So, let's look at why a self-published author should bother with a print book?

Though the ebook revolution has created an entirely new marketplace, it still has not become the largest category of book sales. The most recent data suggests that, in 2012, U.S. ebooks represented 23% of all trade books sold. (Note: This statistic does not include self-published books) That means a decision to do ebook only, misses potential sales in the other 77% of the market. Once a book is offered beyond the U.S. marketplace, the ebook to print book ratio is lower still. Even if these statistics are off a bit—

some pundits claim ebook sales are closer to 40% in the U.S. when you include indie publishing—why would an author choose to shut herself out of a substantial market by not having a print book available?

With easy uploads to distributors like CreateSpace and Lightning Source (Spark Press), there is little cost compared to the possible return on investment. The cost to upload to CreateSpace and make your print book immediately available for purchase via CreateSpace and Amazon is zero. That's right, absolutely FREE. If you would like that book distributed to Barnes & Noble online, made available to local bookstores in the U.S., as well as Europe, Canada, the UK and other places around the world you pay a fee of $25.00 and your book is picked up by Baker & Taylor and Ingram for the widest possible distribution. This means anyone can order your print book online, or walk into a local bookstore and request your book and have it delivered within a few days.

With worldwide print-on-demand (POD) technology, it is possible for you to have your print book delivered to a fan and pay no shipping cost. The Book Depository provides free shipping on all print books in its catalog, anywhere in the world.

http://www.bookdepository.com/

You will have to pay full price for your book, but you will still earn your forty % commission and you have no shipping to pay.

The Ingram Spark (similar to Lightning Source) alternative works similarly but the costs are a little higher. With the new Spark Press option, you pay $49 and get several options for distribution. Your book goes directly into Ingram's catalog. You discount is automatically at 55%, and returns are allowed.

You also have the option of uploading the same print book to Espresso Book Machines (EBMs) around the world. These are machines that print on demand within a store—usually a bookstore, but they also exist in some libraries, colleges, and universities. You upload your cover PDF and interior PDF in the same way you do for CreateSpace or Lightning Source. To access this resource, go to http://ondemandbooks.com/ Click on the Self-publishing tab for full information on uploading your own books.

Convinced? I publish every novel I write in both ebook and print form. My local booksellers really appreciate it. It allows them to order copies and make them available on their "buy local" shelves. If I want to participate in a signing locally or anywhere else in the country there is no problem getting my books. I have also had fans who bought the ebook first, and loved it so much they wanted to have a signed print copy too. If I only created ebooks, I would be missing a significant income stream.

Final steps in preparing a book for print

Currently all print-on-demand vendors require a PDF file. By following the instructions provided earlier, you already have a professionally formatted book in your word processor. All you need to do is to save it as PDF.

In Microsoft Word and most other word processing programs that entails clicking on the **File** menu item, then selecting **Save As**.

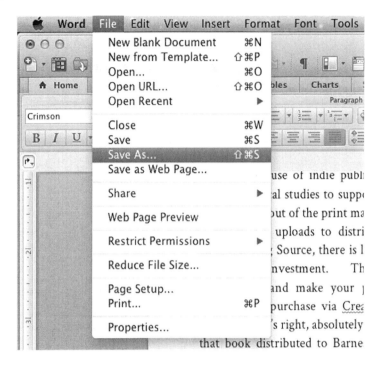

After clicking the **Save As** option you will be presented with the regular **Save** screen. Go to the **Format** line and click on the drop down arrow. Click on the **PDF** option.

I usually keep the name the same, so it is easy for me to find in my file structure. It will append the PDF extension to your file. Be sure to click the **Save** button in the lower right corner of the box.

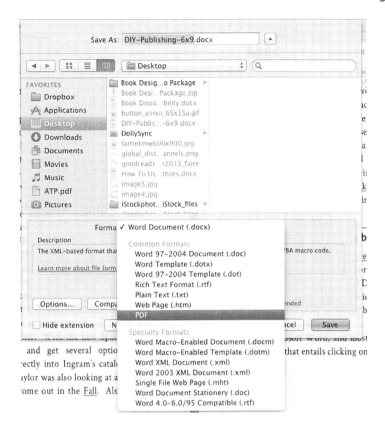

and get several optio[...] [...]sort word, and most
ectly into Ingram's catal[...] that entails clicking on
aylor was also looking at a[...]
ome out in the Fall. Als[...]

In Open Office, the process is to **Export to PDF**.

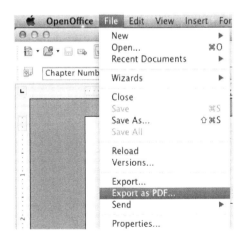

Once the Export option is selected, there are a number of parameters to check in the security dialog box. Be sure that the following are checked in the General tab.

- Lossless compression of images.
- PDF A-1a
- Export bookmarks
- Embed standard fonts

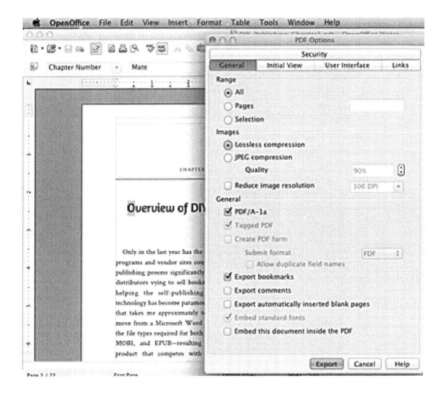

The other tabs default settings are fine. Click the **Export** button to complete the creation of the PDF file. You will have the option to rename the file. I advise keeping the same name as your book. The PDF extension will be sufficient for you to identify it.

However you create your PDF file, be sure to open that PDF file in Adobe Reader and look through it. Make sure that pages are falling in the right order and that there are not multiple blank pages between chapters or sections. One easy way to look at the file as you would the actual book, is to select the **View** menu item in Adobe and click on the **Print Layout** option.

In this way you will see the book displayed with facing pages. Next, scan for anything that stands out. For example, most templates are fully justified. If you didn't hit a return at the end of a paragraph, or did a copy and paste without full attention to where you were, it is possible that your justification will be off.

Your justification will be spread out too far like this.

If you have a large word or a URL as part of the text, it is possible that the justification will have a line where there are only a few words on it.

It might look like this http://www.thecreativepenn.com/2013/02/22/designing-your-book-interior/ because of the long URL. In that case you should look at your sentence and see how to add or delete words to make the justification work more effectively. Another option is to make all long URLs appear on a separate line.

If you have corrections to make, return to your word processing document and make the corrections there, then save again as a PDF.

I will cover uploading your completed book to CreateSpace and other distributors in the chapter on uploading your finished ebook and print files to each distributor (*Chapter 15*).

Another option for book interior preparation– Adobe InDesign

Adobe InDesign has been around since 2002. It has been the premium print publication software since its introduction. Originally designed for corporations to produce newsletters, brochures, flyers, magazines, and annual reports, it has also been used widely by book publishing professionals. In the past three years Adobe added functionality for interactive and web-based publications, including various ereader devices.

As expected, the software delivers tight integration with other Adobe applications, like Photoshop, Dreamweaver, Flash, Illustrator, and Fireworks. In the 5.5 version of InDesign, some new tools help reduce design tasks to fewer steps. Over the past two years, Adobe InDesign has kept relevant by focusing on built-in support for publishing pages anywhere—in print, on the Web, to Adobe PDF, and ebook formats. (see notes about ebook format difficulties below)

This is a great professional program. It is also a one with a very steep learning curve. It can do so many different things, and has multiple parameters you can set to have a print perfect publication. If you are familiar with print publishing concepts like leading, kerning, bleed, layers, text and graphic boxes, auto column calculation, etc., and like to control all these parameters, then Adobe InDesign is definitely the program for you. If you are a regular Photoshop user and love all of the functionality it provides, then you will be familiar with how Adobe approaches the user interface and the types of customization options that may be available.

If you are challenged by graphics programs, photo programs, and having too many choices to make, Adobe InDesign is not the program for you. Personally, I find it far too time consuming for creating my print and ebooks. I can easily become lost in the myriad of design decisions one can make. Even though I have a good technical background, my focus is on spending the majority of my work hours writing the next book. I prefer to purchase a good template and use it as the foundation for a professional book interior. It allows me some control, without expending a great deal of time.

Evaluate where you fall on the design continuum regarding your own needs for control and perfection. What is the balance between seeing a specific vision for your book and giving up some control of that vision in order to have more time to write? If you are not sure, then download a free trial version of Adobe InDesign and see how it feels. You may find you love it.

http://www.adobe.com/downloads.html?promoid=KEWBH

CHAPTER 5

Ebook Preparation

There are three major ebook formats an author needs to be concerned with producing. These three formats will work on 99% of the devices readers use to access your books.

- **EPUB.** This is an open standard—a specification determined by a group of developers and provided free of charge for anyone to use in their personal and commercial products. The EPUB standard is supported by all non-Kindle reader devices.

- **MOBI.** Also known as Mobipocket, this is a proprietary format, based on many of the EPUB standards but changed to be specific to the Amazon Kindle. Mobipocket is also supported on other devices like tablet computers.

- **PDF.** The Portable Document Format is an Adobe proprietary format supported by most devices. It has been around since 1993. Each PDF file encapsulates a complete description of a fixed-layout flat document, including the text, fonts, graphics, and other information needed to display it. Because of its fixed layout, it is sometimes preferred by those who enjoy reading on tablets or desktop computers. However, PDF files are not compatible with most single format ereader devices and are very difficult to use on small devices like smart phones.

Note: All major ereader vendors (e.g., Amazon, Barnes & Noble, Kobo) provide free viewer applications that can be loaded into any type of computer or mobile device. This allows readers to easily synchronize their reading across multiple devices and to purchase books from that vendor.

There are other formats, including plain text and HTML. However, any ereader device developed in the last two years will accept one or more of these file types. In addition, older Nooks, Kindles, and some Sonys will also accommodate at least one of these three file types.

As self-publishing opportunities increased and authors began putting up more books, both new and old software companies rose to meet the various formatting needs. You no longer need to know HTML or understand CSS in order to create your own ebook- formatted files. Let's look at a few options before we talk about my preferred option, Jutoh.

Calibre

The first free and still widely used software for converting ebooks to other formats was Calibre. This program was designed to help readers convert their purchased ebooks for use in different devices they might own. http://calibre.com. Quickly, several indie authors realized they could also use the program to convert their manuscript files to other formats without having to learn HTML or understand CSS.

Calibre always worked decently for Amazon files and for EPUB files at Barnes & Noble. However, my experience with the software is that in order to keep up with constant changes and new distribution outlets, I needed to constantly download new versions. This was particularly evident as Nook made several quick changes and Kobo came into the market.

I do not fault the creator of Calibre for this. When you consider it is a FREE option and the only money collected to reimburse the creator's time is from donations, I applaud his ongoing efforts. You can still use Calibre for most things, but I have not found it reliable in the way it maintains the display for other devices. In addition, most Calibre converted files have validation problems in several device types—particularly with Apple, some Nook, and anything where DRM might be required (such as uploading EPUB files to NetGalley or Overdrive).

Calibre was not designed as a primary conversion tool of original content for authors and publishers. It contains a viewer, which is very forgiving for readers, but does not always contain all the formatting and metadata content providers would want to include in their books. In addition, the viewer is not a replica of the viewers each device would use. It is completely separate.

InDesign

In terms of producing good ebook formatted files, Adobe InDesign does a nice job with MOBI—the Amazon Kindle format—and an amazing job with PDF. At this writing, it continues to have problems with the EPUB format. It will validate in the open source EPUB Checker. However, I have found continued problems validating with Apple and Sony. Also, the way the pages display in the newer Nook devices is not consistent.

Because the learning curve required to be effective with InDesign is challenging, along with the continued difficulties with EPUB validation, I rarely recommend this software for the average indie author/publisher. However, if you enjoy having perfect control over the entire look of the publication and you are willing to learn the product, InDesign is an excellent tool.

Direct Upload of Word Files

Both Amazon and Kobo allow you to upload a Microsoft Word document and they do the conversion for you. Unfortunately, those conversion engines tend to leave out a great deal of formatting and you have no control over the metadata that is included with your file. Your metadata is relegated to whatever is entered on their product screens.

In addition, these conversion engines change on a regular basis depending on which device the vendor wishes to feature the most. For example, if Amazon has recently released a high-definition tablet device, they may tweak the conversion engine so that ebooks will look the best on that device. Those small changes to the conversion engine will then render your content not as attractive on the devices people purchased a year or two before.

Every option, whether vendor direct (like with Amazon and Kobo) or through a software process like Calibre, InDesign, or Scrivener must do a conversion to the native file type. No one software solution is perfect.

Jutoh

After evaluating several options, I recommend Jutoh http://jutoh.com. Jutoh is a product created by Anthiom Software Ltd., an independent software house based in Edinburgh, Scotland. What I like about this product is that it is designed to do one thing, to create clean files in a variety of ebook formats. It is not designed to be a word processor, a file indexer, a print book creator, or any other ancillary duty. It only does ebook file conversion and, in my opinion, it does it better than any other software program.

You can create a project within minutes by using the Project Wizard and importing existing files. Alternatively, you can write your book from scratch using the built-in styled text editor. The cost is a mere $39 for the basic software.

There is also a Jutoh Plus download option, which supports scripting and HTML templates, primarily used by small publishers who want to automate ebook production or add custom code. I do not recommend the PLUS version for the average indie author. To take advantage of the PLUS features, you would need to be familiar with custom coding, scripting, and other programming protocols to make it work for you.

Jutoh is particularly excellent for preparing EPUB files that validate across all devices, but it can also create first-rate Kindle files (Mobi), and several other formats used primarily with older ereaders or web pages.

In the next chapter I will take you through the five easy steps to formatting an ebook file in Jutoh using the Word document you've already created with styles. I find it takes me approximately 10 minutes to complete the entire ebook creation process. That includes upload, reorganizing sections for ebooks, adding active

URL links, then exporting to each file format I need for distribution.

Things that will change from print to ebook

Authors are usually surprised when they first view their ebook in the ereader devices. When compared to the fixed-format PDF document, it can look quite different. The first question I'm often asked is what happened to all my beautiful formatting—the swirly font in my chapter titles and the special scene shift spacers I selected?

Each ereader has a certain set of default fonts installed. When it receives your file, it will match the fonts you selected as best it can with the fonts installed within the device. As newer devices are released, a much larger font selection is available. However, for older devices, some of them have only one or two fonts. So, it is possible that your document will look different from one device to the next. In addition, most ereaders give the user the option to select a different font and to make it larger or smaller to fit their specific reading needs.

Though fonts are regulated by the ereader device and the user, the author still has some control of the reading experience. Based on formatting selections, you can still define the relative size, position and other typographical features of the text (italics, bold, etc.). This is why using styles is so important.

Section breaks will still cause the next chapter to start on the next screen, preserving the flow of the book as you would expect. Again, depending on the device, chapters may begin at the top of the screen or in the middle of the screen based on the sophistication of the device. Other styles will also be retained, such as spacing between chapter numbers and titles and a larger font for chapter titles. However, it is likely that special fonts, drop caps, and certain text symbols will not render as expected due to the way each ereader device interprets those specialized elements. Finally, if bullets or numbering were used without a specified style assigned, they may not show up at all. The words will still be there, but the bullets and numbers will not.

As mentioned previously, ebooks are designed not to use set page numbers. When you consider that users can choose the font and the size it makes sense that pagination is not retained. Add to that the different device sizes, ranging from the two inch screen of a mobile phone to a 10" iPad, and it would not make sense to plan for pagination on each device.

In late 2011, Amazon decided to respond to the desire for a reference to physical page numbers by creating an algorithm that will supply them on certain books. This service is only provided for books that are bestsellers, in the Kindle top 100 lists, or from certain publishers who pay for the service. In other words, the average self-publisher cannot access this service, and other ebook distributor's devices do not provide page references at all.

It may be frustrating to those authors who want their books to be as visually perfect and similar to the print version. However, the ereading experience was designed with customer choice in mind—as a means to peruse text in the way the reader prefers.

I know there are still some who will insist they must have page numbers or they must have a picture or table on a particular page or the book won't work. For those instances, I suggest you only distribute the book electronically as a PDF file. Just be aware that those who do not like the way PDF files render on their device will not purchase your book, or will likely return it.

There is a way to force a fixed format for MOBI and EPUB files. It is used for children's picture books and technical manuals. However, other than those two instances, I strongly recommend against it. This will stop the user from being able to resize fonts, and it will stop the natural page flow. This means that some users won't be able to read your book because the font will be too small in order to fit an entire page on their device, or too large because you chose to go with a 14 point text font and 18 point headers which take up the entire page. Or the readers will have to scroll horizontally in order to see everything on the page. In other words, it will be a big pain for readers and that is the last thing you want to happen.

An option for Book Design Templates specifically for ebooks

Joel Friedlander's Book Design Templates also offer an ebook bundled option for the print templates you purchase. The ebook bundle provides a rendering for most of the styles you have in your print book using a style template that is compatible most ereader devices. This is done by making a number of choices in the new style sheet provided. One choice is to use the Times New Roman font throughout—the native font of most ereader devices. Another choice is to forgo most fancy header and chapter number styles, choosing instead to render them in something simpler yet unique.

CHAPTER 6

Jutoh in 10 Minutes

I found Jutoh through the recommendation of another indie author. After seeing how straight-forward it was to use, I was surprised this program is not better known. Its capabilities, ease of use, and consistent performance in generating good, clean code and metadata for ebooks is unparalleled by any other ebook generation and conversion tools I have evaluated. I suspect this best kept secret will soon be unleashed.

To fully understand the capabilities of Jutoh, I think it is important to know what it can do in the context of the needs of the novelist or non-fiction book author. Lets begin with a quote from the Jutoh publishing guide. *Creating Great Ebooks Using Jutoh,* in order to understand the vision of Jutoh from the creator's perspective, Dr. Julian Smart.

Jutoh is an editor for creating your ebooks; you can create a book from scratch in Jutoh, or you can import an existing book. ... Unlike most word processors, Jutoh divides ebook content into sections, which is more naturally suited to the way ebooks work. Jutoh is a bit like a word processor in that it supports content formatting, but it is geared towards generating a variety of ebook formats, with various tools to help with this task. You can add images to your documents, and (experimentally) sound and video where supported by the ebook reader.

I am very impressed by the way Jutoh exports several different ebook file formats while embedding important metadata in the file structure. Jutoh will automatically create the table of contents and bookmark links to chapters. For non-fiction books, Jutoh can compile a linked index, as well as assemble references at the end of a section or in a separate reference section at the end of your book. The program can create internal links within an ebook, and links to external web sites such as an author page, social media, or buy sites for subsequent books.

Jutoh works on Windows, Mac OS X and Linux. You only need to pay once. One license is good for all platforms, which is handy for most of us who move our work from a desktop to a laptop and perhaps to a tablet for travel. In my home, my husband uses a PC desktop and a PC laptop. I use a Mac Laptop that I can also hook up to a monitor and keyboard to pretend it's a desktop. I anticipate we will have an Android tablet in the near future. Jutoh can also be run from a USB drive instead of installing it on each device you own.

The quick and easy Jutoh import from Microsoft Word or Open Office

For those who work in a word processor, like Microsoft Word or Open Office, the beauty of Jutoh is that it will import the file and automatically parse it into chapters and sections. That is, providing styles have been used consistently as I described in previous sections of this book. To get a sense of how smoothly and quickly things can go once you understand the Jutoh software, I will explain my ten-minute ebook conversion process.

Do not get frustrated if it doesn't work easily for you the first time. Every computer is different and the way you selected styles or used a template may have created some problems. Following this introduction, I will provide step-by-step information that will allow you to set up your own process for consistent ebook creation. In addition, Dr. Julian Smart has created a thorough guide for using Jutoh. The guide contains many screen captures with additional detailed information, including advance functionality. You can download the guide for free here:

http://www.jutoh.com/book.htm

The ten-minute process makes a few assumptions about your preparation for converting you document to an ebook.

- You have a finalized book description.
- You have used styles appropriately to define all chapter and section headers
- You have used section breaks at the end of each chapter or section
- You have a book cover already prepared and ready to be inserted.
- You have already installed the Jutoh software.

Step 1: Create a New Project for this book

Open the Jutoh application. At the top, click **File** and **New Project**. Every book should be created as a new project.

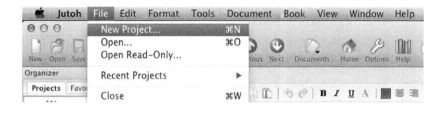

Step 2: Provide information about your book

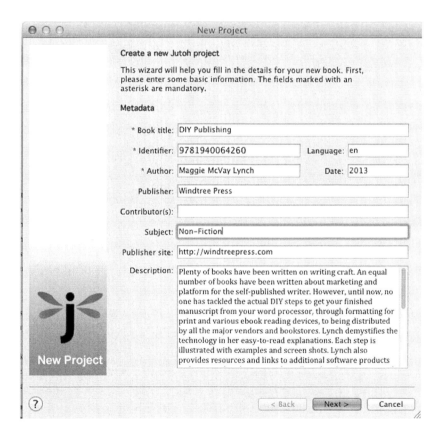

Once you see the New Project window, you need to complete this form. Accuracy is very important, as every piece of data on this form may be used in search engines to help readers or reviewers find your book. Let's work through each of the fields.

Book Title. Type in your title here.

Tip: If your book has a subtitle DO NOT input that here. It may provide difficulties when uploading to vendor sites. Most vendors catalog books with the subtitle separately. Also, do not use a colon following the book title as some vendors will read anything following the colon as a subtitle.

Notice, as you type in your title it simultaneously enters your title into the **Identifier** field. This works fine if you are not planning to use an ISBN for your ebook. However, I strongly suggest you **do** use an ebook ISBN and type that ISBN number in the identifier field. (See *Chapter 13* on the importance of ebook ISBNs and the different ways to obtain one, and *Chapter 15* on how those ISBNs impact your distribution options.)

Author. Type in the first name and last name of the book author. If you are using a pseudonym for your book, type it here. Jutoh will automatically input whatever name you used when you purchased the Jutoh software. Change it to the author name for this particular book. Be sure it matches *exactly* how the name will appear on the book. For example, this book is published by Maggie McVay Lynch. If I only enter Maggie Lynch then the author name will not provide all the details about my name. Some people may type in Maggie McVay (those who know previous books I wrote by that name) and thus will never see this book because I didn't include the entire name.

Date. This field reflects the publication date of the book. The current year is automatically entered for you. Even though your book may have been previously published in print, you will want the date the book is being offered in ebook format. If your book was previously published in ebook by another publisher, and now you have the rights back, then you *still* need to provide a new date. This is the second edition of that ebook and it is considered a new book. (Note: You cannot use the same ISBN your previous publisher used. You must have a new ISBN.)

Contributor(s). This field can be complicated for some books. A contributor is an individual or group of individuals (like an organization) who have a controlling interest in the copyright. If you have a co-author, this is where you would list that person. Although you may have many contributors to the book (e.g., cover designer, editor, typist, etc.) this field is usually not for those individuals as they have no legal interest in the copyright. If you paid your cover artist for the art, she is not listed as a contributor. You may include her in your copyright page to provide credit. The same rule applies to an editor you paid to edit your book. That individual is not a contributor unless you have given her some controlling interest in the copyright (e.g., you've agreed to split sales proceeds with her). However, if you wrote a children's book and have an illustrator AND you are splitting the earnings of the book with that illustrator, then you definitely want to list that person in the **contributor** field. If you have more than one contributor, like in an anthology, then you should list each of them. I will cover how to add additional contributors in the Metadata chapter of this guide.

Subject. This is a complex and very important field. It tells libraries, booksellers, and online retailers how to index your book. This is another field that needs to match how the distributor views subjects in their catalog. If you live in the United States and/or distribute in the United States, it is wise to stick with the BISAC definition of subjects (http://www.bisg.org/what-we-do-0-136-bisac-subject-headings-list-major-subjects.php) as these are the most commonly used by vendors to create their search categories. In this field, enter either Fiction or Non-Fiction. I will come back to this area in the Metadata chapter of this guide.

Publisher. If you have a separate company name that you are using to publish your books, enter that name here. If not, type your name in the space. It is up to you whether to use your author name (if it is a pseudonym) or your legal, given name. As an indie author, you are a publisher. Do not enter distributors (such as Amazon, Kobo, Barnes & Noble, Sony, Apple, etc.) as your publisher. As a self-published author, *you* are the publisher.

Tip: If you plan to publishing several books, it is wise to set up a publishing company as the controlling entity for these books. It helps to establish a separate business for bookkeeping and tax purposes, and it allows you to publish under several pseudonyms with one entity. In the United States you can do this with a DBA (doing business as) for an average cost of $50. The cost may vary by state. In other countries you may be required to set up a limited liability corporation or other corporate structure. Check with your state or country small business guidelines.

Description. This is where you enter your book blurb. This is the same description that is often found on the back of print books. Remember to write this in an active voice. This description is a marketing tool. You want it to be interesting and exciting, so when someone reads it she will want to pick up your book and read more. It is best to get this set exactly how you want it in advance and then copy and paste the completed blurb into this section of Jutoh.

Click the **Next** button to go to the second screen in the wizard.

Step 3. Tell Jutoh where to save your project files and what ebook formats you want to distribute.

Jutoh will put in your project name in the first field. The Project Folder, where all your projects and files are saved, will default to a folder in your computer called **Jutoh Documents.** Personally, I let it default to this folder. However, if you prefer to set up your own Project Folders in your file structure, do that in advance in your file management system. Then click on the button with the three dots (ellipses) in it. This will allow you to choose the folder from your file management system.

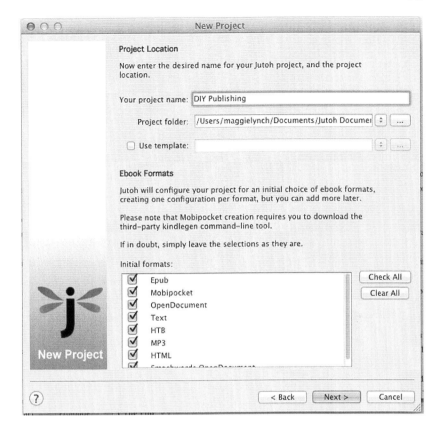

Do *not* select **Use Template** on this screen. This refers to templates that Jutoh provides with the software. As you already have a template embedded in your Microsoft Word or Open Office document, you do not want to use a Jutoh template.

Ebook Formats. By default, Jutoh selects all the ebook formats the software is able to provide. I suggest you leave all of these marked. Even if you ultimately only use a couple of them for this project, it doesn't hurt to have additional options here should you make a different decision later.

Click the **Next** button to go to the third screen in the wizard.

Step 4. Select Import Options.

On this screen, I advise accepting all the defaults and clicking **Next.** As you are importing a file with styles already, there is nothing to change on this screen.

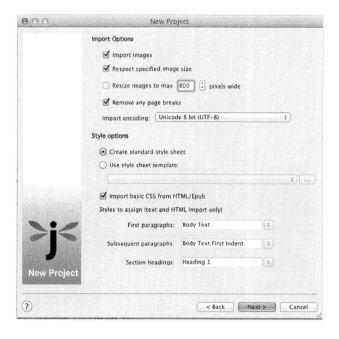

Step 5. Tell Jutoh how to find your completed file and to use all the styles that come with it.

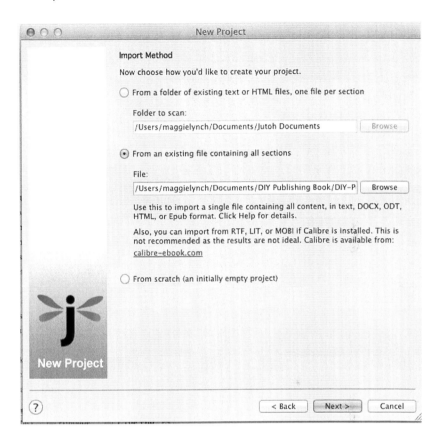

Import Method. Be sure to click in the circle next to the item that states *"From an existing file containing all sections."* This is what tells Jutoh that you already have a file ready to go—your Microsoft Word or Open Office file with styles embedded.

Next, click the **Browse** button to locate your manuscript file in your computer file management system. Once you have selected that file it will provide the path and name in the input box.

Remember: Your file MUST be a .DOCX (Word 2007 and above) or .ODT (Open Office) file. Earlier versions of Word will not work because the styles and information about your document will not be embedded.

Click the **Next** button to import the file.

You will quickly see a processing frame. If your book is short, it may happen so fast that you'll barely notice it. This screen shows Jutoh processing each of your chapters and, if you have them, images related to those chapters.

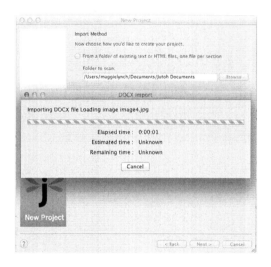

Once the import is completed a confirmation screen is presented. A small **preview** window with your chapter headings is displayed. If all went well with your styles—which it should if you used the purchased style sheet or designed your own as discussed in the previous chapter—you should see that Jutoh maintained the style of your chapter titles and headers.

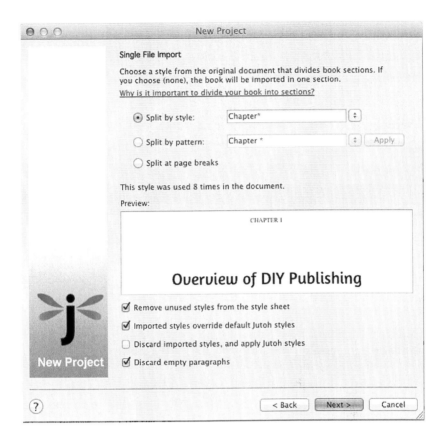

It may be that a few styles have changed. For example, in the screen shot above you will notice that the style for Chapter Number in the print book included a horizontal line underneath the chapter number. This did not translate in the Jutoh import. However, the Chapter Title styles came across without incident.

The reason that Jutoh ignores certain styles is to make sure your book is compatible with the largest number of ereaders.

If you purchased the ebook bundle with a Book Designer template, as described previously, and copied your print document into that ebook template, then everything will be imported into Jutoh exactly as depicted in your Word document. However, if you take styles directly from a print template, as I did in this example, then horizontal lines and some special characters will not be the same. This is because the way they are coded in Word does not translate to most ebook readers. You can decide if it is worth the time to transfer to an ebook template or if you can live with the few things that are not transferred directly from a print book template.

For now, don't worry if it is not exactly the same as your Microsoft Word or Open Office Document. You will have an opportunity to change it later if it is important. Once again click the **Next** button.

The next screen allows you to import your cover file, if you have one. You also have the option of creating one in Jutoh. If you have a cover file, click in the circle labeled **Use an existing file**. Then click the **Browse** button and locate the cover file in your file management system. If you do not have a cover yet, you may skip this step and come back to it later.

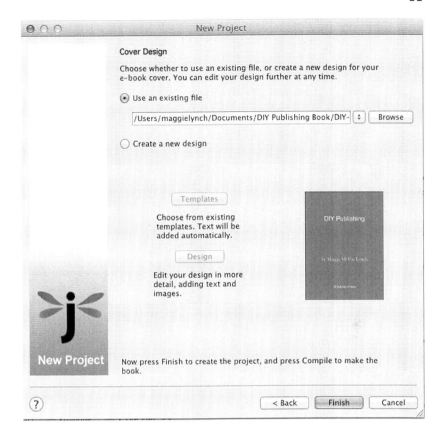

Click the **Finish** button.

Again, you will be presented with a processing screen as it compiles all the sections of your book, based on the style sheet embedded in your manuscript. When processing is completed you should see your sections listed vertically in the top left window. Your cover (if you uploaded one) will be displayed in the lower left window along with the configuration defaulted to EPUB in the bottom left. In the center pane will be the beginning of your book.

*Tip: If you do not see a screen configured like the one below, it means the items are not selected to display. Go to the **View** menu item on the top of the page. Make sure a checkmark is next to Main Toolbar, Status Bar, Organizer, Control Panel, and Log Window. To create a checkmark next to an item, click on it. This will provide the view below that is most helpful when working within Jutoh.*

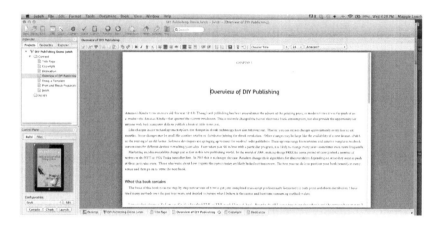

Click through the items—primarily chapters and sections—displayed in the organizer on the top left side. Make sure each one is a new section or chapter. On your first try with this process, it is not unusual to find that some of your front matter ran together. For example, it may be that the title page and copyright page ended up in one section together, or that your dedication was appended to the title page. This happens because most authors do not provide headers and styles for the front mater. Fortunately, it is very easy to correct.

The Concept of Book Sections

Once your book is imported, Jutoh automatically puts it into sections. These sections (shown in your upper left organizer pane) are also the same sections that will be linked and bookmarked within your ebook when you create the ebook files. You can change the order of these sections, add additional sections, or delete sections.

The easiest way to fix the front matter is to create the new sections you need. If you were using the template, this is usually a copyright section and a dedication section. Let's go through that process.

To add a new book section, select the item you wish for the new section to follow. For example, if you wish to add a copyright section, select the **Title Page** in the left pane. New sections are always added *below* the currently selected item. Next, click on the **Document** menu item in the top menu, and select **Add a Book Section** from the drop down as illustrated below.

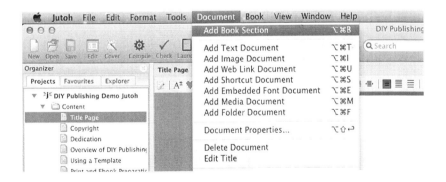

This action will pop up an input box asking you to enter the name of this new section. In this example, you would type in **Copyright** and click the **OK** button.

The new section will appear on the left in the organizer pane, and a blank page will appear in the main window. Next, return to your Title Page and highlight the copyright information. Execute a *cut* (CTRL X on the PC, COMMAND X on Mac). Select your new Copyright section and *paste* the information into it. (CTRL V on PC, COMMAND V on Mac). Now your new section should have all the copyright information in it.

Repeat this same procedure for any other information that needs to be put into new sections.

There are many other manipulations you can do with the sections and the styles, some of which we will cover in the next chapter. Let's complete the process now to turn this manuscript into an ebook file.

Normally, you would not execute this final step until everything is complete and meets your approval. For the purposes of this introduction to Jutoh, it is good to practice completing the process. You can always run the process again after you have made corrections.

Tip: Just because you've created an ebook file does not mean it is set in stone. That is the beauty of self-publishing and of doing your own formatting. If you find errors, you can always go back and correct them, then export the file again.

The final step in creating an ebook file is to click on the **File** menu item at the top of the screen and select **Export** in the drop down menu. The next menu displays all of the options for ebook file types. For the purpose of this introductory tutorial, select **Epub**.

This step will generate a window for you to rename the new EPUB file, if you like, and to select where you want to save this file. I prefer to leave the file name the same for every ebook file type. It makes it easier to find later and to replace should I need to correct mistakes and create a replacement file. Jutoh will automatically retain the current name of your file, and append EPUB as the extension. This extension will identify the file type to browsers and operating systems, as well as to specific ereaders. Jutoh will also default to placing the file in the **Jutoh Documents** folder. Click the **Save** button to save your ebook file in the EPUB format.

The final step is the actual creation of the EPUB file. Click **Save** on the screen, and the export compile will begin. You will get the processing screen that looks similar to other processing screens you've seen before.

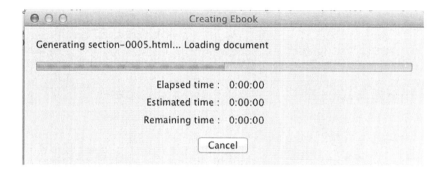

When it is completed you will have an EPUB file that can be uploaded at all vendor distributor sites except Amazon. Amazon requires a MOBI file type. If there are errors in the file, you will see them listed in the bottom pane (see example below).

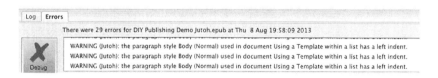

For most novels, which are primarily text with few styles, you will not generate any errors. If you are including images, charts, tables, lists, etc. then there is a higher likelihood of errors. The errors almost always have to do with style problems. This occurs when you do something within Jutoh that is not associated with a style.

In the illustration above, all 29 errors relate to the same problem: "Body (Normal) used in document. Using a template within a list has a left indent." This means that the author likely created a bulleted list and indented it. The style defined for "Body (Normal)" does not accommodate this. The error is a warning to tell you that if you use this EPUB file it may not display with those indents in all ereaders.

There are three options when seeing an error: go back through the manuscript and fix the problems; change the style definition for Body (Normal); or ignore it and see how it looks in the ereaders you are targeting. It may work fine.

If this happened to me, I would go back and fix this by removing all left indents for bulleted lists. Alternatively, I would create a specific style for bulleted lists that includes the left indent (see discussion of how to create a style in *Chapter 2*). Then go through the document and apply my newly created style to each bulleted list. Either of these solutions would solve the problem and I would know that the newly generated EPUB file would be clean in all ereaders.

In the next chapter we will talk more about configuring the outputs, how styles are used in Jutoh, and what you can do to minimize errors. However, we will not talk about the code level of fixing errors, as that is beyond what most authors are prepared to do for their books.

Jutoh comes with an excellent 180 page guide that covers many more details. The company also has a wonderful support network to respond to your questions, should you have a problem you can't resolve on your own.

Some Considerations in File Naming

Why would you want to rename the book file? The primary reason is that many authors like to specify which vendor has which file. This is particularly important if you are adding buy links to additional books at a specific vendor. (We will talk more about that in the marketing section of this book.) If that is the case you might want to label each export file differently. For example: *DIY Publishing Kobo.epub; DIY Publishing Sony.epub; DIY Publishing Nook.epub;* etc.

One thing to consider is how much you want to track and maintain these different files as you create and publish more books. The more books you publish, the more time consuming it becomes to maintain separate files and buy links for each book. If in a year you decide to make changes to a book (perhaps your readers found several errors you wish to correct) it is much easier to make changes to the epub file and the mobi file once than to make changes to multiple epub files. The same difficulty arises if you are providing buy links that are vendor specific at the back of each book. Does this mean you need to go back and update those links with every new release?

I recommend creating only one EPUB file for all venues. At the back of the book, link to your website or publisher site where all your books are displayed with links to your book at each distributor (e.g., Amazon, B&N, Kobo, Apple, Xin Xii, Sony, etc.). I find it easier to maintain a single website and its links for each book than to maintain multiple copies of the same book in Jutoh. However, you may wish to make a different choice.

CHAPTER 7

Metadata

Metadata has become the buzz word for visibility of books on the web. When most authors hear this word, they begin to shake or close their eyes and take a deep breath. The word itself engenders nightmares of being lost in esoteric coding. I've heard authors say to me: "I just can't do it. It's too complicated."

The good news is Jutoh provides many options for metadata, and it can be as simple or complex as you wish to make it. In fact, by creating a title, a description, and an author name some metadata is already created for the book. In this chapter, I will explain about the importance of other metadata and demonstrate ways to include that within each ebook file. The chapter following this one will be devoted to a specific type of metadata—keywords.

What is metadata?

Metadata is officially defined as "data about data." I've always found that definition unhelpful. Metadata is also known as tags, descriptions or properties, and keywords. Metadata helps identify information about a product, in this case books. The easiest way to understand this is to think of your book—all the words, the cover, the pictures—as information. Readers want to search for books based on specific criteria. You can help them find your book by providing descriptions regarding the content.

How search engines work is not easy to understand. Most people type something into the Google search box and expect that what comes up will be the best resources available on the subject. Librarians will tell you that this is a fallacy – there are plenty of things Google doesn't pick up. Just because a searcher doesn't find it, doesn't mean it's not there.

In the case of books, much of that "discoverability" has to do with a book's metadata. Not simply title and author, but the BISAC codes, the description, the table of contents – anything that describes what the book is about. If a self-publisher is not paying attention to metadata, it will be much harder for readers to find that publisher's books.

The good news is that you are providing metadata without even knowing it. Every time you fill out a form about your book, you are providing metadata. Every time you write a blog or a Facebook post or a tweet, you are providing metadata. Search engines use all this information and attempt to index your book into categories. The bad news is, if you aren't careful how you are providing all that information, the search engines won't find your book when a reader looks for it—at least not in the first 200 hits or so. Most readers won't look beyond the first ten to twenty hits.

Print books also need metadata associated with them. Though you cannot embed that data within a print book, you do provide it through other means. If you purchase ISBNs from Bowker, the official registrar in the U.S. and its territories, or from the registrar in your country, you are required to provide a certain amount of information about your book. The title, price, description, format, and category placement are all pieces of information that end up becoming metadata for search engines.

With technical advances in indexing, some companies have the capabilities to sort through metadata inside books if you provide the entire text. Bowker is one of these. The site gives you the option to upload a PDF of the entire book. They do not sell or make your PDF available to anyone. However, their software will scan the text in order to generate additional keywords and indexes of the content. For example, if your book is a historical novel set in 1942 it would come up whenever someone included the year 1942 in a search request. How high it places on the list would depend on how many other elements from your book match the request.

Every retailer and product manufacturer provides metadata in order to get the most visibility for their items on the Internet. You need to compete with that both in print and in ebooks. With ebooks you have the additional advantage of embedding that metadata in the file you send to each vendor.

Before you begin entering metadata into forms on every vendor site, or into Jutoh to embed in your ebook files, it is helpful to think about some of it in advance. Below is a list of items you may wish to prepare prior to completing a form or entering metadata fields. We will talk about each of these in detail.

- Title
- Author

- Publisher
- Contributor
- Subject or Category
- Abstract of 70 characters (including spaces)
- Short Description of 255 characters (including spaces)
- Long Description (usually called the blurb)
- Audience
- Keywords
- Country of author
- Regional code
- Reviews
- Links to excerpts
- Awards / Prizes

The above list is what I would term the "basic" list of possibilities. Traditional large publishers use a system called ONIX (ONline Information eXchange) to transmit book metadata to all vendors involved in selling, distributing, or organizing books. ONIX offers an extensive list of data fields (as many as 200) that can be used to describe a book. In addition to title, author, and ISBN, publishers regularly include availability, pricing, publisher name, reviews, blurbs, territorial rights, and jacket images and can include much more. To see the entire list of ONIX codes go to: http://bit.ly/15pb11k

To compete with these publishers, you will want to provide at least the basic metadata mentioned above, and to provide that metadata using the correct terminology and codes so that they are recognizable and will be indexed in the same way as other books. Let's look at how to use Jutoh to create metadata that is embedded with your ebook files. Going through this process will also help you to understand what types of metadata you will want to provide when completing forms at distributor sites for both print and ebooks.

Providing Your Book's Metadata in Jutoh

In *Chapter 6*, you set up a project for a book and went through the quick ten minute process for getting from completed manuscript to ebook file. In that process you already completed some metadata: book title, language, ISBN (if you had one) author, publisher, one subject, and your book description. Now, let's return to the Metadata Panel and provide even more information to help get your book discovered.

To access the Metadata Panel, go to the menu item **Book** and select **Project Properties**.

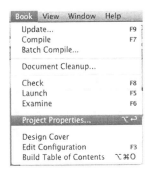

The project metadata panel will be displayed. As described in *Chapter 6*, to change an element simply highlight and type over what is there. The next step is to add enhanced metadata to your project by providing additional information for each element, or adding new metadata entry fields.

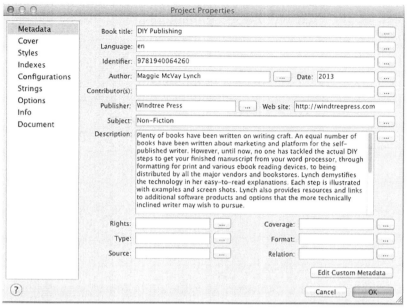

The first field to tackle is the **Subject** field. Currently, you will have typed either Fiction or Non-Fiction in that field. Next is the opportunity to include additional subjects. The subjects give you a standardized way to tell retailers and the general book trade about the primary and secondary store sections where a title will fit best–and, hopefully, sell best. In addition, they help retailers get your titles on the shelf more quickly (or online in the appropriate category), and they provide an electronically compatible method for describing the content of a book. In order to follow the standards and expectations of these groups it is best to use the categories defined by BISAC (Book Industry Standards and Communications).

Developed to standardize the electronic transfer of book information, the subjects are contained in an industry-approved list of descriptors (or headings), each of which is represented by a nine-character alpha-numeric code. The list has 50 major sections, such as Computers, Fiction, History, and True Crime. Within each major section, a number of detailed descriptors represent subtopics that the BISAC Subject Heading Committee has deemed most appropriate for the major topic. A complete copy of the list can be found at: http://www.bisg.org/what-we-do-0-136-bisac-subject-headings-list-major-subjects.php In order to determine the hierarchy of major and minor subjects, you will need to first click on the major subject and then peruse all of the possibilities for minor subjects. For the purpose of the instruction in this book, I will use a fiction example to illustrate each step because the majority of self-publishers tend to be fiction authors.

If you are an author with a fiction book that is single genre, your use of the subject field is straight forward in that you will only need to enter two categories. However, many authors today write fiction books that cross multiple genres. In that case, you will want to generate a subject code for each possible category. Though the forms of some vendors may limit the number of categories you select to two or four, within your ebook file you may include as many categories as needed.

Tip: Though you may be tempted to select every possible category that even slightly relates to your book, I recommend not doing so. You need to find the balance between what is the most representative of your book and the ability to put it in the appropriate category for sales. Consider the bookseller. If she has sections in her store for Mystery, Paranormal, and Romance and you mark your book as all three, how is she to determine where to place your book?

It is important to look at the BISAC subject headers first and try to fit your book into the header that best describes the primary tone of your book. In other words, evaluate which category reflects the majority of your book. Cross-genre authors often find it frustrating that BISAC frequently does not provide a subject header for each of the cross-genre possibilities. For example, if an author has penned a story which contains mystery, paranormal, and romance elements she would need to identify where to place the book. There is no Fiction / Paranormal category. In Mystery all categories assume a detective, and then the author must select a specific mystery detective type (e.g., hard-boiled, historical, women sleuths, etc.). If the Romance is central to the story, the closest BISAC category may be Fiction / Romance / Paranormal.

Select the category that is closest. If there are two categories that fit, then list them both within the metadata. Don't worry if it isn't exact. There will be other places you can describe the exact content.

To provide multiple options in Subject with Jutoh, click on the ellipsis button to the right of the field. This will display a new data entry window.

You should already see displayed an element named **Subject 1** and an Attribute with the value of **Fiction**. In the Preview box you will see the coding for that metadata. The "dc" stands for Dublin Core, a metadata standard. The easiest way to add multiple subjects, in order of importance, is to copy and paste the code in the **Preview** box for each subject you wish to add. Then change the information as I did in the example here to include Fantasy, Teen, and Young Adult. Remember, you want to put the subsequent categories in order of importance. This is because some search engines may only index two categories whereas others may read more.

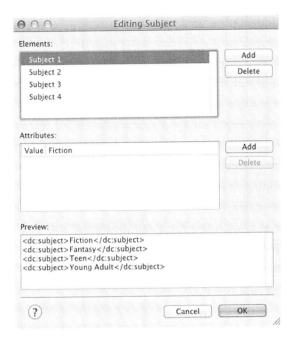

If you are selling in the United States. you also want to include the BISAC designators. Personally, I prefer to put these following the first subject and prior to the remaining subjects. This is because they are used so frequently by retailers, booksellers, and librarians in the U.S. In order to do this you will need to add elements and attributes. First click on the **Add** button next to the **Elements** box. This will add an additional subject element. Then click **Add** next to the **Attributes** box. This will ask you to enter an attribute name. Type in the words **BISAC Subject Heading** as in the illustration below. **Press OK.**

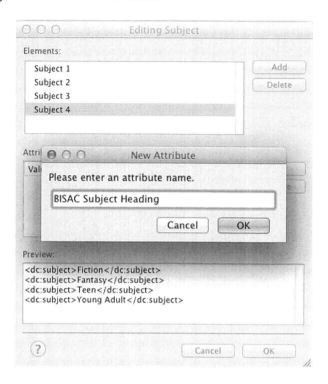

The BISAC Subject Heading will now appear in the Attributes box with a square next to it. Enter the subject, separated by slashes, exactly as it appears within the BISAC standards. In the illustration below I have entered FICTION / Fantasy / Paranormal. I did a copy and paste from the BISAC page. That will assure that it follows the expected categorization scheme.

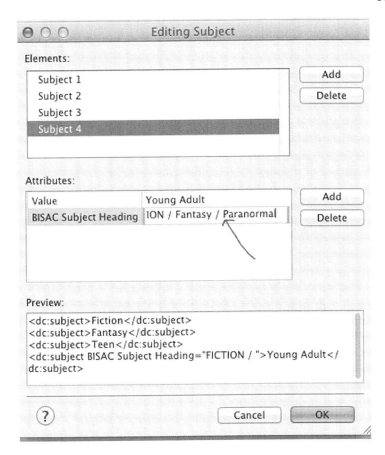

Next, repeat the same process. Begin by adding an element. This time add an attribute named **BISAC Subject Code**. This will allow you to enter the actual combination of letters and numbers that represent that code.

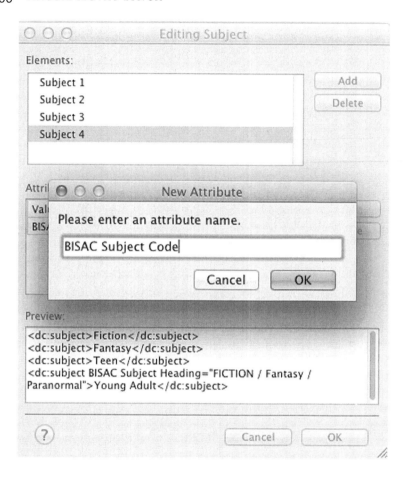

As you can see below, the subject code that relates to the heading above it is FIC009050. These two elements have now described the expected categorization scheme for United States titles.

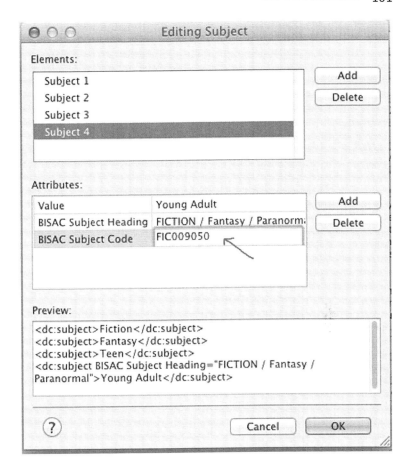

When you are finished with adding subjects, click the **OK** button.

The remaining basic metadata elements defined in the list earlier in this chapter will all need to be added as custom elements. I will demonstrate two of these, Abstract and Keywords, to show you how to create custom elements. You can then follow the same process for each of the metadata elements not already included on the project metadata panel.

The first custom element to add is Abstract. That is the 70-character short description of your book. Most writers will find that encapsulating their book in 70 characters (including spaces) is very challenging. Remember, the purpose of the abstract is to attract the reader. Think of this more as the pitch, the tag line in a movie poster—something that captures the essence of your book but is also a marketing tool.

To build a custom metadata element, click on the **Edit Custom Metadata** button in the bottom right corner of the metadata panel.

A window will pop up for your entry. Click the **Add** button to access the fields in the window. Type in the word **Abstract** as the new metadata name. Click the **OK** button.

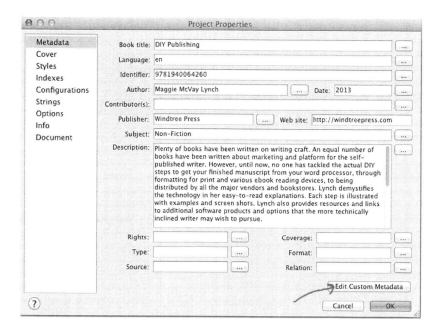

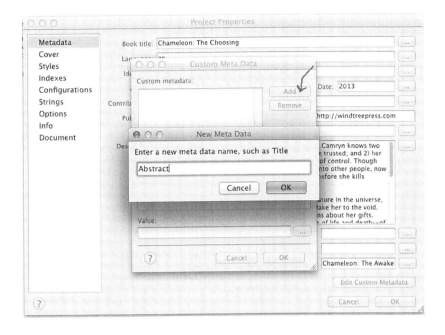

In the example below, I have copied and pasted in the Abstract for my book, *Chameleon: The Choosing*, into the **Value** field. It reads: **Her gifts can save or destroy everyone and everything she loves.** It certainly does not describe the whole book. I didn't need to worry about including the subject: young adult, fantasy, paranormal because that is already in the subject metadata and will be repeated in the keywords. What I needed was a line that reflected the stakes in order to draw the reader into the story.

Abstracts are important in many ways. When a potential reader Googles a book, it is often the Abstract (if designated) that is included with the link. On some ebook retailer sites, it is the abstract that appears when the buyer hovers over the book cover. You can also use the abstract as a header for the book on your website, or when introducing the book on your blog.

CHAPTER 8

Keywords Metadata

Next, let's consider keywords. This is an area that has engaged many bloggers, marketers, and search engine operators (SEO). It is one of the hottest topics of conversation among indie authors around the globe. That is because keywords is one of the few data fields on retailer sites that allow you to finally specify your own categories for your book—ones that may not appear in the BISAC list or in the retailers drop down box of subjects.

Although search engines can quickly sift through millions of pages, they are not very good at parsing bundles of text or images to work out meaning. Consequently, search engines rely on human-designed keywords to know what a book is about, and what is most important. This applies to both external search engines like Google and Bing, as well as to internal ones at retailer or publisher sites like Amazon, Kobo, and Windtree Press.

The name "keywords" is a bit of misnomer. Keywords actually refers to a collection of words and/or short phrases. Depending on the system, keywords are entered on separate lines or all together and separated by commas. My contemporary romance, *Healing Notes*, uses a combination of individual words and phrases for the keywords metadata. Here is part of my list in order of importance: contemporary, women's fiction, sensual, music, fiddle player, rape recovery, forgiveness.

Why this order? My book lies at the intersection between contemporary romance and women's fiction. Most vendor sites will let me select "Romance" as a subject category. However, beyond that selection it varies. Most vendor sites do not have a category called "women's fiction." Yet it is a well-known audience identifier among readers. The designation of "sensual" comes third because romance readers want to know the heat level of the book. With the first three keywords I have identified the the book for a specific audience. With the last three keywords I identify the character (fiddle player), the central theme (rape recovery), and the story arc (forgiveness). This is part of an ongoing series about musicians, so it was also important to include "music" as a keyword.

Selecting Keywords

The trick to selecting keywords is remembering that it's not about choosing the words that *you* think describe your book's subject. It's using the words *other people* use when searching. Keywords need to be selected carefully and placed in a hierarchy of importance. Though you can have many keywords identified in your metadata (rule of thumb is up to 255 characters, including commas and spaces), most vendor sites limit the number of keywords or phrases you can use. Some only allow seven

(Amazon), while others allow fifteen (Apple). The ranked list also helps you to determine how else you will use those keywords in other media as you talk about your book. The reuse of keywords in blog posts, review sites, twitter feeds, etc. will reinforce those words and make multiple connections to your book.

Think about how you might look for a book in a search engine. If you don't know the book name or the author, but someone told you about a book they loved, what would you likely remember? A plot element? A character trait? The genre? These are the very same criteria for choosing keywords and phrases.

Keyword categories to consider:
- Setting (WWII, urban, rural, forest, a different planet, a specific city or country)
- Character types (veteran, career woman, curmudgeon, teen, homeless, mentally ill, wizard, secret agent, femme fatale)
- Career types of characters (housewife, attorney, plumber, CEO, chef)
- Audience (women's fiction, teen, seniors, LGBT)
- Themes (coming of age, forgiveness, love, alienation, betrayal, survival, coming home)
- Story tone (feel-good, happy, funny, scary, mysterious, satirical)

Other keywords to consider are character names if you are writing an ongoing series. Readers may look for a book based on your protagonist's name. If you write under multiple pen names and you want readers to see the cross-over, you can include your other name(s) as a keyword as well. I am in the process of adding a keyword for Maggie Lynch on all of my fiction books. This is because many people know me by this name and, when they go to look for my books, they do not remember my pseudonyms. Those are lost sales for me.

It would be ideal if retailers like Amazon, B&N, Kobo, and Apple provided tools to help you understand their search algorithms, but they don't. Fortunately, there are two ways to help you determine the best keywords to use: 1) Google Keyword Planner tool; and 2) The autocomplete function at most vendor sites.

The Google Keyword Planner was designed for customers looking to use Adwords as part of their marketing campaign. In order to use the Keyword Planner, you will have to sign up for an Adwords account. If you already have a gmail account or a blogger account, you can use that to login. Don't worry; once you get into the Adwords you won't be charged unless you actually elect to start a campaign and set a budget. The tool is found at: http://adwords.google.com

When presented with the screen below, click on the tab titled **Tools and Analysis**. Then select **Keyword Planner.**

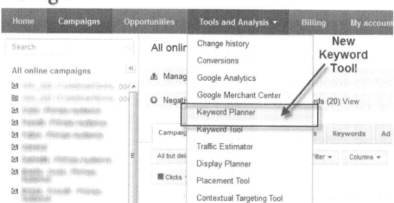

The Keyword Planner has a "wizard" interface. The first step in the process is to determine how you're going to go about creating your ad campaigns and ad groups. You're asked to pick one of four possible paths. You want to select the second option highlighted in the screen capture below: **Get keyword volume for a list of keywords or group them into ad groups.**

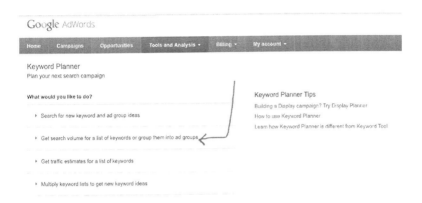

A search volume means that Google will run a search on all the times that keyword was used and tell you how many searches per month are usually conducted. When you click this item, a screen is displayed that allows you to enter the keywords of interest.

Enter your keywords with commas separating each one. Using a phrase as a keyword is also allowed. It doesn't matter whether your words are capitalized or not. In the illustrations below, I've elected to use some of the keywords identified for my young adult fantasy series: fae, paranormal, forest people, lichen, mutation, magic, magick. I chose to use the two popular spellings of magic to see if it made a difference in hits.

When you have entered all the key words you wish to evaluate, click on the **Get search volume** button at the bottom of the screen. In my example, all of the keywords together total 405,600 average monthly searches. This is a nice high number.

Click on the link to see each keyword delineated. In the next screen capture the results for each of the selected keywords are displayed.

Ad group: Keywords like: Forest People

Keyword (by relevance)		Avg. monthly searches	Competition	Suggested bid	Ad impr. share	Add to plan
fae		301,000	Low	$10.83	0%	
fantasy		49,500	Low	$0.88	0%	
paranormal		27,100	Low	$0.14	0%	
lichen		27,100	Low	$0.56	0%	
mutation		18,100	Low	$0.00	0%	
forest people		390	Low	$0.77	0%	

1 - 6 of 6 keywords

In this example, "fae" received the highest number of monthly searches at 301,000. The lowest number of searches is for "forest people" at only 300 searches per month. This tells me that if someone were to enter "forest people" in the search engine it is likely my book would be near the top of the list. However, not very many people search using that phrase. If a vendor site only allows five keywords I would certainly drop "forest people" from my list. On the other hand, the more keywords I am allowed to enter the higher likelihood of getting a good number of hits.

When I did this analysis prior to the release of my first two books, I found that the best keyword for me was "human chameleon" which only generated 110 monthly searches. Though that is a low count, combined with the category information of young adult and paranormal and magic, it creates a count of over 100,000 monthly searches. Those two words together describe my primary character as well as her dilemma, and is the motivational arc for much of the plot. If you can find a keyword like that for your novel or non-fiction work, you will want to use it everywhere possible. With those two words, when anyone enters "human chameleon books" in Google, my books will be on the first page of hits.

Tip: Remember, your keywords become part of the search after the primary metadata (title, author, and category) have already been taken into account. You want keywords that provide additional critical information to searchers.

I use "human chameleon" as the top keyword within my ebook files and in every description of the book I've provided at all vendors, on my blogs, on Facebook, on Pinterest, and on Twitter. In addition, because it is part of the book description, the words "human chameleon" are used by every reviewer. Reviewer blogs and articles also add to the ranking when search engines match words to determine importance or meaning.

Not every book will have such a unique keyword possibility. However, it pays to determine what is an exclusive combination of words for your book that will gain the most potential readers in your genre. Being unique on its own is not a road to riches. But having a concept or character who is intriguing within a genre is helpful and will provide a great keyword or phrase for you to use.

Next, let's look at how to evaluate keywords by looking at search engines at online retailer sites such as Amazon, Kobo, Apple, or B&N. Vendors and most online retail sites do not provide Google-like tools for evaluating keywords. However, most of them use an autocomplete function that provides the top keywords used by customers. These top keywords may change regularly, as the search engines constantly evaluate data and provide the most searched words at any particular day or hour (depending on how often it is refreshed).

In this illustration I'm going to compare the autocomplete keywords for both Kobo and Amazon. I'm going to use the word "paranormal" for both. In the Kobo books illustration below, paranormal brought up the following search possibilities: paranormality, paranormal media, paranormal love, paranormal state, paranormalcy (book 1), paranormal fright, etc. For Kiersten White, author of the book *Paranormalcy*, this is a great result. Her title fits the genre and is high on searches. For myself, it makes me consider if any of these higher searches fits my books. The closest would be "paranormal love." Even though this is a young adult series, there is a love interest. The results would suggest I add "paranormal love" as a keyword to my books at Kobo.

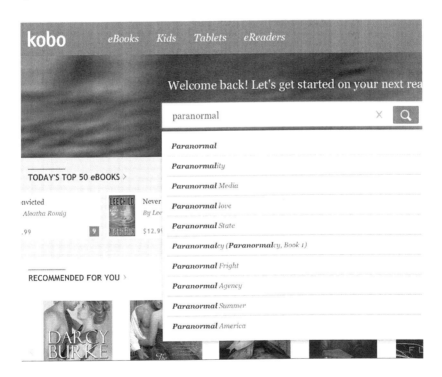

Let's try the same search at Amazon. In this case the results were quite different. As you can see in the screen capture below, "paranormal romance" and variations on it encompass five of the keyword searches. Other options are paranormal erotica, paranormal mystery, paranormal investigation, and paranormal books. As at Kobo, "paranormalcy" is also a highly searched term which when clicked will get Kierstin White's book at the top of the page.

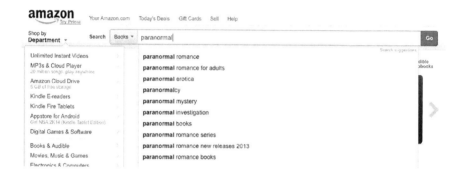

Whereas Kobo books provided insight for me to add "paranormal love" as a keyword for my book series, at Amazon I would make that keyword "paranormal romance."

At Barnes and Noble, the top keywords were paranormalcy, paranormal protection agency, and paranormal activity. At iTunes (Apple) the list contained paranormal witness and paranormal activity.

Tip: At Apple iTunes, searches for books are not separated from searches for and movie titles. Of the major online book vendors, the information gleaned in the iTunes autocomplete function is not as useful for authors.

In addition to evaluating keywords at vendor sites, it is also helpful to look at how bestselling books are categorized at each site. This may give you insight into how to choose categories for your books.

In determining categories, stick with bestsellers that are similar to your book. The easiest way to do this is to use the Amazon bestseller list. Amazon has several bestseller lists. Begin by selecting the one that is closest to how you are planning to categorize your book's subject.

To change things up, I've selected a non-fiction title this time, a memoir that is currently number one on the bestseller list: *I am Malala: The Girl Who Stood Up for Education and Was Shot by the Taliban*. Though it is true that this book has a unique background, lots of media attention, and a natural platform, you can still learn from the subject categorization selections. Many non-fiction writers create memoirs or books based on actual events.

Once I click on the book title, I scroll down to the "product details" where I can see the best sellers rank and the categories in which this book achieved bestseller status.

Product Details
File Size: 7626 KB
Print Length: 352 pages
Publisher: Little, Brown and Company (October 8, 2013)
Sold by: Hachette Book Group
Language: English
ASIN: B00CH3DBNQ
Text-to-Speech: Enabled
X-Ray: Enabled
Lending: Not Enabled
Amazon Best Sellers Rank: #19 Paid in Kindle Store (See Top 100 Paid in Kindle Store)
    #1 in Kindle Store > Kindle eBooks > Teen & Young Adult > **Biography**
    #1 in Kindle Store > Kindle eBooks > Biographies & Memoirs > Specific Groups > **Women**
    #2 in Books > Biographies & Memoirs > Specific Groups > **Women**

Notice the hierarchy of subjects where this book is #1 versus #2 and that the title is #19 overall in the Kindle Store. It is most difficult to achieve bestseller at the top of the subject tree (Kindle Store). This is because there are more titles competing. The Kindle Store has millions of titles, whereas the **Biography** subject under Teen & Young Adult has perhaps only tens of thousands of titles.

Amazon Best Sellers Rank: #19 Paid in Kindle Store (See Top 100 Paid in Kindle Store)

> #1 in Kindle Store > Kindle eBooks > Teen & Young Adult > **Biography**

> #1 in Kindle Store > Kindle eBooks > Biographies & Memoirs > Specific Groups > **Women**

> #2 in Books > Biographies & Memoirs > Specific Groups > **Women**

If I were writing a memoir or a biography, this categorization would give me ideas about subject categorization and keywords. First, I might not have thought about using Biography as a subject. I might have only thought of Memoir. Second, though the book is about a twelve year old girl—a good fit for the **Teen & Young Adult** category, the publisher also selected **Women** as a subject category lower in the tree with **Memoirs** and **Specific Groups**. This indicates that the publisher is looking for cross-over readers. Adults will certainly read this book. Finally, this book is available both in print and ebook. In print, the category where it reached bestseller status did not include teen & young adult at all.

Try this type of search for each of your titles and write down the categories that apply to you. It is very important that you categorize your book as deeply as possible in the subject tree. It is much easier to make a bestseller list online at a lower level in the heirarchy than at the top level (i.e., Kindle Store or Books). Once you've selected the lowest level, the book is automatically included at all levels above that in the tree hierarchy.

Putting keywords in the Jutoh metadata panel

Just as I demonstrated with "Abstract" metadata, you will want to create keywords metadata as a custom metadata field. Select the **Edit Custom Metadata** button at the bottom of the Project Properties Metadtata control panel. Click the **Add** button to create a new metadata tag. However, this time you will type in "keywords" as the tag title and click **OK**.

Type the keywords into the **Value** field. Remember to separate them by commas. In the example below I typed in the keywords associated with my book *Chameleon: The Choosing*. Once you have typed in all the keywords you wish to use, click the **OK** button.

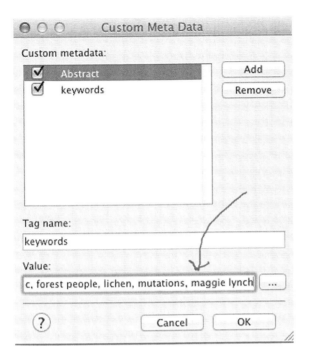

Tip: Be sure to save your list of keywords, and its hierarchy in a text file somewhere on your computer. You will be using them many times as you upload your files to each of the vendors. You will also want to use them as tags on your blogs, in guest posts, and anywhere else you can provide metadata about your book.

CHAPTER 9

Front Matter

Every book contains content prior to when the narrative starts (front matter) and after it ends (back matter). The placement of this content will vary depending on the format of the book. Print books have a traditional way of presenting information, beginning with the title page, copyright page, the dedication, and then the beginning of the primary content. Ebooks do not need to follow that same tradition. In fact, many ebook authors believe that most of the front matter should be placed at the back of the book. It is the author's decision. Let's look at what is included and why, as well as the pros and cons for placement.

Front matter refers to any content that comes prior to the main story or narrative. The traditional types of front matter include:

- Title Page
- Copyright Page
- Author Letter

- Foreward
- Table of Contents
- Dedication
- Acknowledgments

In addition, some publishers and authors choose to include the following in the front matter.

- A one page excerpt
- Advance praise and pull quotes
- A listing of other books by the author

Each of these elements serves a specific purpose. From the list above, the only required pages are the title page and the copyright page. I will discuss each page, its traditional purpose, and what options you might consider in electing to include that page or not and where to place it in your book.

The Title Page

The title page is important to reinforce the book title, author name, and publisher. If it is a print book and the cover has been torn or is missing, the title page still contains the information. If it is an ebook, depending on how the ebook files were constructed or the type of device used to read the electronic file, it is possible that the cover is not a part of the transmitted file. Thus the title page again serves as a means to identify the book.

In print books, the book's title is typically presented on the title page using the same font presented on the cover. If a subtitle is included, it would be centered below the main title. If the book is part of a series, the series title will then follow as the third item.

A number of spaces then separate the titling section from the author's name, which usually appears near the center of the vertical page. Finally, centered toward the bottom is the publisher's name, city, state, and country.

This is not always the case. Take the time to peruse six or seven books by different publishers in order to review the choices they make. You will see that some only include the title on the title page, while others may include the publisher's name but not the location information.

In ebooks the above is also true for the title page, except the font used on the cover is often not available to be used in an ebook or will not display in the same manner. When I create an ebook, I attempt to keep the font as close to the cover as possible simply to make it stand out. However, I do understand that some ereaders will translate the font to Times Roman and there is nothing I can do about it.

Copyright Page

The primary purpose of this page is to describe who owns the rights to the book and what, if anything, a person who buys a copy of the book can do with it. The copyright page also serves as the place where the publisher (you) provides bibliographic and contact information. Select three or four books from your library and examine the copyright pages. As I describe the elements identify where those are in your sample print or ebooks.

Though most copyright pages take up an entire page, the requirements are minimal. According to the United States Copyright office, you must include only three items:

- The symbol ©; the word "copyright"; or the abbreviation "Copr."

- The year of first publication. If the work is derivative or a compilation that incorporates previously published material, the year of first publication of the derivative work or compilation is sufficient.
- The name of the copyright owner.

For detailed information on the requirements review http://www.copyright.gov/circs/circ03.pdf .

The copyright information must appear in one of the following places:
- The title page
- The page immediately following the title page
- Either side of the front or back cover
- The first or the last page of the main body of the work

The most important element is the actual copyright statement which consists of three elements: the word Copyright or symbol ©; the year of the first publication of the work; and identification of the copyright owner (you or your company) by name. Typically, these three elements together look like this.

Copyright 2013 by Maggie McVay Lynch

or

© 2013 by Maggie McVay Lynch

or

Copyright © 2013 by Maggie McVay Lynch

The final example is the one used by most print book publishers. In the case of an ebook, the copyright symbol may not always display correctly. In that case, using the first example without the symbol is sufficient.

Note: Though the above examples are presented in italic font, that is not required and not recommended on your copyright page. I used this technique simply to separate examples from the primary narrative in this section.

Though the three elements on the previous page are all that is required by law to indicate copyright protection, there are other things you will want to include to meet the purposes of clarifying rights and providing contact and bibliographic information. It is also wise to also include the book title, the ISBN, location of publication, reservation of rights statement, and contact information. The contact information may be as simple as an email or as complex as a complete mailing address.

Your new copyright page with this additional information might look like this example.

Copyright © 2013 by Maggie McVay Lynch
DIY Publishing: A step-by-step guide to print and ebook formatting and distribution

ISBN 978-1-19400642-6-0
United States of America

All rights reserved.
For permissions contact: maggielynch@myaddress.com

Given that the above is all that is required and suggested, why would an author want to include anything else? Let's review the additional elements most often found on publisher copyright pages. Some of these may apply to you and others may not. However, it is important to understand what each element is and why you might choose to include it.

Book Edition. If this is the first time the book has appeared in any format, it is the first edition. If the edition is not listed, it is assumed this is the first edition. However, some publishers like to make this explicit. Also, some publishers like to differentiate the format. For example: "First print edition" or "First ebook edition".

If the book was published before by another publisher and you had the rights returned to you, you are now publishing a second edition and that should be included on the copyright page. If you made substantial changes to the book and are now redistributing it (e.g., you added several new chapters or did a major rewrite), the book may be considered a new edition.

Note: *A new edition requires a new ISBN.*

Expanded Rights Statement. Most publishers include an expanded rights statement that is a paragraph of information instead of the simple "All rights reserved" statement. Though this is not required, they want to be sure anyone reading the statement is clear on exactly what "all rights reserved" means. In addition, some ebook aggregators or distributors, like Smashwords, may require you to include them in your copyright page in order to be distributed by them.

Here is a typical example of an expanded all rights reserved statement.

Acknowledgment or Credit to Contributors. This is where you would list your cover designer, editor, interior book designer, or others who were part of creating this book. Though these listings are not required, I believe it is good form and richly deserved to credit those individuals who help to make a difference in getting your book formatted and ready for publication.

Note: This is different from the people you acknowledgment who supported your efforts both emotionally and factually (e.g., critique partners, friends, family, etc.). Those individuals are credited in your acknowledgments or dedication. In the copyright page for this book I acknowledged the cover designer for the book and the template designer for the interior.

Permission Statements. If you were required to get permissions to include certain types of details in your book, this is where those permissions are stated. For this book, because I used screenshots of Jutoh, I asked for permission from the software developer and acknowledged that permission on the copyright page. For a work of fiction, you may have sought and received written permission to use words from a song or specifics about a local restaurant. If you received written permission, this would be the place to acknowledge those things.

Publisher's Address and Contact Information. Larger publishers always want their information on the copyright page. This is a part of branding books and making a statement on quality related to the publisher. It also provides a way for anyone needing rights permissions to contact the publisher.

As I discussed earlier, I am an advocate of authors forming a publishing company entity as the holding place for all their publications. This can be as simple as a DBA, or as complex as creating a corporation. Whether you do that as an individual or as part of a group of authors, it provides a means to separate you as an individual from the public information on location and business correspondence. If you decide to create a publishing entity, you will want to provide that information just below the rights statement.

Return to the title page and copyright page at the front of this book and review how I provided the publisher information following the permission request.

For permission requests, write to the publisher, addressed "Attention: Permissions Coordinator," at the address or email below.

If you don't wish to form a separate publishing entity or join one, then the previous example of providing an email address or your own physical address is sufficient. It is definitely recommended that you provide some means by which you can be contacted for permissions. After all, you do not want to make it difficult for those seeking translation rights, movie rights, or game rights to find you and negotiate.

Ordering Information. This only applies if you are engaging in direct sales through your website or a publishing website. Publishers will provide order information for large quantities or special discounts. Though this applies primarily to print books, it is possible you would also want to make discounts available for multiple orders of ebooks as well. For example, perhaps you wish to allow school classrooms to order your young adult book at a discount. The language for ordering information is typically similar to that below.

Ordering Information:
Quantity sales. Special discounts are available on quantity purchases by corporations, associations, booksellers, and others. For details, contact the "Special Sales Department" at the address above.

The "address above" language refers to the contact information described as the publisher's address.

Cataloging-in-Publication Data (CIP). This is data received from the Library of Congress for participating publishers. (Note: This may differ significantly in other countries and how they catalog data for their libraries) Most self-publishers cannot participate in this program. However, author publishing cooperatives may want to consider this. There is no fee to get the data. The requirements are for a publisher to have a minimum of three titles by three authors in addition to the one being requested for cataloging. Publishers send information to the Library of Congress in advance of publication in order to get the cataloging data. Once the book is published, the publisher must send one copy to the Library of Congress. It is the receipt of this copy that replaces any fees.

If you are part of a publishing company that meets the criteria, definitely consider this. The price is very reasonable (one copy of the book). Once the CIP data is provided the book becomes part of a listing that goes out to all U.S. libraries. It is from that list that libraries order books. This type of easier access to libraries may be important—particularly for non-fiction books.

Most self-publishers are precluded from using this service. However, the Library of Congress does have another option called PCIP or Publisher CIP. This cataloging service is offered by other commercial entities that submit on your behalf. It requires an ISBN. The cost typically runs around $60-$80 per book. The downside is that the Library of Congress does not include these books in their weekly updates to libraries. However, other library entities (e.g., WorldCat) do and, depending on the private cataloger they may have authorization to upload your information to these other entities.

Is it worth it? If you believe your book should be in libraries it may be worth it. Alternatively, you can wait and see if a library purchases your book and creates the catalog entry for it. Once a library creates an entry it is shared with other libraries to use. Then you can use that in the future. Even if you donate a book to a library, or get them to purchase it, it may still take months before the book is actually shelved because of the cataloging requirement. Cataloging often goes to the bottom of a busy librarian's to-do list. Having this information in your book makes it easier for them and more likely to get it on the shelves quickly.

Here are two resources for doing the P-CIP:

http://www.fiverainbows.com/pcip.php

http://www.cipblock.com/

What *Not* to Include on Your Copyright Page. A "stripped book" statement. This is a statement seen on mass market paperback fiction. It is usually at the top of the page and set off in a box. Below is a copy of such a statement.

> The sale of this book without its cover is unauthorized. If you purchased the book without a cover, you should be aware that it was reported to the publisher as "unsold and destroyed." Neither the author nor the publisher has received payment for the sale of this "stripped book."

Most self-published books are in trade paperback or hardcover format. These formats are never stripped. Please do not include this on your copyright page unless you have made arrangements with an offset printer to produce mass market paperback books *and* have made arrangements with booksellers to return them to you stripped for credit.

Author Letter

The author letter is similar to a foreward in that it talks about the book, what to expect, and may include what inspired the author to write the book. It is addressed directly to the reader. This is a common practice in the romance genre. However, I've seen it employed in historical fiction, crime fiction, and in some non-fiction. The primary purpose is to share something with the reader that relates to the content or research of the book.

I used an author letter in a women's fiction novel that included rape recovery as the theme. I wanted readers to be forewarned in case this was an issue that was difficult for them. I also used the letter as a way to draw attention to the problems of rape and how different women react. Author Delilah Marvelle has used author letters in her historical romance fiction as a way to summarize the themes of the story and to express her interest in the research for the era.

Non-fiction authors most often use the author letter to discuss how they undertook the research and why this particular topic was of such importance or interest to the writer. In memoirs or self-help books, authors will sometimes use the author letter as a means to describe their expectations of the reader when they complete the book.

The author letter is usually placed at the front of the book, before the title page and copyright.

Foreword

A foreword is always written by someone other than the primary author of the book. It is often written by someone who is prominent in the field (in the case of non-fiction) or a bestselling author in the same genre (in the case of fiction). The narrative typically includes a story of how the foreword author and the book author know each other and why the foreword writer believes this book is worth reading. Later editions of a book sometimes have a new foreword which appears before an older foreword, if there was one. The new foreward might explain in what respects that edition differs from previous ones.

The primary purpose of a foreword is for marketing. An opening statement by a well-published author gives added credibility, a "stamp of approval" for the book. The foreword tends to appear after the table of contents but before the first chapter of the book.

Table of Contents

In a print book, the table of contents provides a quick index to all of the chapters. This is very important in a non-fiction book where a reader may skip chapters and move foreward and backward within the text.

Tip: Both Microsoft Word and Open Office have an automated means for generating a table of contents from headers within the book. See instruction links below for each platform. This can be a real time saver.

Microsoft Word: http://bit.ly/fhVMak
Open Office: http://bit.ly/JWsHDz

A fiction book rarely has a table of contents. Fiction is usually designed in such a way that the reader must engage with the earlier chapters in order to be caught up with the action and characters in later chapters.

Ebooks for both fiction and non-fiction have a type of table of contents. That is, they provide a linking and bookmarking system for chapters that helps readers to more easily stop and start without losing their place. When the reader returns to the book, she is placed within the chapter last read. It also allows readers to skip to different sections in the ebook. If you are using Jutoh to build your ebook files, you do not need to manually provide this table of contents. Jutoh automatically generates it for you, along with the bookmarks, from the chapter sections. If you are creating your files through HTML you will need to manually create these links yourself.

Dedication

This section is where you select a person or group to which you dedicate the book. The narrative tends to be short and personal. Authors frequently dedicate books to family members or friends who were particularly supportive. However, often a book is dedicated to someone who may never read it or may not even be alive. I've seen dedications to English teachers, parents, pets, or even to another author who inspired the writer.

The dedication is different from the acknowledgements section (see Acknowledgments below). The dedication tends to be more inspirational than practical. It is also possible to dedicate the book to someone and include him or her in the acknowledgments. For example, I dedicated my first published book, *Expendable*, to my husband because without his belief in me I would never have finished it. However, I also mentioned him in the acknowledgments specifically for his moral support and, because it involved military protocols that he knew and which helped me fashion the story.

Acknowledgments

This section is significantly longer than the dedication and includes all those who had some impact on getting the book completed. It includes practical assistance such as critique partners, beta readers, editors, and other authors who perhaps helped guide the work. It can also include friends and family who offered moral support, did housework during deadlines, or took the kids for a weekend while you recovered.

Similar to the dedication, the acknowledgments are definitely personal. It is up to the author to determine how short or long to make the acknowledgments. However, it is recommended not to exceed two pages. One page is preferred.

When acknowledgments are in the front matter, they typically appear after the dedication. However, in the last three to five years I have more often seen acknowledgments placed in the back matter following the last chapter.

Marketing Related Front Matter

The remaining types of front matter are all marketing-related materials. These are pages designed to convince the reader to buy the book. All of these tend to come before the title page.

A one page excerpt is used to draw the reader immediately into the story. It is rarely from the first page. The page is usually one with action and one which is typical of the genre. For example, in romance the excerpt might be a first kiss or a lead-up to sexual tension. In a thriller or suspense novel, the excerpt will be an action scene where the protagonist is put in jeopardy. The excerpt may come from any part of the book, but should not reveal a major turning point or the climax of the story.

Praise or pull quotes from advanced reviews are also used to convince the browsing reader to purchase the book. If this is the first book by the author, it helps to get some advanced reviews and include them in the front of the book. If it is a second or third book, you can also use the reviews from a previous book to draw readers in. This is particularly true if the second book is part of the same series.

When using advance praise, it is most helpful to get quotes from well-known authors in the same genre. In the case of non-fiction, getting quotes or reviews from experts in the field or other authors who have written on the same topic is critical. The key to using these quotes is not to provide an entire review, but to pick out parts of the quote that are most likely to pull in a reader. Adjectives like top-notch, fast-paced, true-to-life, and insightful are all good ones for fiction. For non-fiction, look for quotes with words like comprehensive, practical, applicable, and invaluable. Of course, any words that capture the nature of the book and the excitement in reading it are great to have.

The final type of marketing front matter that is often included is a listing of other books by the author. Depending on the purpose, some writers prefer to put this listing at the back of the book instead of the front. The decision whether this should be front matter or back matter has to do with where you are in your writing career.

In fiction, if you are a fairly new author—perhaps with only two or three books—it might be advantageous to have them at the front. This alerts potential buyers or reviewers that you are not a one-book author. Also, if the book is part of a series, it helps to have the entire series listed at the front of the book. In this way, the potential buyer immediately knows that perhaps she should go back and get the previous books first to make she enters the series with full knowledge of the characters and the world set up.

If you have written many books, or books that are unrelated to each other, consider moving this section to back matter.

The question to ask yourself in making decisions about all the marketing front matter is: If a reader is finding my books for the first time, what will most impress him or her about me and this book? The answer will help you decide where to place your book list and other materials.

CHAPTER 10

Back Matter

Back matter is all of the materials that come after the end of the narrative. As discussed in the previous section, an author may choose to place some typical front matter text in the back. Some things to include in the back matter that I've already discussed are acknowledgments and a list of other books by the author.

The primary purpose of the back matter is to get readers to purchase another book by the author or the publisher. It does this by focusing on two areas: marketing additional books by the author; and convincing readers to learn more by signing up to receive newsletters or emails about upcoming books. Let's look at each of these techniques. Whether you have only one book or many books, both of these techniques can increase your future sales.

Marketing Additional Books by the Author

Previously, I've discussed providing a listing of additional books. For a print book, it is helpful to provide a list divided by genre and series relationships. With an ebook, you can provide a link directly to where the reader can buy each book. It is easiest if those links are on your website so you can provide a single link for each book that has all the vendors who distribute your books.

If you only have a few books to offer, you may wish to include a very brief description for each book (three to four lines) along with a thumbnail cover to entice readers to try them. If you have more than three or four books, a simple listing of the books is sufficient. If the book that has just been completed is part of a series, you definitely want to include all other books in the series as part of your list—including unpublished titles if you know the titles and approximate release dates.

Another very popular tool to tempt readers to buy the next book is to offer a "sneak preview" by providing an excerpt or the entire first chapter in the book you are marketing. This is particularly important if you are doing a series and something difficult or horrible has happened to the main character at the end of your book. You want readers to know that in the next book, either the main character or those close to her will be looking to resolve the problem. Even if the next book isn't finished, it helps to provide this first chapter to let readers know it is scheduled and coming soon.

If you don't have another book to offer or your other books are in a different genre with a different reading audience, consider partnering with another author to exchange "sneak peeks." Perhaps you know someone who writes dragon stories similar to yours. You can feature the first chapter from one of her books in exchange for her featuring the first chapter from one of your books. You both win and you've already begun some cross-promoting and marketing together.

I'm doing an exchange with this *DIY Publishing* book. My fiction titles don't serve as good preview candidates for this book on publishing. Furthermore, my previously published non-fiction books about technology and distance learning also do not have the same audience as this book. So, I am partnering with author Jamie Brazil and her non-fiction book geared to newer writers. We will both feature first chapter excerpts of our non-fiction books in the "sneak peak" back matter of our books.

Jamie's non-fiction book for writers titled *Some Writer's Deserve to Starve* is a great companion piece to my book because we cover similar concerns but from different places in a writer's career. I focus on the self-published writers whose manuscripts are ready to be published; her book is aimed at authors pursuing traditional publication through agents and editors. Where my book focuses on formatting and distribution, Jamie's book helps the writer to market to agents and editors through techniques like the proposal, the abstract, the tag line, the pitch and queries. The skills that writers will aquire in both books will help them to achieve their career goals.

Getting the reader invested in learning more

Two things that every writer needs to gain sales are reviews of the book and readers who wish to learn about upcoming books. Reviews helps readers who are browsing determine what other readers liked or disliked about your book. Inviting readers to join a mailing list provides you with a built-in means of providing information every time you publish. The best way to get both of these is to ask for it.

At the back of every one of my books, print and ebook, I do two things: I ask readers to consider leaving a review and I ask them to sign up for my mailing list. In the ebooks I provide a clickable link to my mailing list.

Let me share with you ideas about how to make these requests. I present both requests on the same page. These requests are the positioned on the page following the end of the narrative and before any other back matter. When a reader finishes your book and feels satisfied, it is the best time to get him or her to act. The best way to determine exactly what you want to say is to read several examples from other authors and determine what fits your voice and style. Below is mine. Feel free to use my words, or some variation, in your own books.

Example at the back of each book in my
YA Fantasy series.

New Release Mailing List
Want to find out what happens next to Camryn and the rest of the forest people? Sign up for my mailing list http://maggiefaire.com/mailing-list.html *to be the first to know when the next book comes out. I do not spam anybody and I do not release your name or email to anyone else. You only receive an email when the next book is within one month of availability. Also, any pre-release deals or special sales for the books will go first to those on the mailing list.*

Consider Writing a Review
Word-of-mouth is crucial for any author to succeed. If you enjoyed the book, please consider leaving a review on Amazon, or on GoodReads. GoodReads reviews are imported to many places including Kobo, Apple,

and Windtree Press. If you are a librarian and subscribe to LibraryThing or Shelfari, please also consider leaving a review there. Even if it's only a line or two, it would make all the difference and would be very much appreciated.

Example from Jamie Brazil's YA Historical Fiction, *The Commodore's Daughter.*

I can't give you permission to use this one because it definitely reflects her personality and style. It is also specific to this book. However, I wanted to offer it as an example of how you can insert your own voice into your requests.

And now, a personal appeal from Jamie:

Thank you for reading The Commodore's Daughter. I hope you enjoyed the story as much as I enjoyed writing it. Commodore Perry's journey of 1853 has been widely documented. There are genealogical accounts of the Commodore's wife and daughter, Caroline. However, Caroline did not have a sibling. While this novel has elements of a historical event that dramatically transformed two countries, Jennifer Perry is a fictional character.

She was also a labor of love. This novel took over five years to complete. And I swore to never write another historic novel again... except... well... I'm fascinated with the past and history has a way of seeping into my brain and leaking out my fingertips. In flawed, but perhaps interesting ways.

You be the judge. Which is what I'm asking you to do.

Strike asking. How about begging? Please, please, please share your thoughts in the form of a review. Reader reviews are the engine of independent publishing, and your opinion – whether you loved this novel or hated it – helps shape the future for digital books and indie authors like myself.

The future is at your fingertips. Please share your thoughts!

Sincerely,
Jamie Brazil

Example of providing incentive for a review instead of a direct request.

Please tell other readers why you liked this book by reviewing it at one of the following websites: Amazon, Barnes and Noble, or Goodreads. If you do write a review, please send an email to author @gmail.com. I would like to gift you a copy of the next book in the series as a way of thanking you.

Other Back Matter

Book lists, sneak previews, and requests for readers to do reviews and join mailing lists all meet the criteria for using marketing in backmatter. There is also back matter that relates to the book itself and helps the reader to engage or learn more about the story or to use a non-fiction book more effectively. Those things would be:

- Index - Only used in non-fiction, the index provides an easy way to find terms in the main body of the text. It is a type of navigation guide to the book.

- Glossary – For fiction, this might contain foreign words or phrases used in the story. For non-fiction, it would contain specialty jargon relating to the content (e.g., a list of computer terms).
- Maps of relevant areas.
- Links to additional references or more information.
- Afterword – Similar to a foreword, the afterword explores how the book came to be written or how the ideas were developed. It is written by the book's primary author. In later editions, the afterword might be written by a well-respected individual who comments on the book's impact.
- Appendix – Only used in non-fiction, it provides supplementary materials to the book that usually add details, tables, raw data, or updates and corrections to earlier material.
- Bibliography or Reference List – Primarily used in non-fiction books that are research intensive. Memoirs, self-help, or opinion pieces that attempt to consolidate "common knowledge" on a subject rarely contain a bibliography, though they may contain footnotes or links to additional information.

Finally, you should always include links to your website, blog, and social media. If you have a publishing company and a site that represents your books, you should include that on the final page of the book.

CHAPTER 11

Cover Design

An attractive cover can convince someone to buy your book without knowing anything more than the genre. A bad cover will just as surely cause a potential buyer to turn away from all your hard work. I am the first to admit that I do not prepare my own covers. I learned early on that just because I have a good eye for selecting images and know my way around Photoshop does not mean I can create an eye-catching and effective cover. It is more than technique and more than "I'll know it when I see it." It is art; and because covers are so critical to sales, I've chosen to always have a professional cover designer create mine.

However, even if you hire a cover designer, it still helps to understand what makes a good cover. A designer will ask what you want, ask you to point to covers you like, and may ask you to send stock image comps for her to use in your cover.

Cover design consists of marrying image, color, and typography in a way that not only captures the reader's attention but also conveys the genre and story theme. That is a lot to accomplish! So, what is it that makes a great cover? I've narrowed it down to four important first-impression items.

1. It looks professional. In other words, it looks like something NY would put out.
2. It fits genre expectations.
3. The author's name is easy to read, even in thumbnail view at only 150 pixels tall.
4. The title is easy to read and the typography is indicative of the genre.

Let me share a few of my own covers and talk about what works and what doesn't. I've learned this over the past three years and I hope to save you some of that trial and error.

First the good. My cover for *Chameleon: The Awakening* has drawn in readers beginning with my first cover reveal several months before the book was available. It is the only one of my book covers that booksellers, readers, and other authors always tell me they love. Many reviews of the book have begun with "I was drawn in by the cover."

After my first book signing for this series, the bookseller loved the cover so much she had it made into a giant poster and hung in the window in order to intrigue buyers to come into the store.

Of all the covers I have loaded on Pinterest, this cover gets the most interest and re-pins. In short, having a great cover will get you exposure in a lot more places than in an online catalog. Is it surprising that this book has done better than any other so far?

What works with this cover? First it has a central image that is appealing. Most YA fantasy and paranormal books feature the protagonist as the central image, so this meets the genre expectations. The typography says "fantasy book." The title and author's name are all easy to read. The series' title is also clear. In other words, it hits all the reader's buttons.

Now let's look at a not-so-successful cover and its replacement to understand what went wrong.

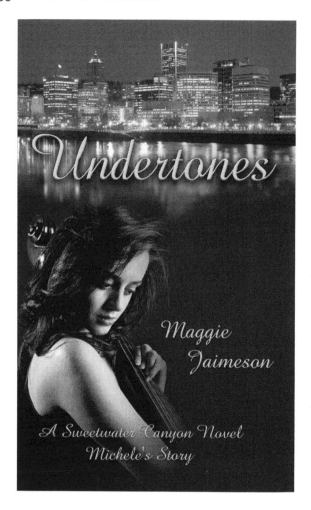

Looks gorgeous, doesn't it? It is professionally done and it has all the elements I asked for. When I received it, I immediately fell in love with the composition, colors and "feeling" of the image. However, I now know there are two major problems and a minor problem with the cover: 1) This is a romance and the romance genre expects a couple on the cover. I only have the protagonist. 2) The author's name and the series name are too small. In thumbnail you can't read the author's name at all. 3) It is too dark.

This is not the artist's fault. She was following my rules. However, contemporary romance readers expect lighter backgrounds. Now, let's look at the revised cover.

The image of the protagonist is the same, but now the male romantic interest is there as well. My name is easily seen and the series name has been moved to the center of the page. Though there is still a lot of black in it, the cover feels lighter because of the window and the blue sky background. Also, the use of the window grounds the primary image in a room instead of floating in front of the water. In the thumbnail all the important elements can be seen and read.

The best way to understand covers is to go to a large bookstore or surf online at publisher sites. Do a search on the genre where you believe your book fits and look at the top selling novels (25-50). See what patterns you can define. A good example is YA paranormal books. They almost always have a single teen as the focus of the cover. In contrast, middle-grade paranormal books almost always have an animal or magical person/creature as the focus of the cover. Very different approaches.

Women's fiction may not have a person on the cover at all. It may be a place instead. If there is a person, it tends to be a woman alone, often without her face showing. A suspense or a thriller cover needs to be ominous and dark. Most suspense protagonists are often depicted in silhouette or in shadow. Historical novels have a definite sense of the period—castles, period dress, and antique items feature regularly on covers. Literary novels tend to be all over the map. Science Fiction novels must indicate the science part of the novel on the cover. Space ships, robots, and computers are all popular cover elements.

Non-fiction also has genre types. Memoirs echo much of women's fiction covers—places or single individual pictures. Self-help books are light or saturated with primary colors designed to make the reader feel confident and positive. Non-fiction tends to stress a single image or frequently uses just words and color.

A mistake authors often make is to try to recreate a particular scene on the cover. The difficulty with this approach is that the scene can quickly get busy and there is no room for the author's name, the title, or other details that need to stand out.

Similar to the important one-scene mistake, authors try to capture the entire plot of the book on the cover. For example, I knew an author writing a mystery set in the 1920's. As part of unraveling the mystery the protagonist had to find a special candle, was stabbed by the bad guy, and ended up in a cobblestone alley. She wanted the protagonist dressed to the nines, slumped in the alley with her pearls, candle, and a knife in a circle around her. Though it meant a lot to the author, the reader picking up the book wouldn't have a relationship to all the objects. Once again it becomes too busy. Selecting the same cobblestone street with only a bloody high heel surrounded by pearls could still invoke the sense of history and danger that the author wants while leaving much more space for typography and focus.

Frequently, the best image is the simplest image with one central focal point. The concept is not to depict scenes, but rather to capture a feeling. Look at covers that draw you in and write down what feeling you get when you view that cover. Then consider how your cover can represent something similar and yet relate to your unique story.

A great resource for studying cover design is the monthly book cover design awards at Joel Friedlander's site. http://www.thebookdesigner.com/2013/09/e-book-cover-design-awards-august-2013/

Each month he takes 50-80 covers that are submitted by independent authors and designers. He comments on what works and what doesn't. Every time I look at his site, I realize how important it is for the typography and image to work together and I count my blessings that I have a good cover designer who understand my genres.

Branding

The primary purpose of your cover is to sell more books. Assuming you understand the genre expectations, the next thing to consider is branding. There are three elements to consider in cover branding—author, genre, and series. If you only write in one genre you are in an easier branding situation than authors who write in multiple genres like me.

Writers never know what is going to hit first in branding. For some authors it is their series. They begin a series and somewhere around book three it starts to take off. That is a brand to capitalize on. Branding a series involves more than using the series title somewhere on the book, it also requires using the same look and feel for every book in the series. You want readers to immediately recognize your book while flying through online catalogs or review sites. It needs to stand on its own and shout, "This is your series!" before they see the title or the author's name.

My YA Fantasy series is about "the forest people." Therefore I've made the choice that every book will have a background of green forest or moss. Lichen plays a major role throughout the series, so it is also on every cover in some way (usually on the protagonist). I am using the name "Chameleon" in every title to help readers immediately connect with the series. They may not remember every book title, but they will know the primary character is a human chameleon. You already saw the font I use. It is distinctive. I'm sure someone else has used that font on a book, but it's not one I see often on fantasy and paranormal titles. All of these elements are series branding.

Author branding on a cover is also achieved through distinct typography. Are you known as an author who writes "dark" narratives or "light" homespun stories. author. It makes a difference in how your readers perceive you and find your books. The typography for your name needs to reflect that brand from one book to the next. Again, writing only in one genre simplifies matters. If you are writing in two or three genres, consider a typography that is cross-genre for your name.

The CAP rule – contrast, alignment, proximity

I admit, I made up the acronym CAP. I like mnemonics that help me remember principles. Stacie Vander Pol, owner of Cover Design Studio, talks the "rule of thirds" and the "golden triangle" in graphic design. I was never trained as a graphic designer, so I highly recommend reading her two part tutorial on cover design at her website.
http://www.coverdesignstudio.com/layout-rule-of-thirds-diagonal-scan-and-more/

Stacie also provides two well-organized YouTube tutorials for designing your cover using Gimp and Photoshop Elements.

Gimp http://www.youtube.com/watch?v=CONohk1H684

Photoshop Elements
http://www.youtube.com/watch?v=YZ3o7Z02aLM

I will summarize her "rule of thirds" and how I believe it also illustrates the CAP rule. Stacie states that elements on the page should be divided into thirds, either horizontally or vertically. This makes the image more appealing and fits the **alignment** part of the CAP rule. The center third is the focal point and thus usually where the highest **contrast** occurs—where you want the eye to look first. The horizon of the image should appear in the the upper or lower third rather than straight through the middle. This relates to the **proximity** part of CAP.

The Western eye views images from the top left to the bottom right. Composing the image and typography to take advantage of this comfort zone feels "right" to buyers.

Below is an example of a simple but eye-catching cover from William Hertling that uses the rule of thirds well. Consider whether this meets the expectations of his SF readers.

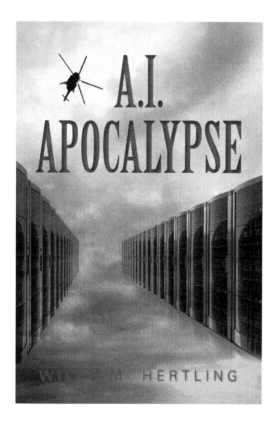

Proximity places the central image—the banks of servers—in the center third of the page. Alignment places the title in the upper third and the author name in the lower third. The contrast of the red typography with the black and white picture not only makes the title and author name stand out, but also frames the central image while suggesting the possibility of fear and destruction. Placing the helicopter in the top left helps the eye track from left to right and balances the slightly off-center diminishing horizon in the primary image. The only thing I would suggest changing on this cover is to make the author's name larger. I suspect that in thumbnail, his name is unreadable.

I don't know if William Hertling did the cover himself or not. I do know it is a self-published title that has done well in the market. The image, titling, and typography also match the science fiction genre in which he writes.

Typography

The title, author name and series title are absolute musts for all books. In addition, you may wish to include tags—a descriptor or modifier to the title or author's name. The key is not to use every bit of space on the cover. The eye needs rest. If the tags overwhelm the central focus the cover appears busy and distracting. On the other hand, tags can make great points and help readers make the decision to buy.

Bestselling authors (i.e., USA Today or New York Times Bestselling Author) definitely want to include that tag on every cover. The placement should be near your name—either above or below. Tags should be identified with the part of the typography it modifies. Your bestselling status is part of your author brand.

I have seen many books that simply have "Bestselling Author" or "Award Winning Author" as the tag on the cover. Carefully consider what that says to readers. The fact that the bestselling or award winning status is not defined is a red flag to many readers. Unfortunately, too many independent authors have been putting those undefined tags on books in an attempt to compete more effectively. All it takes is one or two readers to research your claim and if it turns our your award was for an unpublished manuscript or a paid position on a small list your reputation is sullied.

If you have won a major published book award in your genre, by all means say so. RITA Award Winner does garner respect from romance readers. Hugo Award Winner is important to science fiction readers. Winning an Edgar or Agatha in mystery is also something worthy of putting on the front cover.

However, if your award was won in a contest where you submitted three chapters prior to publication, I'm not sure that is the best use of your brand. Certainly, you should be proud of it. But save those types of awards for your author biography.

The same reasoning applies to tagging yourself as "Bestselling Author" on the cover. If you aren't willing to state how or where you are a bestseller it should not be on the cover. Again, readers are wary of this title. It seems that every indie author is a bestseller somewhere which makes the tag useless if it isn't associated with a known list like USA Today, New York Times, or Publishers Weekly. Being in the Amazon Top 100 when you put your book up free downloads does not count. Being a bestseller at a small press where bestselling means you sold thirty books in one month or even 100 is not worth the possibility of tainting your author brand.

What if you are an Amazon bestseller or a Barnes & Noble bestseller on the paid list? Honestly, I'm not sure how that works as an author tag. Personally, I would consider using that as part of my excerpts and quotes in the front of the book rather than on the cover. Of course, it is up to you what to put on your book. Just remember the trade offs and possible consequences.

You don't have to have "Bestselling Author" or "Award Winning Author" on your cover to sell books. In fact, that is far down readers' lists of how they find you or choose to take a chance on you. Readers identify they find new authors first because of an interesting cover, then by reading a good blurb, and finally by being drawn into an excerpt or viewing the first chapter. Seeing "Bestselling Author" on the cover falls somewhere around number nine on a list of top ten items.

Be proud of who you are as a published author and confident in what you write. Let your name and the work speak for itself. Don't allow desperation for sales now create false impressions of your author brand that will haunt you in the future. If your cover is inviting and the book is interesting, it will find a readership. Your popularity will build. When you win a major award or make a major bestseller list is the time to make it part of your author brand and tag the cover.

Another tag often used on covers is a pull quote or short review blurb. This type of tag should be placed near the title. In this case, a quote or blurb is modifying a particular work. Pull quotes work best when they are from a major reviewer or a bestselling author in your genre. If your quotes do not meet that criteria, leave them off the cover. Instead, use them in the interior as part of the front matter.

Below are two covers that use all of these tags while maintaining author, genre, and series branding.

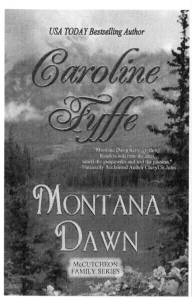
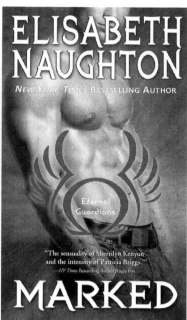

Note that both authors have their bestselling tags near their name. In Fyffe's instance, she has placed it above her name. Naughton put the tag below her name. Both work because the placement is in a section of the image that is not too busy. These novels are part of a series and the series branding is obvious. The McCutcheon Family books all have the small badge at the bottom. The Eternal Guardians novels always display the omega symbol and the name inside as a series tag.

Both authors also have pull quotes on the cover. On *Montana Dawn,* the quote is more centered, instead of pulled closer to the title. On *Marked*, the quote is obviously tagged to the large title. Finally, on both covers the title and author names are easy to read at this size and at thumbnail size.

One more possibility is to use a "tag line" that represents the book or series instead of a pull quote. Below is another example from Elisabeth Naughton. Above the title she has placed a tag line to capture the essence of the story arc. It reads: "He lost her once. He won't lose her again." Along with the cover images which meet romance genre expectations, good typography on the title and author name, this short tag line adds one more draw to move a potential reader toward a buy decision. It must have worked. *Wait for Me* was Elisabeth's first book to make the New York Times Bestseller List. It stayed at number one and two for a long time.

Selecting Art

Few writers are photographers or artists. This means that it is most likely you will be using licensed photography, also known as "stock photography." There are many stock photography sites. The key is to find one or two that seem to meet most of your needs. Below are the ones I'm personally familiar with using.

iStockphoto http://www.istockphoto.com/

Fotolia http://us.fotolia.com/

Dreamstime http://www.dreamstime.com/

Getty Images http://www.gettyimages.com

Most sites require you to pre-purchase "credits." These are usually sold as one dollar equals one credit. The cost per credit decreases with the more credits you purchase. Because of this you want to be sure that whatever site you choose is one that is likely to have many images you can use. Images include photographs, original art work, videos and vector art.

Be cautious when using art from a non-stock site. For example, many authors may fall in love with a particular piece of original art from a site like Deviant Art. It has certainly happened to me. The difficulty with sites like that is that they are set up primarily as a portfolio showcase for the artist. They are not set up as an ecommerce site, nor does it have standard licensing. This means the author must negotiate with each artist separately. Some of the artists are familiar with licensing and have contracts ready to go while others do not, which leaves the onus on you. Furthermore, artists may leave art up for long periods of time but be virtually unreachable as they haven't checked into the site for years.

The key to finding stock images that meet your needs is using search terms at these sites. In addition to searching by descriptions (e.g., female, brunette), also search by moods (e.g., sad, happy, pensive) and by locations (e.g., Scotland, Maine, New Zealand, urban, rural).

Once you have located something that is close, also search the artist's portfolio. You can usually do this by clicking on the artist's name. Some sites also have a link titled "more of this model" or something similar. This means it will look for additional images that were part of the same photo shoot, as well as pictures of the same model.

It is easy to fixate on a particular model because he or she matches the character in your mind. For me, that often happens on some of the more expensive images. Because my budget is limited, I always look for model images that are under $5 for the size I need. On special occasions I might go as high as $10. I'm not willing to pay $50 or $100 because I like to keep my per book costs down as much as possible and I know my cover designer will make the model into what I need. Your budget and choices may be different.

Consider partial images. Though it is wonderful to find a single image you love, often covers are made up of two or three images blended together. Also remember, if you are working with a cover designer, or have the skills yourself, things like hair color and eye color can be changed. Skin tones can be lightened or darkened, and a certain amount of clothing can be added or modified. In other words look for the big ideas.

Once you have selected images, download the comps. These are images that are smaller and tend to be watermarked with a copyright symbol or the photo distributor name in it. The purpose is for you to play with them and see if they will really work for you. Ignore the distracting watermark and mock-up a cover, by placing the images in the positions and proportions you were considering. Once you are sure the images do what you need, go back and pay for the appropriate license.

For example, on my cover for *Chameleon: The Choosing*, I provided three different images to the cover designer. One was an image of a cave with a waterfall. There were people in the cave and outside. Another was an image of a girl walking in a forest of brown trees. The third was an image of a young man lying face down in a grassy water area. The cover designer was able to take the individual images and manipulate them, then blend them on the cover into a single image. This takes time, skill, and talent. If you don't have these skills or time, contract with a professional.

Below, see thumbnails of the original three images given to the cover designer, and then the finished product. Total cost to purchase the stock images from iStockphoto was 23 credits. Because I had previously purchased a large batch of credits on sale, the actual cost for me was $12.00 for all three images.

In the first image, notice that the model is walking in a brown forest and is facing in a different direction. On the final cover design, the designer increased the hair color to be a more vibrant red and changed the eye color to be blue. The hair and eye detail matches the model in the first book of the series, even though we did not use the same model. The designer also changed the direction the model faced and placed her in the cave. She added lichen growing on her arm, which is a feature of the protagonist in each book. Lichen gives the forest people special magical powers.

In the second photo, the male model is in a very different environment than the cave where he was placed on the cover. The stock photo shows him in a flooded grassy and the full nude body is exposed. In the cover, the lower half of the body is covered in moss and the model is placed on a slope. Also, like the protagonist, lichen was added to his body.

A good cover designer can take parts of photos and manipulate them to fit the needs of your novel. You do not have to find the exact model in the exact location that matches your novels story. Models can be cut out and put elsewhere, images reversed, hair color changed, clothing added or taken away to a certain extent, clothing colors changed, skin color lightened or darkened. In the same way a makeup artist for movies can create a different creature or make an actor look unrecognizable, so can I good cover artist.

The cave image above is the primary background photo for the cover. Though it is hard to see in this thumbnail, there were people hiking both inside and outside the cave that needed to be removed. In addition, the cover designer added more moss throughout the picture and darkened the clouds and sky to increase the ominous mood I wanted to portray. The completed cover design is below.

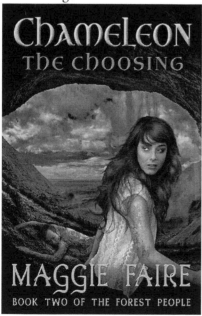

Though your cover may not be as complex as this one, I hope this example helps you to see that an image does not have to be perfect when you purchase it. It needs to be close to expressing the idea you want to convey. With photo manipulation, highlights, contrasts, and color changes the cover can become unique, eye-catching, and meet your needs with a little work.

Stock Photo Licensing

Be sure to read the licenses associated with the photos you wish to buy. You pay by the size of the photo and the license type on the photo. Remember, that for print books you need 300 dpi quality. This usually means you need files that are approximately 2200 pixels on the long side. In most stock photo purchase sites this file size is labeled "large" or "extra large."

For images to be used only for ebooks, 72 to 150 dpi will be sufficient for most displays. However, you do need to worry about the requirements at each vendor. It seems that size standards increase every year or two as tablet and ereader technology advances. Amazon is now requiring 1200 pixels with 2100 pixels on the long side preferred. I would go for the largest size you can afford.

When you evaluate licenses, look for the following items and make sure they are covered to meet your needs.

- *Time Limits* – What is the cost and what does that buy you? You want to make sure you can use that image in perpetuity. A time-limited license (i.e., 2 years) is not helpful when it is likely your book will be available for decades.

- *Use Limits* – Does the license only allow you to use it on your cover? What if you want to put the cover on your website or use it in a marketing campaign? Make sure the license allows that. Sometimes you will have to pay more for that privilege.

- *Model Release* – Does the license include a release from the model and what does that entail? Most licenses do include model releases of some type. However, some models include restrictions on the use of the image. For example, the model cannot be clothed in certain types of outfits or posed within certain scenarios. Most of these restrictions are sexual in nature. If you are looking for sexy poses for your book be sure to select models who are already posed in that manner in the original image. Their release will likely be unrestricted for that type of use.

Though stock photo licenses can contain a variety of restrictions, most sites have three types of licenses available: royalty-free, rights-managed, and extended. The royalty free license is the most common and affordable. I always look for those licenses first. Some sites call this royalty free license "standard license."

Royalty-Free License. Royalty free means you can use the image multiple times, without paying a royalty. The downside of royalty free is that the images are non-exclusive, meaning anyone can purchase and use them. This sometimes results in seeing a particular image on lots of book covers (e.g., a man and woman kissing). When choosing a royalty free image, you may wish to scan a number of book covers in your genre and make sure that particular image is not being used on very many of them.

Because all of my book covers use only parts of images and often change them significantly (e.g., hair color, location, clothing), I never purchase an exclusive license. The book cover with a variety of art becomes a separate image that is unique. Unless you are using a single image for your cover, and it is important to be exclusive, I don't recommend paying for exclusivity. Exclusivity costs hundreds and often thousands of dollars. Royalty free images are often as little as $2 to $5 and have the most lenient permissible uses for both commercial and personal projects.

On the other hand, if you are planning a series of books and want to be sure the same model is available for all of them, you might consider working with a professional photographer and doing an actual photo shoot. If you are a professional photographer this is a great way to get exclusive photos. If you are paying a photographer, this may cost you $300 to $500, depending on time and model fees. Amortized over many books in a series, it may be worthwhile in the end. It all depends on your budget and how important exclusivity and having the same model are to you.

Rights-Managed License. A rights-managed license offers exclusive, time-limited use of a stock image. This will cost more than the royalty free license. The license is granted on a pay-per-use basis. That means the image can only be used for one particular project *and* for a set period of time. Some licenses are specific to a geographic area (i.e., only in Oregon or only in the United States). This type of license is rarely used for book covers. It is more often used for a specific marketing campaign.

Extended or Enhanced License. An extended or enhanced license is usually a license that "extends" permissions for a royalty free license. For example, most royalty free licenses allow you to use the image in many venues—on your cover, on your website, in marketing campaigns, etc. However, they do not allow you to resell the image in other products, such as on a calendar, t-shirts, greeting cards, or a print-on-demand image of your primary character. If you anticipate selling the royalty free images beyond the use in your book cover, then you will need the Extended or Enhanced License.

In most cases, you can purchase a standard license and if your needs change, return and purchase a different license to meet upgraded needs. This is more costly than purchasing the correct license the first time. However, if you are unsure of your use beyond the book cover, I suggest purchasing the license that best meets your immediate needs. That is the least expensive option.

Aspect Ratios

Another important part of cover design is understanding the expected aspect ratio of the finished design. Print books and ebooks have sightly different preferences. A professional cover designer understands this and therefore gives you different cover aspect ratios for print and ebooks.

What is an aspect ratio? It is a graphic term that describes the relative horizontal and vertical sizes. For example, if a graphic has an aspect ratio of 2:1, it means that the width is twice as large as the height. When resizing graphics, it is important to maintain the aspect ratio to avoid stretching the graphic out of proportion.

Books tend to be significantly taller than wide. For example a book designed for a 6" x 9" trim size would have an aspect ratio of 1.5. In other words the height is five times times the width. A different trim size selection would have a different aspect ratio.

Ebooks tend to follow a similar aspect ratio design. Some vendors definitely recommend a 1.5 aspect ratio, while others simply list pixel minimums for longest side. So what does that mean when the recommendation is to go above 2,000 pixels on the longest side? Below are three typical sizing possibilities that match this 1.5 aspect ratio.

- 1400 x 2100
- 1667 x 2500
- 2500 x 3750

You don't have to do these calculations yourself. Most graphics programs have the ability to expand or reduce the size of the graphic while maintaining the proportion.

Working with a cover designer

If you are like me, either your design skills or time are limited. Like writers and editors, cover designers come at a variety of costs and skill levels. When looking for a cover designer I suggest doing the following.

1. Look at books that have a cover style you like. Go to the copyright page and see if the cover designer is listed. If not there, go to the acknowledgments.

2. Ask your author friends who they use and what the relationship is like.

3. Type "cover design" into a search engine and a number of companies will come up.

4. Go to the designer sites you are considering and look at their portfolios. It is important to evaluate whether all their books look good or only a few. Even bad designers get lucky once in a while. But good designers will have many great covers and will display them in their portfolio.

5. Make sure the designer has created covers in your genre. Understanding the reader expecta-tions for a genre is critical in a cover design. A science fiction cover designer may not do a good job on a romance. A designer who primarily works in non-fiction may not understand the expectations of genre fiction.

6. Look at the costs and determine if they are within your budget. Costs typically range from $100 to over $1,000. You can get a good design for between $100 and $300 if you are careful who you choose. The higher-cost designers tend to be people with decades of experience and a reputation in publishing. If you need something unique and have the budget and time, a higher-cost designer may work well for you.

Once you have selected a designer, make an appointment to speak with him or her on the phone. It is important to get a feel for how your relationship will work and if you feel comfortable asking questions. You also want someone who is confident and experienced enough to be honest about the viability of your cover ideas. If the designer believes your cover vision will not provide the most effective marketing, he or she should be able to explain the reasons the cover won't work and offer alternatives. You do not want a designer who will implement your cover vision knowing that it will be ineffective.

Here are some questions to consider asking the designer during your telephone or in-person interview.

1. How many covers have you designed in my genre?

2. What do you believe must be included on my cover to meet genre expectations?

3. What is your typical timeline for a design project? Are the additional fees if I need it sooner than that?

4. What is your preferred communication? Phone, email, text message?

5. How many mock-ups do you provide?

6. How many changes are allowed with the standard pricing?

7. Do you pay for the stock photos or do I?

8. What type of information do I need to provide about my book and what I see as the cover?

9. Is there a discount for multiple books, such as a series? If so, do the books need to be contracted within a specific period of time to obtain the discount?

10. If we disagree about what to include on the cover, what will be the result?

11. If I cannot accept the final design, is there still a cost I 'm obligated to pay?

12. Assuming we both love the cover, will you be including my cover in your portfolio?

Once you have established a relationship and a timeline, it is important to articulate your vision for the book both in words and images. Many designers will ask you to send them pictures of book covers you like and that reflect your expectations for the look and feel of your book. This helps them get an idea of your taste. Some designers will also ask what colors you see as important to the book. Remember, this is not necessarily your favorite colors but the colors that will meet genre expectations.

Nearly all designers will ask for a summary of your book. Your back cover blurb or the blurb you put up for an ebook provides this information. Some designers will go further and also ask for you to describe your main character(s) in terms of gender, age, hair color, eye color, etc. This helps them to look for stock photos and models that may come close.

I've found that if I have a clear vision for the book cover, it helps to provide specific stock photo images to the designer. Again, no need to purchase them yet. Simply send the comps. As I detailed earlier in how the *Chameleon: The Choosing* book came together, I found the images and sent them to the designer with a description of what I envisioned. In this way, the designer is not spending time looking for images that I will ultimately not like because it doesn't fit what is in my mind.

I do not always have such a clear vision. On a different cover, the third book in my romance series, I was not as clear. I knew I wanted a couple on the cover because it was a romance. I also knew it needed to be in the country and my protagonist would be playing the guitar. Other than that I did not have an idea of the composition or what the character needed to look like. In that instance, I sent three model comps of the female that worked for me and two model comps of the male along with several background comps. I left it up to the designer to determine which things went together most effectively.

If you don't have any idea what you want, then a written description is sufficient. However, your description needs to communicate more than plot. Be sure to describe the mood, tone, and themes of your book as much as possible. Then keep an open mind to what the designer presents. It is unfair to say, "I don't have any idea what I want" and then get upset because the designer didn't give you what you secretly had in mind.

Even when you have a clear vision and provide all the images, you need to still be open to suggestion. Remember, the reason you are hiring a cover designer is because you don't have the expertise or time to do it yourself. This means the designer may present things in a way you didn't expect. This is because she understands proportion, typography, focus, and genre. You need to listen to the reasons she made those choices and carefully consider them.

Whenever you get a draft design or several mock-ups back, do not immediately accept or reject them. Take a day or two to live with them. If you are unsure, ask trusted author friends to look at them and give you an opinion. Sometimes a cover that rubs you the wrong way might be exactly what you need because it invokes a certain uncomfortable emotion. Other times a specific concern about a pose or lighting or colors may be legitimate.

If your designer gives you two or three drafts and they all appear equally appealing to you, consider posting them on your blog or Facebook page and asking people to vote. Again, open your mind to options. You do not need to make the decision alone.

It is rare that a draft cover will be exactly what you want the first time. Do not be afraid to ask for changes. However, do it with respect. Remember, if you really hate the draft design, your upfront communication of expectations might be as much to blame as the designer's interpretation of your description.

Creating your first book cover with a designer is often the most difficult. Once you have established good communications, having a cover designer you trust is an invaluable asset.

Changing designers in the middle of a series will often result in having to redo all previous covers in the series. It is very difficult to copy the exact same aesthetic from one designer to another. So, take the time to carefully choose your cover designer. Staying with a designer can ensure that your author brand, series brand, and genre brand are all cohesive and well-maintained throughout multiple books.

CHAPTER 12

Book Blurbs and Author Bios

You've completed your manuscript and have exported it for print and ebook. You have a magnificent cover that will draw readers to open the book and read the first chapter. You probably already have a great back cover blurb. Now you are ready to upload your book to a print-on-demand (POD) printer like CreateSpace or Lightning Source and to all the ebook distributors. You are ready to start selling.

Before you take that final step, however, it is important to look at your book description (blurb) and your author biography in terms of marketing. What you present on vendor sites may be different from what you present in your book. The purpose of distribution sites is to sell, sell, sell. The best way to do that is by making sure your blurbs and bio are short, consistent, and enhance your author brand on every site that features your books. This includes vendor sites, your website, blogs, Facebook, and anywhere else you might be providing that information.

The book blurb that sells

Most authors are not very good at writing marketing copy. When I write non-fiction I am focused on the details of instruction and the overall structure of how the information is delivered. When I'm finished with the book, the last thing I want to consider is how to write a sales blurb. When I write fiction, I am caught up in a world of my own creation. I am living with characters and places and details that are not real. When I finish a novel it is nearly impossible for me to write good marketing copy.

Tip: Consider writing your marketing copy before you start your book. Even if it's not perfect it will help you to focus the plot and themes. Writing your book blurb first will help you envision the arc of the story and the most important elements to entice a reader. It can help you to start stronger and finish sooner.

Back cover book blurbs follow a tradition based in print publishing. They are written to encapsulate your novel in two to four paragraphs. They are designed for readers browsing a bookstore shelf to quickly ascertain if the story is enough to entice them to open the book and read, then to buy. The blurb paragraphs tend to describe the goals and motivation of the primary character(s); the stakes of the story; and to end with something to entice the reader to open the book. Even if you are not doing print books, ebooks still use the equivalent of a back cover blurb as a long description of the story.

The book blurb you use at distributor sites and in other websites is different from the back cover blurb. First, it is signficantly shorter—usually under 100 words. Think of it more like a pitch you would hear on a 15-second commercial for the movie of your book. There is no time for the voice-over actor to read three or four paragraphs. You must capture the tone of the book and the imagination of the reader in four to five sentences.

Most distributor sites today ask for the "short description" and then also provide space for the "long description." Depending on the site, usually the short description is what is displayed with the book. The longer description is reached either through scrolling down the page or clicking on a tab or link.

If the site only allows one description, you should use the short description. This is because when a reader is browsing a book, she will not linger to read four paragraphs. She is evaluating several options and wants to make a decision quickly. If you don't capture that reader in one short paragraph, you may lose her.

I am the first to admit that I am not very good at writing these marketing book blurbs, though I am getting better with practice. I always ask for help. A great resource is finding friends who are scriptwriters or have had scriptwriter training. Their training tends to include a lot of pitches to Hollywood. If you don't know anyone with that background, find an author whose descriptions always pull you in and see if you can get some mentoring.

When I had worked my back cover blurb to only be four paragraphs I was ecstatic. It had started at six. But the idea of getting it down to 100 words was mind boggling. I turned to writer Jamie Brazil who enjoys the challenge of this and provided me with some excellent options. Below is an example of how the back cover blurb for my YA Fantasy novel, *Chameleon: The Awakening*, changed to a shorter marketing blurb to use on all vendor sites.

Print Back Cover Blurb

No identity. That's what it's like to be a human chameleon, and sixteen-year-old Camryn Painter wonders if she'll ever figure out who the real Camryn is—or should be. Just looking at someone else will cause her body to change into that person. Her parents called it her gift. She calls it her curse.

Then Ohar, a man with impossibly good looks and an ethereal manner offers her a way to claim her birthright by joining the Mazikeen as part of the Forest People. He says she is "the chosen" of the Forest People. The prophecy indicates her powers are beyond any others and she will save their world.

Camryn had always loved the Redwoods at her back door. The stories her mother spun of its inhabitants kept her entertained for much of her childhood. The problem is the stories are real. The forest people are real, human yet not human. They are faery and beasts, evil and angels, mutations of humans and animals over thousands of years. Then there's Dagger, a young man who distrusts the Mazikeen and Ohar, but admits to being a thief and only interested in his own pleasure. All of them want the Chameleon for their own agenda.

With the help of Ohar and Dagger, Camryn learns to control her identity so that she can walk among more than one world. Yet the more Camryn learns, the more she suspects there are too many secrets — dangerous secrets. There are no easy answers, and every decision she makes puts someone's life in danger.

Yes, it's too long even for a back cover. If I had known then what I know now, I would have combined the first two paragraphs and cut the blurb length in half. But it followed all the blurb writing conventions. Below is the single paragraph blurb that I now use at all vendor sites, on my website, and whenever I'm writing an article or doing a guest blog.

Short Marketing Book Blurb

Camryn Painter is a 16-year-old freak of nature. Or possibly the savior of a civilization that isn't supposed to exist. She's a human chameleon... one who transforms into the image of whoever she sees. Escaping from a medical research facility, Camryn discovers a magical forest world. Not that she's welcome. Her new home is filled with faeries and beasts set on destroying her. Striking a tribal alliance between what she once believed were mythical beings is her only chance of survival... if she can just control her power and figure out who to trust.

Notice how the marketing blurb still captures the tone of the story—young adult and a little dark. It also captures the cross-genre inclusion of both fantasy and paranormal elements. Though it doesn't discuss the protagonist's specific goals and motivations or any backstory, it clearly suggests the stakes—her survival.

In *Chapter 7, Metadata*, the importance of a 70-character abstract was discussed. Think of the abstract as the movie poster tag line. The marketing blurb expands on that tag line. Strive to keep your marketing blurb under 100 words. To add emphasis, consider combining the tag line as a lead-in to the 100-word blurb. On the Amazon page my description looks like the one below. The combination of the tag line and the marketing blurb gives it the most impact.

Her gifts can save or destroy everyone and everything she loves.

Camryn Painter is a 16-year-old freak of nature. Or possibly the savior of a civilization that isn't supposed to exist. She's a human chameleon...

one who transforms into the image of whoever she sees. Escaping from a medical research facility, Camryn discovers a magical forest world. Not that she's welcome. Her new home is filled with faeries and beasts set on destroying her. Striking a tribal alliance between what she once believed were mythical beings is her only chance of survival... if she can just control her power and figure out who to trust.

Need more help in writing blurbs? Here are three blog articles that provide practical help and examples. The first one is from bestselling, thriller author and writing teacher Mike Wellsindie. He has a five part blurb building method. Be sure to take his fun quiz for distilling longer blurbs into two sentences for practice. http://ht.ly/bNzmd

The next blog post is from bestselling historical Scottish romance author Marti Talbott. The first book in her Highlander series has sold over 50,000 copies. http://maritalbottstories.blogspot.com/2013/05/how-to-write-book-blurb-that-sells.html

The final article I'd recommend is from writing workshop instructor Marilyn Byerly. What I like about this article is that she gives examples from different genres and explains what needs to change in the blurbs to meet reader expectations in each genre. http://marilynnbyerly.com/blurb.html

---

The Author Bio

Just as there is a differences between the back cover blurb and the marketing blurb used to sell the book, the author bio you use at the back of your novel may be different from the author bio you present on vendor pages or attached to articles and guest posts.

Depending on the genre of your book, your author bio at the back of the book might be more personal or friendly. For example, the tradition in romance is to present the author as someone who could be a friend—someone the reader can identify with. Because romance explores some of the most intimate topics in readers lives, it make sense that the author bio is written in this tone. Science Fiction, however, has a different tradition. SF readers value an author who has a science background. Highlighting a job in a scientific research facility or at NASA gives the author great credentials in the eyes of readers. Science fiction readers don't necessarily care about the family background or other more personal details because the books are not written to capitalize on that identification in the reader.

Whatever your genre or the style of your current author bio, the key to writing one for marketing purposes is to depict those parts of your biography that indicate you are the best expert to write this book—that your unique background and knowledge gives you inside information. This is particularly critical for non-fiction. And it is an important selling point for fiction. If you write in multiple genres, you might fashion an author bio for each one. On the other hand, if you deal with similar themes in all your books, one bio might be sufficient. Let me share some examples from my own background and how they have changed over the years.

I write in multiple genres and my books often cross genres. My adult novels have elements of contemporary romance, women's fiction, suspense, science fiction, and paranormal. My current young adult novels are in the juncture between contemporary fantasy and paranormal. I also have a non-fiction book publication career going back to 1998.

Given these disparate genres, until recently I have maintained three separate websites, three distinct author personas, and three different biographies—one for adult fiction, one for young adult fiction, and one for non-fiction. My biographies on each site were far too long. I've provided a shortened version of each one below.

Adult Fiction Bio

My educational background is in psychology, counseling, computer science, and education. Yes, I have far too many degrees. I just couldn't make up my mind what I wanted to be when I grew up. Somehow I found a way to satisfy both my left and right brain and fashioned a career that could do that by choosing positions that would use my people skills, my love of adaptive technologies, and my desire to be a teacher and mentor.

I am fortunate to now spend the majority of my time journeying into the world of my imagination and writing novels that reflect my passions and my belief that strong women can do anything, that the good guys win in the end, and that love will conquer all.

Young Adult Fiction Bio

I am the oldest of nine children. This means I can always raise an army to fight off evildoers whenever they appear. It also means I'm a control freak and like to be the boss. Throughout my many career choices, the one constant was writing. The other was never letting reality intrude too far on my fantasy life.

I've finally found the perfect profession. One where I have complete control of entire worlds and the people in them. One where fantasy and reality do more than coexist, they embrace each other. One where I can still induce people to listen to me, to pay attention, and to give me money. Really, what's more fun than that?

Non-Fiction Bio

Dr. Maggie McVay Lynch is an acclaimed technology teacher and academic computing executive who spent over 30 years in education and computing.

After initial careers in corporate technology training, she spent eight years in executive management with two major software companies.

Later in life she completed a doctorate degree in education, allowing her to transfer her technology and teaching skills to academia where she served in positions from Professor to Dean and eventually Chief Information Officer. Maggie ended her career by consulting for both large and small universities, working with teachers and executives to identify appropriate technology for their needs.

Dr. Lynch has previously authored four textbooks by major publishers in London and New York. Also a fiction writer, she has now turned her efforts to helping other authors learn to use technology effectively in their writing business.

Certainly, for the back of a completed book, each of these biographies serves a purpose and meets reader expectations in the genre. The voice for the young adult fiction bio is designed to appeal to both teens and adult readers who like young adult books. It is written as a little more fun. The adult fiction bio attempts to provide enough information to please readers at both ends of the spectrum—those who want a more personalized approach and those who are more interested in specific subject knowledge. Because my books tend to be dark or issue driven, it is written more as a reflection and philosophical approach. The non-fiction bio is exclusively subject knowledge based and designed specifically to market educational books.

Of these three, only the non-fiction bio meets the marketing test. My background in teaching and technology matches my non-fiction publications. However, the fiction bios are too "friendly" from a marketing perspective. They do not capitalize on subject matter expertise and they do not offer an incentive for the reader who doesn't know me to take a chance because they don't speak to my qualifications as a career writer.

If I were a USA Today bestselling author, that would be a great marketing lead. It speaks to popularity. If I had won a literary prize, it would speak to quality even if I wasn't popular. If I won a genre book award—the RITA, The Edgar, the Hugo—I would have something to tout. Alas, like the vast majority of authors I can't claim any of these. Without a bestseller or a major award, for the vast majority of authors the question becomes: "What can I say about myself that convinces a reader to try me?"

The key to the author bio is to sound interesting. When I first began writing novels, I thought I would never find anything interesting to say about myself. I didn't want to talk about my education because I felt it had nothing to do with what I was writing—particularly the romance novels. I definitely didn't want to talk about my family life. No one cares if I am an only child or the oldest of a brood to challenge the Brady Bunch. Add to that I don't write about big families.

When I discussed my dilemma with multi-published author Dean Wesley Smith, he said: "Everyone has something interesting to share. Whether you are a stay-at-home mother who writes in between diaper changes or a librarian who catalogs books, there is something interesting in your life that relates to what you write. All writers include parts of their life in their books. It's all in how you say it."

Dean found my educational background interesting. Where I saw it as appearing that I couldn't make up my mind about a career, he saw it from a marketing perspective that I was well-rounded and can write on almost any subject. He loved that I came from a big family. After all, what better way to understand how to negotiate politics and the psychology of communication. It's like having my own little town. The bottom line is that what I found boring, uninteresting, or just down right bragging, might be exactly what a reader would find fascinating. It is all in how you say it.

When evaluating your own background, consider some of these things and how you can tie them into the books you write.

1. *Hobbies* – Do you run marathons? That shows persistence and the ability to overcome adversity. How about flower arranging? Watching movies from the 1940's?

2. *Work History* – Even working at McDonald's can provide a plethora of experiences to tie into your subject matter, both humorous and serious. My first job was with Carl's Jr. –a fast food restaurant. After three years I had plenty of stories that became parts of science fiction shorts. Work for a small town newspaper? What incidents did you cover that might relate to your book? Be creative.

3. *Where You Live* – Your hometown or current location can be a good marketing focus. If you live in a rural area, and your books take place in the country, capitalize on that. The same goes for urban living. If you've moved around a lot there may be something to tie in there—a story about coming home or finding home perhaps.

4. *Travel* – Have you traveled to exotic places that relate to your book? Exotic is in the eye of the beholder. Perhaps your romance takes place in Hawaii and that was where you took your honeymoon. There is a tie-in to romance there. Perhaps your paranormal world or SF planet is filled with geysers. Tie that to your trip to Yellowstone National Park.

5. *Series* – If you are a writing books in a series, once the first book is out you can tag yourself as "the writer of the X series" in your bio. Even better, describe the series with a

modifier. "The author of the popular Dark Fae series which challenges the rules of right and wrong."

6. *Pull Quotes* – Reviews, particularly from well known reviewers or magazines in your genre, can be used in your bio. "Next Magazine said Maggie Jaimeson's *Sweetwater Canyon* series is like vinegar and oil, the perfect combination of tart, painful situations wrapped in soothing romantic relationships that leave the reader wanting the next book."

Always write your marketing bio in third person. Pretend you are the publicist for an up-and-coming new talent. What would you write about you? Use active words throughout. As much as possible match the writing to the voice in your books. If you write humorous books, your bio should have a humorous tone. Dark books or issue books are echoed in a more formal or reflective bio. Ask several people to look it over. Most important, update it when something major happens. Your book has now sold over 100,000 copies? Include that in your bio. If not one book, but all your books together have reached that mark, word your bio to reflect that. Released another book? Update the number of novels you mention in your bio.

What if you've decided to have one bio for all the genres? That does it make it difficult, but it might be wise. Due to changes in the publishing landscape and marketing realities, the old idea of having a different pseudonym for each genre has changed. Now authors are advised to encourage as many cross-over readers as they can. In that case, you want one website with all your books and one bio that reflects all that you write. In other words, you want a supersite.

I'm facing this dilemma myself. I've decided to combine three websites into one in order to capitalize on any cross-promotion for those readers who may move between genres. Those who prefer to only know me in one genre can still find me under the pseudonym that relates to that genre So what did I decide to take from each bio? Below is my combined bio.

Not that the example below is the perfect biography, but it demonstrates how I brought the three personas together into one marketing author bio.

Long Combined Author Bio

With degrees in psychology, counseling, computer science, and education, Maggie Lynch never missed a chance to learn something new. After early careers as diverse as family and marriage counseling and software development, she found a way to satisfy both her left and right brain and fashioned a career in academia that included teaching, faculty leadership, and eventually university executive leadership. Her desire to share her understanding of educational technology has afforded her opportunities to travel around the world, including Europe, Australia, and the Middle East.

Science fiction was Maggie's first love. She sold a number of short stories to SF fiction magazines and tabloids in the mid 1980's and early 1990's. Her focus changed to non-fiction when she joined academia, where she published four textbooks with major NY and London publishers between 1998 and 2007. In 2005, Maggie returned to fiction and her first novel was released in 2011, a romantic suspense. She now writes romance and science fiction under the name Maggie Jaimeson, and young adult fantasy under the name Maggie Faire.

Fortunate to now spend the majority of her time journeying into the world of her imagination, Maggie is happy to be writing novels that reflect her passions. Her novels and her non-fiction reflect her belief that strong women can do anything, that the good guys win in the end, and that love and helping others will conquer all.

Short Combined Author Bio

Maggie Lynch has never missed a chance to learn something new. With degrees in psychology, counseling, computer science, and education she has opportunities that have taken her around the world, including Europe, Australia, and the Middle East. Her current publishing credits include five non-fiction books, a number of science fiction short stories, and seven novels. Now able to spend full time journeying into her imagination, Maggie writes romance and science fiction under the name Maggie Jaimeson, and young adult fantasy under the name Maggie Faire.

Just as with the book blurb, the shorter, marketing bio should be under 100 words. In this instance I focused on the things I hope readers will find most interesting in both non-fiction and fiction of different genres. I focused on my education, my travel, and my publishing credits. Although I can't say I've made a bestseller list or won any major awards, I believe the bio is sufficient to let a reader or media reviewer know that I am a serious, career-oriented writer.

Whether you are releasing your first book or your twentieth make your bio interesting. The nice thing about the short bio is that it leaves room for you to add a line to customize it for particular events. For example, if I'm going to be reading from my YA Fantasy series, I might change the last line to read"…and her popular young adult fantasy series, about a human chameleon and the forest people, under the name Maggie Faire." If I were signing a book in my romance series, I would change the line to reflect that. Because my short bio is only 85 words, I've left room to add enhancements to fit the particular marketing need.

CHAPTER 13

ISBNs

All print books sold through bookstores and online require an ISBN. Though some online retailers do not require ISBNs to distribute ebooks, it is still highly recommened that you have one. In this chapter I will discuss the purpose of the ISBN, the reasons you should obtain ISBNs for both print and ebooks, as well as the costs and trade-offs for where you purchase them and how you use them.

The International Standard Book Number (ISBN) is a unique identifier used around the world to identify, purchase, and sell books. ISBNs first appeared in 1965 as a nine digit number. Since January 1, 2007, ISBNs have contained 13 digits. A different ISBN is assigned to each edition and variation of a book. A paperback, hardcover, ebook, and audiobook edition would each have its own ISBN. A second edition of a book requires a new ISBN. Reprinting the same book does not require a new ISBN.

The graphic below, downloaded from Wikipedia, provides a nice explanation of what each of the digits in an ISBN identifies. It also includes the barcode, which adds the EAN information (Electronic A Number). Bookstores rely on the ISBN for ordering, stocking, and point-of-sale. A number of online retailers of ebooks also rely on this number—particularly Sony and Apple.

To get more specific information go to:
http://en.wikipedia.org/wiki/International_Standard_Book_Number

You do not need a different ISBN for every country. The country is encoded in the "group" digits. You *do* need a different ISBN for each language in which the book is distributed. If the book was published previously by a different publisher, and you have the rights back to the book, you will need a new ISBN. The book is then published as a second edition.

In the digital age of book creation, some authors become concerned that they must have a new ISBN every time they make a change to the book. This is not the case. If you are correcting typos, adding one or two sentences on a page that went astray, or changing the book cover, you do not need a new ISBN. It can still be sold as the same edition. However, making substantial changes such as adding chapters, adding new characters, changing the arc or theme of the story requires a new edition of the book. That edition must have a new ISBN.

In the United States, ISBNs are managed by Bowker, a private for-profit company. You can purchase one ISBN or hundreds of thousands of ISBNs online at http://myidentifiers.com/ The cost per ISBN decreases if you buy multiple ISBNs at one time.

In some countries, like Canada, there is no cost to get an ISBN because the country wishes to encourage local authors and the government funds the service for managing ISBNs. In those countries, ISBN assignment and management is often run through the Ministry of Culture or through the library system. Other countries are similar to the United States (e.g., the United Kingdom, Ireland, and Australia) and have appointed a private company to do this work. Check with your country's ISBN management authority to determine what costs and paperwork are required to obtain an ISBN. IF you don't know which agency or company manages ISBNs in your country, you can get that information at the non-profit International ISBN organization:

http://www.isbn-international.org/agency

Free Versus Paid ISBNs

Most everyone would prefer not to pay for an ISBN. It is particularly tempting to get a free ISBN when you have no idea if your book will ever make back the costs. There are options to get free ISBNs, even in countries that have a paid service. However, there are tradeoffs when you do that.

First, let's look at why you should make the investment in purchasing your own ISBNs if your country does not offer them for free. There are three important reasons to purchase your own ISBN.

1. You are the publisher of record. Your name or your company name is what is listed on all sites and bibliographic reference feeds.

2. You want full control of the ISBN and the content provided to all bibliographic feeds.

3. If you decide you want to have your book printed elsewhere (e.g., move POD printing from CreateSpace to Ingram Spark or to a mass market printing company) you can move it without getting a new ISBN. It's your ISBN as a publisher.

What is the cost? If you are purchasing from Bowker, buying a single ISBN is outrageously priced at $125.00. Therefore, it is wise to purchase at least a group of 10 ISBNs at $250.00, which brings the price down to $25.00 per ISBN. Ten ISBNs represents five books in both print and ebook format. With a plan to write five books during your career, it is worth buying that block of ten. ISBNs do not have an expiration date.

What if you are only writing one book or you can't afford the $250.00 to purchase ten ISBNs? There are alternatives to purchasing from Bowker. You can acquire a free ISBN from a POD publisher like CreateSpace. Other POD printers offer ISBNs ranging from $2.00 to $10.00 each. Each option has a trade-off and only you can decide it it's worth it. Also, once you have made a decision to go with a free or low cost ISBN from a middleman, you can still later change your mind, purchase your own ISBN, and put up a second edition of the book. A number of authors elect to do this when their author sales increase sufficiently to make the financial investment more appealing.

Aggregators are companies that provide services to authors and then directly interface with retailers. Before the ebook revolution, those services were companies like Lulu and Xlibris. Now there are many companies specifically designed to help authors interface with markets for both print and ebooks. Smashwords, Draft to Digital, CreateSpace, Book Baby, Fast Pencil, and Xin Xii are examples of ebook aggregators.

Some author service companies require you to use their ISBN in order to take advantage of the services. Other companies allow you to use your own. Still others, like CreateSpace, allow you to use your own ISBN but it limits your distribution options.

The most important disadvantage to using an ISBN from an aggregator is the coding of the publisher identification digits. ISBNs have a prefix that is permanently associated with the publisher who purchased the ISBNs from Bowker.

For example, when CreateSpace purchases a block of a hundred thousand ISBNs from Bowker, the company then assigns those ISBNs to authors who wish to have a free ISBN. As Bowker is the official manager of ISBNs in the United States, it assigns all numbers in this block to reflect CreateSpace as the publisher. When you accept an ISBN from CreateSpace, it means that CreateSpace is listed as the publisher on all systems around the world and in all bookstores. Is this a problem? Some bookstores have a policy of not dealing with Amazon. CreateSpace is an Amazon subsidiary company and therefore they will not order books from them. For other bookstores it is not a problem.

CreateSpace also offers a $10.00 ISBN purchase option. This allows you to be an "imprint" of CreateSpace. On the surface this sounds pretty good. Big publishers have imprints too. For example, Bantam, Dell, and Spectra are all imprints of Random House. The good news is with the $10.00 ISBN purchase option you or your company is listed as the publisher on all Amazon and CreateSpace sites. Also, in the extended distribution through Ingram and Baker & Taylor (see *Chapter 14* on Amazon Distribution for more information), Amazon will transmit your imprint name as the publisher.

The bad news is that using this option still reflects CreateSpace as the publisher in the group digit. The ISBN itself does not have a separate code for an imprint. According to Bowker, their database and the bibliographic publications they produce do not reflect "second publishers" (imprints) that may be created by the primary publisher to which they originally issued the ISBN prefix. In other words, the *Books In Print* bibliographic publications that Bowker transmits to booksellers and librarians around the world will always point to CreateSpace as the publisher.

CreateSpace recently began offering a $99.00 ISBN purchase option. They claim this ISBN can be used with "another publisher." Whereas the free or $10.00 option would require you to do a new edition of the book if you wanted to publish elsewhere, the $99.00 version is transferable.

To be honest, that phrasing is confusing to me. Because this is very recent, I have not had a chance to research exactly how this might happen. If CreateSpace is still using the block of ISBNs it purchased from Bowker, then the publisher code will still reflect CreateSpace as the publisher. In general, once an ISBN is issued under a publisher it does not transfer to another publisher. There is no commercial publisher I know that will accept another publisher's ISBN.

One other way to obtain an ISBN at less cost is to join a publishing cooperative. This is a group of authors who join together and agree to publish under the same publisher name. Windtree Press and Book View Café are two examples of this. Cooperatives are different from a commercial publisher in that titles are not purchased or contracted, and the cooperative does not employ full-time editors, cover designers, and formatters. A publishing cooperative allows a group of independent authors to share costs and resources in their publishing efforts.

For example, at Windtree Press the cooperative purchases a block of ISBNs to be shared among all the members. Each member then pays a pro-rated cost for the ISBN. Purchasing a block of 100 ISBNs reduces the cost for each ISBN to $5.75. A larger cooperative with 100 members may be able to purchase a block of 1,000 ISBNs. In theory, the cooperative could choose to then make each ISBN available to members at a reimbursment cost of only $1.00. In larger cooperatives it is common for them to mark up the actual ISBN cost in order to pay someone to enter the book information in Bowker's database. But even at $5.00 per ISBN, members realize a great savings.

Members of co-ops still face some of the same disadvantages as they do to purchasing ISBNs from an aggregator like CreateSpace. The publisher of record is the co-op press name (i.e., Windtree Press or Book View Café). Depending on the bylaws of the co-op, if a member leaves the co-op she may need to purchase another ISBN and redistribute books as a second edition. Even if the co-op allows the ISBN to transfer with the member, as Windtree Press does, it is likely she will still want a different publisher identified for all her books.

Ebook ISBNs

The ebook version of your title must have a separate ISBN from the print version. This is because an electronic book is a substantially different format. Some people call this ISBN an eISBN. Technically, there is no such thing as an eISBN, just as there is no such thing as an aISBN for audiobooks. All identifiers for different book formats are simply ISBNs. If you see the term eISBN on a form, it means the vendor is asking for the ISBN assigned to your ebook.

You only need *one* ISBN for all ebook formats. Some authors have chosen to purchase an ISBN for each file type (e.g, one for Amazon's MOBI format, another for EPUB, another for PDF, and yet another for HTML). This is not necessary. In fact, if you go to Bowker and complete the form, you will notice there is not a separate identifier for each ebook file type. Instead the selection is only for ebook as the "medium" and "electronic text" as the type.

In the early days of electronic publishing some authors also purchased a separate ISBN for each vendor—one for Amazon, one for B&N, one for Apple, etc.). They did this to allow for tracking sales by ISBN. With modern sales reporting now available at all vendors, this is not necessary.

It is true that some large ebook distributors in the United States do not require that you have an ISBN in order to have your ebook listed in their online catalog. These vendors are Amazon, Barnes and Noble, Apple, and Kobo. If you choose to upload your ebook without an ISBN, these vendors assign an internal inventory control number in order to track your books and your payments accurately.

With Apple and Kobo, uploading without an ISBN will severely limit your distribution. For example, Kobo works with independent booksellers around the world. Most of those booksellers, including many in the United States, rely on ISBNs to track inventory, sales, and payments. The inventory tracking number assigned by the vendor is not sufficient to interface with all the bookseller systems. Apple also has independent partnerships in several countries that require an ISBN in order for the book to be represented there.

In addition, an ISBN is required in order for any distributor to send sales information to organizations that track book sales and report on them. Many lists, such as the New York Times Bestsellers, USA Today Bestsellers, Wall Street Journal, and Publisher's Weekly are now reporting on ebook sales. Without an ISBN for your ebook, your book will not be tracked for those lists and thus not reported to booksellers and libraries, in newspapers and magazines, or to other media.

Sony requires an ebook ISBN. There is no option for uploading an ebook without one. Most aggregators who distribute to Sony, Apple, or Kobo will assign an ISBN to your ebook. If that happens, you have the same difficulty described earlier in the CreateSpace scenario. The encoded publisher in the ISBN will be that of the aggregator, not you.

How to use Bowker Effectively

If you have decided to purchase your own ISBNs and you live in the United States, you will need to use the services at Bowker. You do all of this online via the site at http://myidentifiers.com

The first step is purchasing the ISBNs. You can buy a block of ISBNs without having to provide any information except you as a publisher and your credit card information. Once you access the myidentifiers.com site, click on **Buy ISBNs** in the menu.

A screen appears with several options ranging from the purchase of a single ISBN for $125 to pricing on blocks of ISBNs at 10, 100, and 1,000. Click on the item that represents the number of ISBNs you wish to purchase. Once selected, you will be taken directly to the shopping cart screen.

*Tip: If you are purchasing more than one ISBN be sure that the number entered in the shopping cart represents the bulk group. In the example below, the author elected to purchase the 10 ISBN package. In the shopping cart it shows the number one. That is correct. The author is purchasing only one package. Do **not** put the number 10 in this section.*

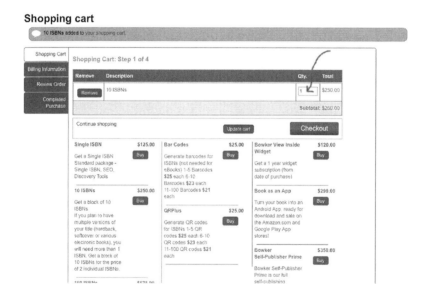

Click on the **Checkout** button to complete your purchase.

On the checkout page you will see a number of other offers. I advise you *not* to select any of these. Bar codes can be generated for free at http://bookcovers.creativindie.com/free-online-isbn-barcode-generator/ Also, if you are using CreateSpace as your print book distributor, they will put the barcode on your backcover automatically. Widgets and Apps can be developed in other venues for significantly less money. The best course of action is to purchase the ISBNs at Bowker and nothing else.

Like all ecommerce engines on the Internet, the checkout process will require you to create an account, choose a password, provide your credit card information, billing address, and phone.

After the payment is processed, the ISBNs are immediately added to your account. To view them go to the **My Account** menu option and select **Manage ISBNs**.

Once those ISBNs are displayed in your account, you can assign current and future titles to them. At any time between the purchase and the release of your book, you can go in and fill in the required fields to make sure your book information is associated with a specific ISBN number. Most authors choose to do this very close to their book release date because that is when they have all of the information for the book. You may go back and change things at any time until you click **Submit**. At that point you can no longer change the title or the publication date. However, you may change other elements.

When you first go to **Manage ISBNs** in your account, a screen with each ISBN you purchased is presented and a button to Assign Title.

Assign Title	978-1-940064-28-4		Upload	Generate	Buy Widgets
Assign Title	978-1-940064-29-1		Upload	Generate	Buy Widgets
Assign Title	978-1-940064-30-7		Upload	Generate	Buy Widgets
Assign Title	978-1-940064-31-4		Upload	Generate	Buy Widgets
Assign Title	978-1-940064-32-1		Upload	Generate	Buy Widgets
Assign Title	978-1-940064-33-8		Upload	Generate	Buy Widgets
Assign Title	978-1-940064-39-0		Upload	Generate	Buy Widgets
Assign Title	978-1-940064-40-6		Upload	Generate	Buy Widgets
Assign Title	978-1-940064-41-3		Upload	Generate	Buy Widgets
Assign Title	978-1-940064-42-0		Upload	Generate	Buy Widgets

If you have purchased a block of ISBNs and already know titles for books, you may wish to enter them all at this time. However, that is not required. You may return to this screen at any time in the future and enter the information as the book is ready for publication.

Tip: Enter the information for your print book and ebook in the same sitting. This will be more efficient allowing you to clone information and then make changes that apply to that format.

Bowker provides numerous opportunities for you to enter metadata that will be transferred via their *Books in Print* publication and feeds to booksellers and libraries. However, only a few of those fields are required. It is up to you how much information you wish to provide. Remember, the more information you provide, the easier it is for booksellers and librarians to find your titles in a search. All *required* field entries are marked with a small red asterisk.

Begin the entry process by clicking on the **Assign Title** button in the **Manage ISBNs** section of your account. This will take you to the first screen in the data entry process. Notice that next to each field is a question mark button. This is context sensitive help relating to that item.

The first screen in the data entry process is the **Title Details** screen. The only required field on this first screen is the **Title**. However, there are several other fields I recommend you take the time to enter.

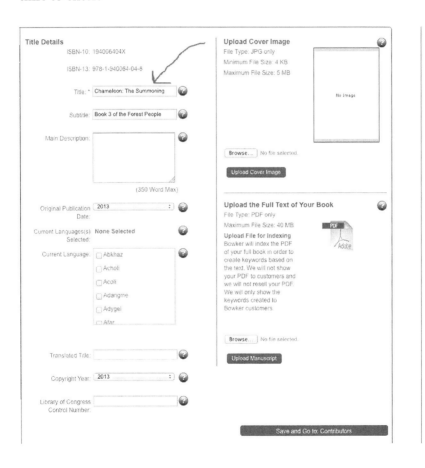

For non-fiction books with a a subtitle, be sure to enter the subtitle exactly as it appears on the book cover. For example, the title of this book is *DIY Publishing*. The subtitle is *A step-by-step guide to print and ebook formatting and distribution*. In this instance the primary title is entered in the **Title** field. The subtitle is entered in the **Subtitle** field exactly as it appears on the book cover. In this case The "A" is capitalized but everything else in the subtitle is lower case. If the subtitle on your book cover contains initial caps, then that is the way it should be entered in the **Subtitle** field in Bowker.

Fiction titles work the same way, though few fiction titles also have a subtitle. If the fiction title is part of a series, I have a work-around suggestion: Enter the series name in the **Subtitle** field. This is because the data entry screens provide no place to enter a series title. If your book has a subtitle and is also part of a series, you have a choice to make. You may include the subtitle in the title line as I did in the example, or you may decide to put it in the **Subtitle** field.

In my YA fantasy series, each of the seven books has the name "Chameleon" as the first part of the title. This maintains continuity between books and references the primary character. This is similar to how the Harry Potter books were presented. My subtitle then refers to the next step in the series: *Chameleon: The Awakening* and *Chameleon: The Choosing* for example. The series title is *The Forest People*. To include all of the information that is on the cover, I put the title and subtitle in the **Title** field. Then I put the series title in the **Subtitle** field with the book number: *Book 1 of The Forest People; Book 2 of The Forest People*.

Tip: When including the subtitle with the title, do not use a colon as the separator. Though Bowker accepts a colon in the title field without *incident. CreateSpace does not. The CreateSpace software reads a colon in the title as a subtitle. This then causes an error when CreateSpace tries to match the ISBN with the Bowker record. Therefore, in both the Bowker record and the CreateSpace record use a hyphen,* **Chameleon – The Awakening**, *instead of a colon.*

The **Main Description** field is where you will enter the short blurb (100 words) you worked on in the previous chapter. Although Bowker allows you to have a description of up to 350 words, it is best to use the marketing description here just as you will in all other places on the web. In that way, it will match wherever a reader or bookseller encounters your title. You will have an opportunity to provide a longer description on many vendor sites.

The **Original Publication Date** is for this particular edition and format of the book. If you are planning your books in advance, use the drop down arrow to select the year in which you anticipate publishing this work.

In the **Current Language** box, scroll down to select the check box next to **English**. Be careful *not* to select **Middle English** which is right under the word English. If you are uploading a book in another language, select it here.

The **Copyright Year** should match the original publication year. Again, just like the publication year, the copyright is the year this particular work in this particular format existed as a whole unit.

The **Library of Congress Control Number** (LCCN) can be entered after you release the book. Because you are required to send a copy of the book when you register the copyright, most authors do not complete this entry until after the book is released and a LCCN has been sent to them. (See the next chapter on Copyright Registration for this process).

On this same data entry page, you may also upload your book cover. This is highly recommended. Notice the file size limitations. I suggest uploading the same book cover size that will be used for all vendor sites. That is typically about 2100 pixels on the long side. Those files tend to be well under 5 MB. To complete the upload, click on the **Browse** button to find the book cover file in your computer. Then click on the **Upload Cover Image** button to complete the upload.

The final option on this first data entry page is to upload a **PDF** file of your completed manuscript. This allows Bowker to scan the entire manuscript and generate search terms. There is no place within the Bowker system to do keywords or other description types as were described in the Metadata chapter of this book. Scanning the PDF file is the way in which Bowker indexes keywords for the manuscript.

Bowker does not make a copy of your manuscript available to anyone. The company does not offer your manuscript for sale. It is simply used to create an index of subject headings and keywords for search. Again, I highly recommend uploading your completed manuscript. To complete the upload first click on the **Browse** button to locate the manuscript file in your computer. Then click on the **Upload Manuscript** button to complete the process.

When you have completed all the fields you wish to complete on this screen, click on the **Save and Go To: Contributors** button. Don't worry if you didn't have all of the information to enter. Remember, the only thing you cannot change once you submit is the title and publication date.

The contributor screen is used primarily to enter the author information. The only required field on this screen is to enter one contributor. If there are multiple authors, you have the option to enter each one. If your book has other contributors you wish to include, such as an illustrator for a children's book, this is also the section in which you would add that person under the **Add More Contributors** button.

Begin the process by entering your author name in the designated fields marked **First** and **Last**. If you are using a pen name that is what is entered here.

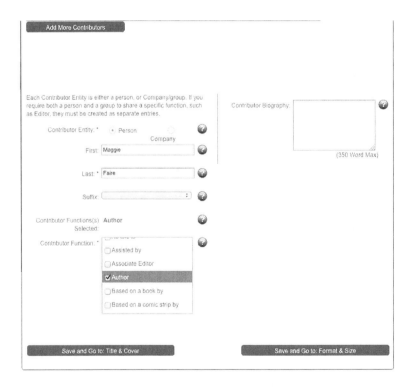

By default the **Person** option is selected as the **Contributor Entity**. If your book was authored by a company instead of an individual, then click on the button above **Company**. This is rare for novelists, but not uncommon for non-fiction work. It is possible, for example, that an organization focused on health issues might author several books on health as a company.

In the **Contributor Function** box, scroll down to select **Author** by clicking in the check box to the left of the entry.

If there are multiple author contributors to the work, as in an anthology, you have the opportunity to enter each one by clicking on the **Add More Contributors** button above the first and last name. Be aware that the order of contributors is important in this instance. The first contributor entered is guaranteed to be displayed in the *Books In Print* publication and feed.

Though not required, it is recommended that you complete the **Contributor Biography** field. This is where you would enter the short bio (under 100 words) you completed in the previous chapter. Remember, the *Books In Print* product is sent to libraries and booksellers. It is what they use to determine which books to purchase. From the *Books in Print* listing, the library or bookseller has several options to purchase the book from their vendor of choice (e.g., Ingram, Baker & Taylor, Kobo, etc.)

The third data entry screen describes the book type. This is where the medium and format of the book are detailed, as well as the subjects which suggest how to categorize the book.

The required fields are **Medium, Format,** and **Primary Subject.** Each is selected by clicking on the up or down arrow in the right side of the entry field.

Format and Size

Medium: *	E-Book
Format: *	Electronic book text
Packaging Description:	
Trade Catalog:	
Primary Subject: *	
Secondary Subject:	
File Type:	
File Size:	

Editions and Volumes

Title Volume Number:		Point Size:	
Total Volume Number:		Previous Editions ISBN:	
Edition Number:		New Editions ISBN:	
Special Edition(s) and Version(s) Selected:	None Selected		
Special Editions and Versions:	☐ Abridged		
	☐ Acting edition		
	☐ Activity Book		
	☐ Adapted		
	☐ Adult		
	☐ Alternate		

Medium describes what type of a book it is: print, ebook, or audiobook. Let's look at entering a print book first.

If the ISBN relates to your print book, select the **Print** option under the **Medium** field. Next, move to the format field. The choices are **Hardback** or **Paperback**. Most self-published authors will select **Paperback**. Finally, scroll through the **Format Details** box to select **Trade paperback (US)**. If you are in the UK or a country that uses UK sizing, select **Trade Paperback (UK)**.

Most authors do not fill in the height, width, and weight of the book. This is used to calculate shipping costs when libraries or booksellers order the book. However, it is not critical for you to enter, as most libraries and booksellers order print books from Ingram or Baker & Taylor. Your POD printer (e.g., CreateSpace, Lightning Source, Ingram Spark) will send the actual final dimensions and weight to distributors like Ingram and Baker & Taylor if you have selected that option.

If the ISBN relates to your ebook, select **Ebook** in the **Medium** field. In the **Format** field there will only be one option to select; **Electronic Book Text**. There are no options for size with an ebook.

The next important field is **Primary Subject**. This is your opportunity to define the subject for your book. Bowker subjects are a proprietary schema used within the *Bowker Books In Print* product. It uses the same phrasing and structure as the Library of Congress Subject Headings (LCSH). There are over 80,000 subject possibilities available. However, the drop down options present only the highest level descriptors.

Authors may find this restricting. However, these selections are only temporary until the book is indexed (another reason to provide that PDF copy). Then catalogers will create the permanent subject descriptors. In order to have the subject changed, you will need to email Bowker support and request a change.

When you have completed all the options you wish to provide on this screen, click on the **Save and Go To: Sales & Pricing** button at the bottom of the screen.

Sales & Pricing is the final data screen prior to finalizing and submitting your book to be placed on the *Books in Print* list.

Bowker provides options for sales and pricing in six countries: Australia, Canada, New Zealand, Spain, the United

Kingdom, and the United States. Enter the sales and pricing information for each country in which you wish the information to be distributed. I recommend entering the information for all six countries. Though you may put all pricing in US dollars, it is much easier for international buyers to calculate costs and budget if it is in their own currency. This screen is also where you must enter the actual publication date and a target audience.

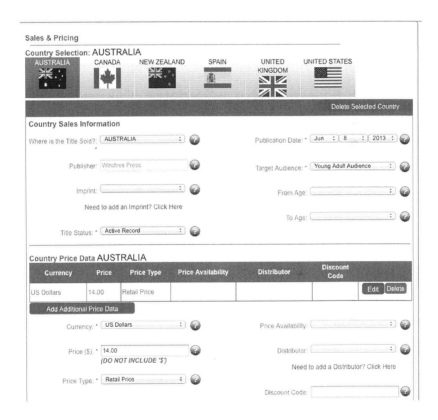

You must enter the required fields of **Where is the Title Sold** (Country), **Publication Date, Audience, Currency, Price,** and **Price Type** for each country. Use the drop down arrows to select a country under the **Where is the Title Sold field**. When a country is selected the appropriate flag appears in the top bar. This allows you to make changes to fields depending on the country selected. For example, a publisher might choose to release a book in the United States in one month and in other countries two or three months later. Personally, I prefer that the book be released in all countries at once. Most authors uploading to distributors select all possible venues at the same time. Once you have entered the first country data, all fields will remain the same until you select a new country.

Let's look at the fields that may not be as obvious.

Title Status for most authors will be **Active Record**, which is the default. However, you do have the option of making other selections based on your planning calendar and how you wish to handle availability. Other popular options include forthcoming, inactive, and out of print.

Target Audience is fairly easy for **Young Adult** audience books (ages 12-18). For an audience under age 12 choose **Juvenile Audience**. You can limit that further with the **From Age** and **To Age** fields. Confusion sometimes occurs, however, in the adult audience options. In the illustration below there are four possible options for an adult audience. The only one that works for fiction is **Trade**. The other options are for non-fiction audience designations.

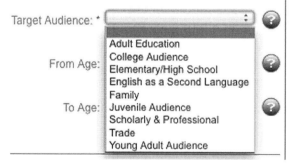

The pricing and currency fields should be carefully evaluated. As I stated earlier, it is best to provide your books in the currency of the country. For this reason you may want to have a currency calculator open in another tab while entering these fields. My favorite one is the one that is at the top of the page in Google when you enter "currency calculator" in the search field. You enter the price in **US Dollar**, then select the next box drop down arrow for the country you wish to calculate. It immediately provides a price.

Most consumers expect pricing to be at an even dollar amount or in the 95 or 99 cent category. Pricing a book at $4.50 instead of $4.99 looks unusual in comparison to larger publisher pricing. In foreign currency round up or down to reach the even dollar or 95 or 99 cent equivalent.

Tip: Canadian, Australian, and New Zealand dollars all tend to run within fifty cents of the same price in US dollars. Instead of putting in an odd price (e.g., 4.62 Australian dollars), consider simply making the price the same across all of these countries. You may gain or lose a few cents, but the pricing looks more professional.

Once you have completed all the fields on this screen, and you are confident in your all entries, click the **Submit** button to make the record with this ISBN permanent. That means you may not change the title or publication dates. However, if you are not prepared to submit yet, then select the left button: **Save and Go To: Format & Size.** This will save all your entries on the **Sales & Pricing** screen but not yet submit the record for finalization.

I recommend doing the final **Submit** the day before your release on other platforms. In that way, you will be certain of the publication date and the title will certainly have been permanently enshrined on your cover.

CHAPTER 14

Copyright Registration

Some writers mistakenly believe that getting an ISBN for a book automatically registers the copyright. **It does not!** They are two different processes. ISBNs are obtained in the United States through a private company, Bowker, that manages the database for all books identified by ISBN. The purpose of an ISBN is simply to have a unique identifier for a book so that it can be sold and tracked globally. Think of it as an inventory code that is the same for every retailer around the world.

Copyright registration has nothing to do with sales of your book or making it available to retailers. In fact, you can register a copyright for a book you never plan to sell or make available outside your immediate family. You are not required to have an ISBN to register a copyright.

Copyright registration is managed through the United States Copyright Office, which is part of the Library of Congress. It is the official United States government body that maintains records of copyright registrations. It is used by copyright title searchers who are attempting to clear a chain of title for copyrighted works.

An analogy I like to use when describing copyright registration is the one most people understand for obtaining title for property. If you own a car in the United States, you receive title to that car from your state government. That title is in the form of a certificate which proclaims you are the owner. The title includes a description of your car, including the vehicle identification number (VIN). If you rent the car out or loan the car to someone else, you still own it and can have use of it. However, if you sell the car you must transfer the title to the new owner. Once that happens, you no longer have use of the car and no say in what happens to the car.

If there were no car titles, a thief could steal your car and claim it was his. You would have little recourse to get the car back because you would have no proof that you own the car. The proof of ownership is the title certificate.

Registering your copyright provides a certificate from the federal government recognizing that you own the rights to your book. In principle, your work is protected by copyright the moment it takes form. However, without this certificate of registration it is difficult to prove you are the owner if another person brings a copy of your work forward and claims it is hers.

As with holding title to a car, you have rights associated with your written work. Those rights allow you to "rent" your work to someone else. This is what happens when you sign a contract with a publisher. The publisher is paying for the right to use what you wrote to make a profit. However, you are still the owner of that work. Based on the contract, the publisher can only make money from your work for a certain period of time. There may also be ways in which you can end your relationship so that the publisher can no longer use your work.

You also have the right to "sell" your work to someone else. This usually happens when you do a work-for-hire contract or a ghost-writer contract. In these contracts a publisher or individual is paying you for the work as though you were an employee. Once that payment is complete (e.g., a specific fee or royalties over a specified time period), the buyer owns your work. You no longer have the legal right to sell that work again or use it in any way.

In both of these examples—and in self-publishing—registering your copyright is what helps to establish that you are, in fact, the original owner of the work. If a dispute occurs, you will want that certificate of registration and the date it was filed in order to prove you are the owner. If there are two separate registration certificates issued for the same book, by two different people (yes, it does happen), the earlier registration has a better chance of being successful in a lawsuit than the later one.

At this time I must provide a caveat. The above illustrations demonstrate how not having a certificate of registration may cause problems. However, I am not an attorney. Therefore, do not take anything I say as legal advice. As I discuss copyright law throughout this chapter, I will reference quotations from the United States Copyright Office or a website that provides legal advice.

If you are unclear about your own copyright situation or how copyright registration laws apply to a specific book, seek advice from an intellectual property attorney licensed to practice in the your country or jurisdiction. Do not rely on what you find on the Internet or in books such as mine to provide legal advice. The law is complex and interpretations change as cases are tried in court. It is important to analyze what the latest case law findings say when making a decision on your own situation. Only a licensed attorney can give you that advice.

Registering your copyright with the United States Copyright Office is voluntary. The copyright office summarizes the reasons for registration on their website:

"Copyright exists from the moment the work is created. However, if you wish to bring a lawsuit for infringement of a work sold in the United States you will need to have registered. Registered works may be eligible for statutory damages and attorney's fees in successful litigation. If registration occurs within five years of publication, it is considered prima facie *evidence in a court of law."*

(See Circular 1, *Copyright Basics*
at *http://www.copyright.gov/circs/circ1.pdf*)

In other words, even though your work is protected from the moment of creation, you can't bring a lawsuit to recover lost income or assess damages against someone who steals your work unless it is registered.

In addition, registering within three months of publication is advised. According to NOLO, a publisher of legal information:

"You can register a copyright at any time, but registering it promptly may pay off in the long run. Timely registration—that is, registration within three months of the work's publication date or before any copyright infringement actually begins—makes it much easier to sue and recover money from an infringer. Specifically, timely registration creates a legal presumption that your copyright is valid, and allows you to recover up to $150,000 (and possibly lawyer fees) without having to prove any actual monetary harm."

http://www.nolo.com/legal-encyclopedia/copyright-registration-notice-enforcement-faq-29067.html

The least costly and quickest copyright registration method is through electronic registration at the United States Copyright Office website: https://eco.copyright.gov/ The cost for this is only $35.00 per book, and you may send an electronic copy of the book with your registration. You can pay by credit or debit card, or by electronic funds transfer using check routing and account information. Once the payment is accepted you will immediately receive a tracking number and a temporary registration number. Approximately 30 days later (depending on how many registrations the copyright office is processing) you will receive the official registration certificate in the mail.

An alternate registration method is through the mail. The cost to do a mailed registration is $65.00. You may download the form from the copyright office, and you must pay by check or money order. The office does not accept credit card payments through the mail. With the mailed form you must send **two** printed copies of the book to the copyright office. The processing time for this is significantly longer—often taking several months.

Even authors of commercial publishers should check if a copyright has been registered on their behalf. Most small presses, and even some large publishers do not do any copyright registration for their authors unless they are bestsellers. Check your contracts. If your books have not been registered, it is recommended that you register them now.

My personal process is to register my copyright within one week of release. Though I have not yet had a need to file an infringement lawsuit, I want to be sure the registration is as early as possible.

I've heard authors tell me they aren't going to register their work because they don't want to pay the fee, or they don't believe their "little, unknown work" will be stolen, or because they are not in a financial position to hire an attorney and bring a lawsuit if it were stolen. Certainly, registration is voluntary. Personally, I look at it as inexpensive insurance.

I wish we lived in a world where no one plagiarized written work, or outright stole books and put a different author name on it. Unfortunately, it happens far too often, and electronic document transmission has made it even easier for criminals to do this.

In addition, the likelihood of infringement increases with the popularity of a book or an author. You never know when you will become popular. You may work in obscurity for six years and then suddenly a book hits the New York Times list or it wins a major award. Once you become popular, not only is the bestselling book a temptation for criminals, but your entire backlist is targeted as well. Criminals have been known to put a new author name on a book and immediately register the copyright. They will even keep the same title (titles cannot be copyrighted). If you have not registered, what recourse do you have? None.

For me, spending $35.00 and a little time online is a small price to pay for the assurance that I can bring a lawsuit to prove infringement.

Convinced to register? Let's go through the online copyright process.

Go to: https://eco.copyright.gov/ Watch for a notice about pop-ups in the upper part of your screen. Elect to allow pop-ups from the copyright.gov site.

Note: The site works well with Internet Explorer and Firefox Browsers. It may have problems with other browsers, including Chrome.

You should first see the login screen. This is where you can set up an account with the copyright office by creating your login ID and password.

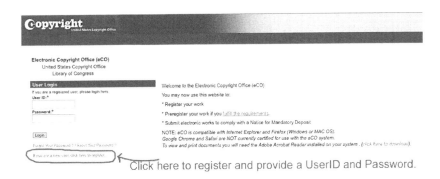

Click here to register and provide a UserID and Password.

Once you have set up an account, you will see a screen with several menu options. To register your copyright, select the **Register a New Claim** option under the **Copyright Services** heading.

Some authors have become confused with the language of registering a claim, mistakenly thinking this means you are claiming an infringement. This actually indicates you are registering your claim as the legal owner of the copyright.

The next screen determines what type of registration you want. A single work, created by one person, solely owned by one person is the default. This is the case for the majority of self-publishing authors. If the statements are all true click in the **Yes** box next to each one. Then click the **Start Registration** button at the bottom.

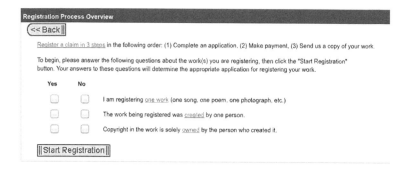

If any of the statements are not true, click in the **No** box and you will be taken to a different form. I will illustrate the process for the default use—a single work, created by one person, solely owned by one person. After checking each Yes box, when you click the **Start Registration** button a window will pop up asking you to confirm your selections.

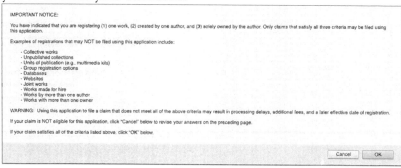

The notice reminds you what you selected and gives examples of the types of registrations that may not be used with the form you will be taken to next. Assuming you still wish to continue, click the **OK** button on the lower right of the screen.

Finally, you will be taken to a screen to start the actual application process. The Copyright Office wishes to be helpful, but unfortunately, the next screen appears confusing. All the links in the center of the screen are to describe the different types of work you may choose and offer extended definitions.

You should go directly to the bottom of the screen and click on the drop down arrow to choose **Literary Work.**

The elements presented on the left will continue to appear on each subsequent screen in the process. This is a tracking system, as well as a menu navigation system. The red arrow on the far left in the navigation tool indicates the screen you have currently selected. In this case it is the **Type of Work** screen.

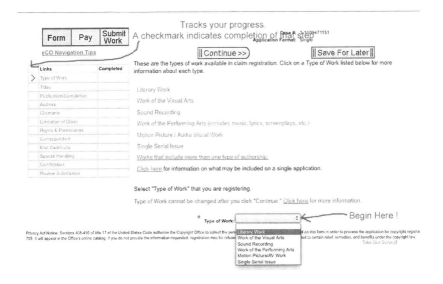

On each screen you have two options presented by the buttons at the top. Option one is to **Continue**. Clicking this will take you to the next screen in the forward navigation. Option two is to **Save For Later**. This allows you to save whatever you have completed thus far and return to it at any time. Now that you have an account, you can log in again and start where you left off.

Once you have selected **Literary Work** click the **Continue** button.

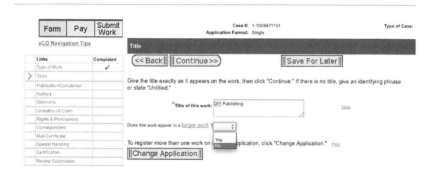

Enter the title of your book exactly as it appears on your title page. The form only allows your title to be one line long. If you have a subtitle, it doesn't need to be put here. The software will think you are trying to register more than one title. For example, for this book I entered **DIY Publishing** and not the subtitle.

The next question asked is: **Does this work appear in a larger work?** If this is a stand-alone book the answer is usually **No**. Click the dropdown arrow to select the answer appropriate for you.

You would answer **Yes** if, for example, this is a short story that was first published in a collection of stories. You would also answer yes is if you had published a novel earlier, then took the first chapter and turned it into a short story. Even though you may have changed a sentence or two, the substantive part of your story was published in the novel previously. Answering **Yes,** generates a screen that requires you to enter information about the copyright and registration of the larger work so that information can be appropriately matched with your copyright registration for the current work.

Once you have selected the appropriate response, **Yes** or **No,** click the **Continue** button.

The next screen will ask about the publication status of the work you are registering: **Has this work been published?** If I am completing the registration after the book has been released for sale, I select **Yes** on this option. You *are* allowed to register a copyright for a book that has not been released or may never be released for sale. Selecting **Yes** to indicate the book has been published, will pop up a screen asking ask for the publication month, day, and year.

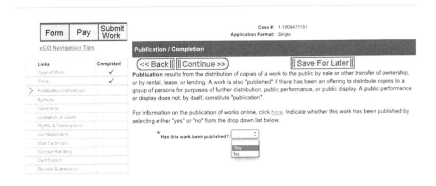

The next screen asks about author information. Only two items are required on this screen (indicated by red asterisks). They are the country in which you hold citizenship or residence, and what contributions the author made to the book. You may select as many boxes as are appropriate to your involvement with the book. I select only the **Text** box because I have someone else who designs the cover and another person who does the editing. Your situation may differ.

Tip: You have a choice whether to use a pen name or not. If your book copyright page uses only your pen name, you will want to type that name in the **Pseudonym** *box. If you do not want your real name revealed in public records, do not fill out the name information in the* **Individual Author** *boxes.*

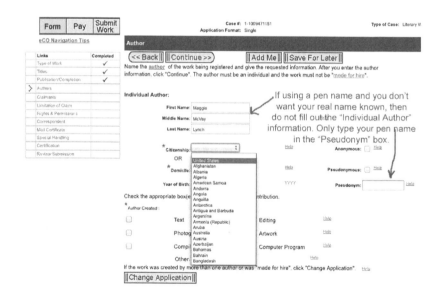

Click the **Continue** button to go to the next screen.

The next screen is where you enter your address. Because you already have a profile related to your account, you can click the **Add Address** button to have the address automatically filled from that information. If you wish to use a different address than what is in your profile, do so here. This information is a public record. Click **Continue** when completed.

The **Limitation of Claim** screen, shown below, is one screen that the majority of self-published authors will not need. It is used only if the work is based on pre-existing work. For example, if your book is an analysis of Grimms' fairy tales and each fairy tale is included in your work, you need to use the limitation screen. This screen allows you to provide the copyright details of the other work(s) and delineate which parts of the book are uniquely yours. It is that unique part that will be registered to you.

Click **Continue** to skip this screen.

The next screen, **Rights and Permissions,** asks for specific contact information should someone request permission to use your work. If you have a publishing entity (highly recommended) that is separate from your individual identity, you would enter that information under the **Organization** column on the right side of the screen. If you do not have a separate company, then enter your legal name and address under the **Individual** column on the left side of the screen. Remember, this is the contact information that would be provided to anyone who requests it. So, be careful when selecting what address you wish to provide. Many authors without a publishing entity will only provide a post office box address. Click **Continue** when you have completed the form.

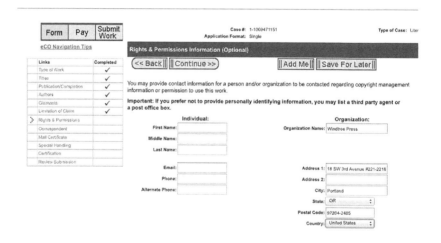

The next screen asks who the Copyright Office should contact with questions. If your publishing company is large enough to have staff or an answering service, you might choose to put that organization name, address, and phone number here. Otherwise, complete the individual contact side and use your personal or author-specific email address and phone.

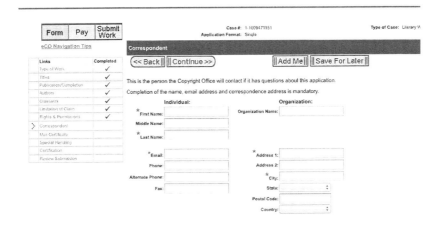

The next screen is another that the majority of self-publishing authors will not use. It is the **Special Handling** screen, and carries a fee of $750.00 if it applies to your situation. It is used by those who are already involved in a lawsuit, have customs issues or have unusual deadline issues. If it doesn't apply to you, simply click the **Continue** button.

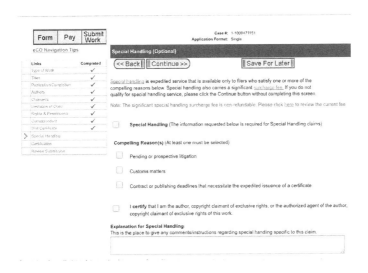

Finally, you have reached the screen where you **certify** that you are indeed the author of this book and that everything you have included on the application is correct. The statement reads:

I certify that I am the author, copyright claimant, or owner of exclusive rights, or the authorized agent of the author, copyright claimant, or owner of exclusive rights of this work and that the information given in this application is correct to the best of my knowledge.

Click in the box next to the certification statement. Then type your name in the box labeled **Name of certifying individual.**

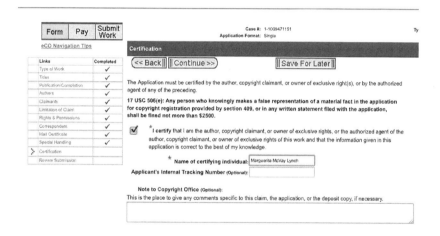

Click **Continue** when you have certified your claim that the copyright should be registered to you.

The final screen before checkout and paying your $35.00 is a review screen. It displays everything you have entered as it appears in the database. Corrections cannot be made on this screen. Click on the appropriate navigation item on the left to return to the screen where you can change the information.

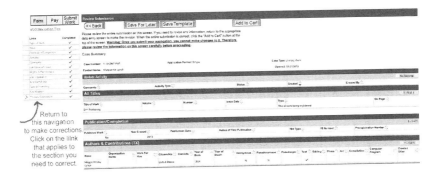

Return to this navigation to make corrections. Click on the link that applies to the section you need to correct.

Once you are satisfied with all of your entries, click on the **Add to Cart** button at the top of the page. This will take you to a check out system where you pay the fee to register your copyright.

If you are not ready to do that yet, click on the **Save for Later** button at the top of the page. This will allow you to save everything you've entered and return to it at another time.

The uploading of the electronic copy of your book comes after you have paid the fee. However, before I illustrate that upload process, let's take a look at how to get back to your application should you decide to **Save for Later.**

First, login to the site at https://eco.copyright.gov/

Knowing where to look for your application is not intuitive. On the left navigation bar, under **Check Registration Case Status**, select **Working Cases.**

This will bring up a screen showing any incomplete applications. Click on the link to the application you wish to review and complete.

Once you click on the link you will be returned to the familiar screens with the navigation on the left and whichever screen you have selected on the right. Continue to work through the application as described above until you are ready for checkout and payment.

Remember: Once you have checked out, that registration record becomes permanent. You cannot return to make changes.

After the check out and payment is complete, click the **Continue** button to upload a copy of your completed book. A payment receipt with your case number will be sent to the email you provided in the application.

Under the **Electronic Deposit Upload** header, click on the link that reads **Upload Deposit**. This will open the file manager on your computer and allow you to browse and select the appropriate file.

The copyright office accepts many file types for upload:

- Microsoft Word Documents (.doc or .docx)
- Adobe documents (.pdf)
- Web page formats (.htm or .html)
- Rich text format (.rtf)

- Text documents (.txt)
- Word Perfect documents (.wpd)
- Microsoft Works documents (.wps)

I recommend uploading a **PDF file** because it retains both the content and the formatting of your book. As you are likely already creating a PDF file for your print-on-demand printer and for electronic download, it is easiest to send this same file to the Copyright Office as the deposit of your work.

The screenshot below from the U.S. Copyright Office's PowerPoint presentation illustrates the upload process.

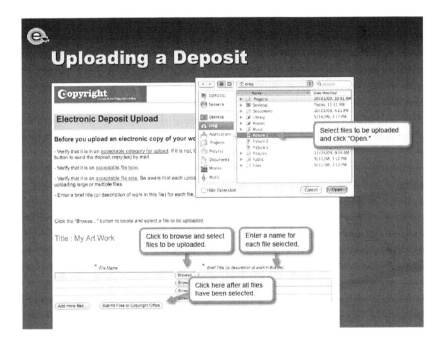

If you completed the form to upload a single work from a single author, then you will only have one file to upload. Note the **Name** field associated with each file. I recommend you name the file with your actual book title (e.g., *DIY Publishing*). Including the author's name along with the book title is suggested if you are publishing under multiple names or are uploading as part of a publishing cooperative with multiple authors. For example: **Maggie Lynch DIY Publishing**. The name is displayed as part of your records to make it easy for you to locate the record associated with this registration. So make sure whatever name you select is readily recognizable to you.

It may take a minute or two for the file to upload, depending on the size, so be patient. Once the upload complete you will get a confirmation screen that says: **The following files were successfully uploaded for service request** (followed by a number).

Click on the **Close Window** button at the bottom of the screen to finish the process. You will then receive an email confirming receipt of your uploaded file. Print out the email and save it. I have a folder marked "Copyright Registration" in which I keep all the emails for each of my books until I receive the actual **Certificate of Registration** in the mail. In this way I have a paper trail of the entire transaction should I need it.

Copyright registration is important. The new electronic registration available at the United States Copyright Office makes it fairly quick and easy. For maximum protection, register every book within three months of its publication.

CHAPTER 15

Print Book Distribution

This chapter discusses the two primary distributors of the print-on-demand (POD) books that most self-published authors and small presses use. The POD printing technology is primarily owned and operated by two large companies: Ingram, through its Lightning Source subsidiary; and Amazon, through its CreateSpace subsidiary. I will discuss the pros and cons of working with each company, and illustrate how to add accounts and upload your work at CreateSpace.

In addition to these two large distributors, there are hundreds of other "author services" companies which will format your print book, create a cover, and arrange for POD printing and distribution. There are significant fees associated with these services, and some will additionally take a percentage of each sale. All of these companies use either Lightning Source or CreateSpace.

I highly recommend that you upload directly to Lightning Source or CreateSpace yourself. You will receive the maximum royalty and control over how your titles are loaded and what data is associated with them.

Let's begin by comparing CreateSpace and Lightning Source. Both are reputable companies that produce library-quality books using a print-on-demand model (i.e., books are printed and shipped to fulfill customer orders). While some services overlap, each company has its strengths and weaknesses. Your preference depends largely on your needs and objectives. In my opinion, the end product is equal between these two sources. In fact, CreateSpace often uses Lighting Source's POD printers when volume overwhelms its own network. However, there are fans on both sides that will shout from the rooftops that their POD printer is better. Let's look at the primary differences between the two:

CreateSpace

- Nice array of trim sizes
- Laminate finish on all covers
- Paperback only
- Setup fee is free.
- Proof copy is your cost for the book. Typical author cost for a 350 page 6 x 9 inch book is approximately $5.00
- You can make changes and reupload the book any time for free.
- One time fee for distribution through Ingram and Baker and Taylor is $25.00.

Lightning Source

- Wider range of trim sizes
- Choice of laminate or matte finish on cover

- Choice of paperback or hard cover
- Setup fee is $37.50
- Proof copy cost is $30-$35 depending on if it's paperback or hardcover
- Change fee is $40
- Author price for a 360 page 6 x 9 inch book is approximately $5.45
- Fee for distribution through Ingram is 12 per book per year in the US and an additional $12.00 per year in the UK.

The above are the basic setup and distribution costs. In addition there are other differences that may impact an author's decision, particularly if you wish to work with a large number of bookstores.

CreateSpace sets the wholesale discount at 20% at the CreateSpace store, 40% at Amazon, and 60% in expanded distribution. Most small bookstores refuse to order print books from Amazon and the actual discount to them is only 25%. Later in this chapter I discuss the math behind expanded distribution and what a self-published author can do work more effectively with bookstores.

Lightning Source allows you to set the wholesale discount yourself for each vendor. The minimum discount is 20%. In this scenario, you decide what discount to assign to Amazon or Barnes & Noble, or bookstores. However, be aware that the decisions you make may impact actual distribution. If Amazon doesn't get 40%, the print books are marked as "not in stock" and flagged as 4 to 6 week order times. Bookstores expect at least 40% and are accustomed to 55%. This means if you set the bookstores at only

20% they will not carry your books, and many will not even order them as a special order because of the shipping costs.

CreateSpace does not accept returns. However, Amazon does. Lightning Source allows authors to determine if they wish to accept returns. Returns mean that if the book does not sell within a particular period of time the bookseller is able to return it to the publisher for a full refund, minus shipping. If you accept returns and are selling regularly this isn't a problem because the returns are deducted from your total sales. However, if your book is not selling well and you accept returns you can find yourself in the position of having to purchase those books yourself because your account will be in the negative.

Three other things to consider are turn-around for proof copies, time it takes to get in distribution once you put it on sale, and over all customer service. Proof copies of the book are handled differently with each vendor. CreateSpace offers two choices: reviewing an online proof copy of both the interior and cover; or having a copy of the finished book mailed to you for proofing. Mailing time varies based on what you are willing to pay for shipping. The least expensive is UPS ground which is guaranteed delivery in seven to ten days.

Lightning Source does not provide online proof copies. They are always mailed. However, the $30.00 fee for a proof copy includes priority mailing which makes sure you receive your proof within three days.

Time to distribution is dependent on where your book is being distributed. CreateSpace electronically transfers your finalized book information immediately to all Amazon stores you've elected. Making your book available in the expanded distribution network takes approximately a month. It appears at Barnes & Noble within a week, but other bookstores take up to a month. That's because the files are sent to Ingram and Baker & Taylor for loading and then to Lightning Source for POD printing.

Lightning Source distribution to all bookstores supported by Ingram appears in the catalog with 24 hours. It appears in Baker & Taylor catalogs within two weeks, and at Amazon usually within one week.

Customer service is also markedly different between the two companies. Lightning Source and Ingram were set up to deal with medium to large professional publishing companies. There is an expectation on their part that you'll understand how to navigate the site, what all the selection options and terms mean, and how to upload a book without mistakes. As a result, Lightning Source customer support is slow to respond to individual author difficulties with the system. They respond only by email. There is no phone support. If you are set up as a publisher and have multiple titles, then Lightning Source assigns a publisher representative to you who becomes your liaison with the company.

CreateSpace, on the other hand, was built with the self-publishing author in mind. It has instant phone and email support 24 hours a day. Is CreateSpace sometimes frustrating to deal with? Sure. Not all reps are created equal. Customer support groups have a diversity of talent and people skills among the staff.

Another subsidiary of Ingram has entered the market as well. Ingram Spark was announced in July 2013 to offer a combination POD and ebook distribution model. It uses Lightning Source for printing and Ingram for ebook and POD distribution. Here is what Ingram says about the differences on the Ingram Spark website: http://Ingrampark.com

The same functionality exists with both Ingram Spark and Lightning Source. Both systems offer the same trim sizes and binding types, and print charges are the same for both. Ingram Spark is designed and priced as a self-service model with slightly reduced pricing for title set up. Ingram Spark customers do not have an assigned Ingram representative, and are instead supported by a team. With Lightning Source, a publisher can set a range of trade discounts on their titles, whereas in Ingrampark, a trade discount of 55% is automatically applied, which gives a book the best chance to sell in the marketplace.

Given my analysis of both companies, I've chosen to use CreateSpace for all my POD printing needs. If at a later date I am selling significant number of books, then I may switch to Lightning Source who can also do offset printing in quantity. To sufficiently decrease the unit cost of books, I've calculated it requires a minimum order of 1,500 books.

Certainly, I am concerned that the majority of bookstores will not order my books except when specifically asked by a customer. However, I know many New York published authors who also cannot get their work on local bookstore shelves. The reality is that there are far too many books for any bookstore to stock them all. With shipping within 2-3 days for any book, it doesn't make sense for bookstores to carry everything.

This is where forming relationships with bookstores makes a difference. Many stores like to carry titles by local authors, or authors who have a tie to the area. Bookstores where I live typically agree to carry two to five of my books at a 40 % discount rate.

For authors who are new in the market, or the sales are unknown, some stores will take self-published books on consignment. This means they agree to carry the books for a specified period of time and at a specified discount (e.g., 40%). If the books sell within that period of time you are paid for those sales. If they do not, you must take them back and the stores is unlikely to provide shelf space for that title in the future.

I began selling my small press books on consignment—at first through in-person signings and store events, then through cold calls. Once a title proved to sell regularly every month, the bookstore will take me off consignment and purchase the books directly from me. This resolves the issue bookstores have of ordering from an Amazon affiliated company, or for the limited discount offered. For local stores I simply replenish their stock as needed, driving to deliver the books in person, signing the stock, and reconnecting with the owners. For stores that are not local and pay me in advance, I drop ship the books from CreateSpace to their store. When I'm in the area I always stop by to sign stock.

To summarize, CreateSpace and Lightning Source are the two largest POD printers and distributors. There are other smaller, independent companies that will handle print formatting and distribution for you, as well as other author services for a fee. Some of these companies are excellent partners. Many of them are not.

Should you decide to use an author services company instead of doing it yourself, be sure to investigate the company carefully. Unfortunately, there are many companies that take advantage of unwary authors and charge outrageous fees for little benefit and no guarantee of getting your books anywhere.

Using CreateSpace

I will only demonstrate the process for using CreateSpace. This is because I do not use Lightning Source or Ingram Spark, so I can't speak directly to the process, nor can I download screen captures. I can say that all sources require you to upload a PDF of the interior of your book and a PDF of the cover wrap. The types of data and information you are required to provide to CreateSpace will be similar to the requirements for Lightning Source or Ingram Spark. However the navigation of screens will be significantly different between the three companies.

To begin working with CreateSpace go to:

http://createspace.com

You will have to set up an account before you can do anything with your book. The account set up process is similar to everywhere else on the Internet.

In the drop down box for "What type of media are you considering publishing?" select **Book**. Then click on the **Create My Account** button.

CreateSpace offers you two ways to navigate through the upload process. One is to go one step at a time; the other is to present all the requirements on a single page. Either way you will see exactly the same options to complete.

I will break the selections into different sections and spend time on each. Now that you have been through the Jutoh metadata screens and the Copyright Office screens, you should be well prepared to enter data on the CreateSpace screens.

The first screen asks for **Title Information**. Like many other online software programs, the required entries are labeled with a red asterisk. However, the more information you provide, the more metadata will be generated for your title and passed on to all distributors.

Note that this screen allows you to enter both your **Title** and your **Subtitle** on separate lines. Be sure that the title listed on the **Title** line is exactly the same as it is in your ISBN purchase and Copyright Registration. Any discrepancy in the title may result in errors when the book is released for sale.

In the **Primary Author** field, enter the name exactly as it appears on the book. Do not use a prefix unless it also appears on the book. For example, do not select Dr. Martha Jones if the prefix "Dr." is not a part of the author name. The same applies to suffixes like Jr.

Options for adding more than one author or other types of contributors are available in the **Add Contributors** section. With each contributor added, select the role of that contributor in the drop down box. Then click the **Add** button. The contributor is not added until the **Add** button is clicked.

If your book is part of a series, click in the check box next to **This books is part of a series.** That will unlock the **Series Title** and **Volume** fields. Enter the series name exactly. The volume refers to the book number in the series.

As described in the ISBN and Copyright Registration chapters, enter the appropriate **Edition Number.**

The language will default to **English** unless you change it. The publication date is the month, day, and year the book will go on sale. You may click on the calendar to select the date or enter it in the format of MM-DD-YYYY. You will not be allowed to select a date in the future.

The next section is where you will enter the ISBN. As stated earlier, an ISBN is required for every print book. If you elect to take the CreateSpace ISBN, click in the radio button next to **CreateSpace Assigned.** Otherwise, click the radio button next to **Enter Your Own.** A pop up screen will open to allow entry of your ISBN.

⊙ **Enter Your Own**	If you have an ISBN for this book that you purchased from R.R. Bowker.
ISBN-10 or ISBN-13 *	9781940064277
Imprint Name * What's this?	Windtree Press

Always enter the thirteen-digit ISBN, even though you are presented with an option of ISBN-10. Today, all bookstore online systems use the **ISBN-13** for tracking and integration with Ingram.

The **Imprint Name** is the the publisher. That is you. This must be the same name used when you purchased the ISBN—your name or your author name or your publishing company name.

Note: When you have your own ISBN, CreateSpace is never the imprint. The only time CreateSpace becomes the publisher or imprint is when you use the CreateSpace ISBN. Think of CreateSpace as the printer for your book.

Prior to distributing your book, CreateSpace will run a check of your ISBN against the records at Bowker and other ISBN agencies around the world. If both the book title and imprint name does not match, it will generate an error. You will not be allowed to distribute the book until the error is resolved.

Now that the title information is complete, you can move on to the sections that describe the physical properties of the book, including the trim size (height and width), the type of paper you wish to use, and whether the interior will be printed in full color.

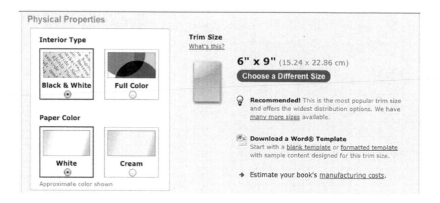

CreateSpace offers a multitude of trim sizes. The two most popular for POD books are 6" x 9" and 5.5" x 8.5". Unit costs are based on the number of printed pages, not the size of the book. Larger books require fewer pages and therefore cost less.

CreateSpace also offers a table which provides the maximum page count allowed for each trim size depending on interior color and paper color. See that at the link below:

https://www.createspace.com/Special/Pop/book_trimsizes-pagecount.html

I personally prefer the 6" x 9" size. It feels substantial and keeps the cost down. However, a book under 50,000 words may also seem too slim to a consumer. In this case you may wish to select a smaller trim size or to use a larger font to create more pages.

The next decision is whether to print the interior in **Black & White** or **Full Color**. Printing in color is significantly more expensive. There is not an option to print only certain interior pages in color and the rest in black and white. Most narrative non-fiction book and novels are printed in black and white. Children's picture books, photography books, and other genres that contain numerous images should be printed in color.

The final choice in this section is the paper color. Choose **White** or **Cream**. Some would argue that, traditionally, genre fiction is printed in white and literary fiction is printed in cream. I don't agree with that. I've looked at a lot of New York books and haven't seen that distinction. However, I would say there is a leaning toward cream in general. Personally, I prefer white because it has higher contrast and is easier to read. The paper is also slightly thicker. There is a slight difference in cost, but it is only pennies. I recommend selecting what matches your aesthetic.

Once the physical properties section is completed, move on to the **Interior** section. This is where you will have the opportunity to upload the PDF file containing the content of the book. Earlier in this book, I described how to use a template and save the completed manuscript as a PDF file. It is that file that you will upload here. Click on the **Browse** button to locate the file on your computer. Then click **Open**. It will place the file name and location on your computer in the field next to **PDF Interior File**.

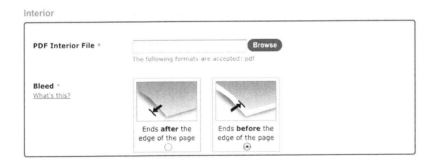

The **Bleed** refers to how much of the printed page will go into the margins. On the majority of books, you would choose the option showing a white margin around the edge. It is labeled **Ends before the edge of the page.**

The only time you would choose the left option, **Ends after the edge of the page,** is if there is an illustration or photograph that takes up the entire page and you want no white space around it. Again, this might be selected in a photography book or an art book or heavily illustrated childrens book.

The bleed gives the printer a small amount of space to account for movement of the paper and design inconsistencies. It is very difficult to print exactly to the edge of a sheet of paper. In order to achieve this, printers use slightly larger sheets of paper and then trim the entire book to the required finished size. For example, a finished book with a 6" x 9" trim, uses 6-1/8" x 9-1/8" paper. Images, background images and fills which are intended to extend to the edge of the page are created to extended beyond the trim line to give a bleed. CreateSpace provides templates with bleed lines for those who need to fill an entire page with color.

The next section provides options for uploading a cover. Though CreateSpace allows you to create a cover using a standard template online, I don't recommend it as it provides a generic cover. As I emphasized earlier, the cover is the number one marketing tool for an unknown author. It is the first thing a reader sees. Therefore having a well-designed cover is critical.

A part of that cover design process is understanding bleed and creating a cover that wraps the front, spine, and back of the book. CreateSpace has a nice template generator that will provide the exact dimensions needed for the cover and bleed based on the page count, trim size, and interior design selections. You can find that template generator here:
https://www.createspace.com/Help/Book/Artwork.do

Do not guess on the page numbers. Put the exact number of pages in your PDF file. This includes front matter and all back matter. The spine calculation changes based on the number of pages. A discrepancy of as few as 25 pages can make the difference between the spine fitting securely or being loose.

Once you have the cover PDF ready to go, click on the radio button next to **PDF Cover File**, and select **Browse** to locate the file on your computer.

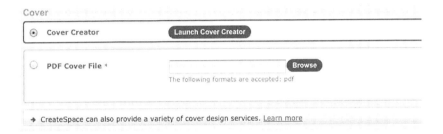

The next section is called **Distribute**. However, it is really descriptive information about the book and you. This information becomes a part of the metadata shared with all sales entities. Assuming you are going to elect to be distributed by Ingram and Baker & Taylor, it is this next section that will appear in the online catalogs beside the book, will categorize the book for search engines, and will provide the author biography.

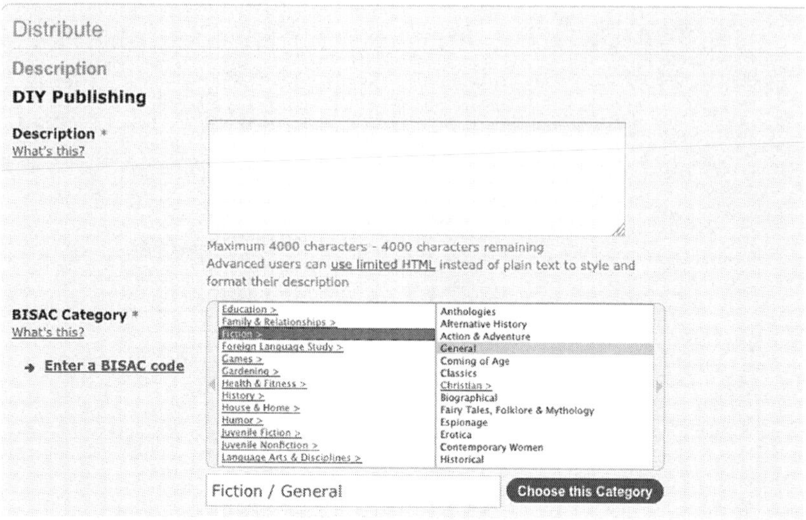

The first box, labeled **Description**, is for your book description. Again, remember this description is what will appear next to your book. I recommend you use the short 100 word description—the one that is geared for the quick browsing reader and is marketing oriented. If you choose, instead, to use your back cover blurb here be aware of the 4,000 character limit which is approximately 400 words.

The next box is the **BISAC Category** selection. CreateSpace does not provide all the BISAC categories here. For both fiction and non-fiction, remember to select the lowest level sub-category that pertains to your book. In that way, your book can be searched in that category and each of the levels leading to that sub-category. For fiction, the category head is "fiction." Select a subcategory following that. You also have the option to enter the BISAC code instead of using the category selection tool. To do this click on **Enter a BISAC code**. I would choose this option if the categories presented in the scroll are not sufficient to describe the book accurately.

Remember: You can find the full list of BISAC subject headers and codes at: http://www.bisg.org/what-we-do-0-136-bisac-subject-headings-list-major-subjects.php Click on the subject header that fits your book and then find the best category description. The BISAC code is next to each line of description.

For example, when I scrolled down the list to classify this book, the closest option was Computers / digital media / general. That didn't quite fit. It said nothing about publishing or ebooks and I doubted readers would search "digital media" to find a book on self-publishing. I went to the BISAC listing at the website above and found a category for Computers / electronic publishing. That was much more accurate. Then I selected **Enter a BISAC code**, and entered the COM065000 from the list. This now provides an accurate categorization for my book and I know that it will be easier for readers to find.

The final part of describing the book is contained in the **Additional Information** section. Here is where you will provide your author biography and keywords in addition to other data.

To include your author biography, click on the **Add** button. This will open a window for you to copy and paste your biography. As I advised in the book description section above, I also recommend this biography be under 100 words if possible. Remember, this is to market yourself and your author brand.

Additional Information (optional)

Author Biography What's this?	Add
Book Language What's this?	English ⇕
Country of Publication What's this?	Choose one ⇕
Search Keywords What's this?	
Contains Adult Content What's this?	☐
Large Print What's this?	☐

The **Book Language** will default to English. To change that, click on the arrows and select the appropriate language. The **Country of Publication** is where the book originates, not where it is sold. This will be used to match the ISBN digits referring to country of publication.

The **Search Keywords** are critical. This is the opportunity for you to provide additional categorization details that you were not able to provide in the single BISAC code selection. CreateSpace limits you to only five keywords or phrases, so select carefully. Because of the five keyword limit, do not use any of the words already provided in the BISAC categories. For this book I choose: self-publishing, formatting, distribution, style sheets, cover design. None of these words were in the BISAC category description of computer or electronic publishing. Remember to separate your five selections by commas just as I did here.

The next button is labeled **Contains Adult Content**. This relates to more than sex or violence. It takes some judgment on your part. CreateSpace describes this selection as: "If the content you provide for your product's detail page is not suitable for minors under the age of 18, your product may be suppressed from some search, browse, and merchandising results to protect customers from inappropriate content. CreateSpace states: *"No modifications will be made to your product's detail page."*

Given ongoing media scrutiny of ebooks in general, and self-published titles in particular, I recommend evaluating your book content carefully when making this decision. Follow this link to learn about the CreateSpace content guidelines.

https://www.createspace.com/Help/Rights/ContentGuidelines.jsp

The final option is to designate if this book is a **Large Print** edition. Large Print is defined as a font size of at least 16 points. Most self-published authors do not provide a large print edition. If you are doing so, definitely click on this radio button. It will allow your book to be included in a special list for sight-impaired readers.

With the availability of ereaders, many sight-impaired individuals have chosen to take advantage of the ability to enlarge print at any time. However, some readers still appreciate a paper copy with large print.

You have now completed the descriptive portions of your book. The next step is to determine pricing and in what markets you would like your book distributed. CreateSpace offers three markets at no cost. The include distribution through the CreateSpace online store; through Amazon U.S.; and through Amazon Europe. The Amazon Europe option includes all countries in Europe where Amazon distributes. I recommend you opt to take advantage of *all* of these markets.

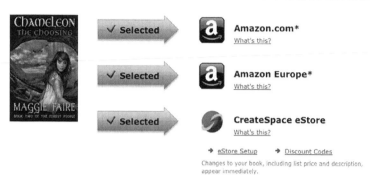

To select a market, click on the green arrow marked **Select** associated with each option. It will confirm your choice by changing color from a green to a blue arrow and marking it as **Selected** as illustrated above.

The next decision is **Expanded Distribution**. CreateSpace no longer charges for this service. This again provides three options: CreateSpace Direct sales; library sales; and bookstores and online retailers. The library sales option is only available to you if you use the CreateSpace assigned ISBN. Later, I will talk about how you can get library sales without using this distribution channel at CreateSpace. Let's evaluate each of these distribution channels.

CreateSpace Direct is the wholesale pricing option that is supposed to simulate what a commercial publisher might offer. However, I do not give much credence to the value of this channel. Many self-published authors report they have received no sales from CreateSpace Direct. Bookstores will not order direct from CreateSpace because the discount is only 20% and that is too low to be profitable. In addition, the majority of bookstores refuse to order from an Amazon subsidiary.

What makes **Expanded Distribution** worthwhile is the "Bookstores and Online Retailers" channel. This is the option that provides distribution through Ingram. It provides you access to over 28,000 bookstores around the world. Your book will be available in their online catalogs at large stores such as Barnes & Noble, Books A Million, and WH Smith, as well as at your small local bookstore. There are also a number of large online retailers for print books such as The Book Depository; Abe Books; and Powell's Books which feature the Ingram catalog.

Choosing expanded distribution does not guarantee your book will actually be stocked in any of these stores. Nor does it guarantee your book will actually be purchased by any library. All it does is make your book available through the purchasing network that bookstores and libraries use.

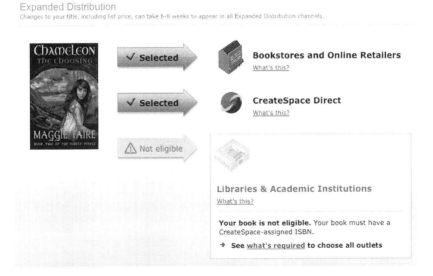

Expanded Distribution
Changes to your title, including list price, can take 6-8 weeks to appear in all Expanded Distribution channels.

Selected — Bookstores and Online Retailers
What's this?

Selected — CreateSpace Direct
What's this?

Not eligible

Libraries & Academic Institutions
What's this?

Your book is not eligible. Your book must have a CreateSpace-assigned ISBN.

→ See what's required to choose all outlets

The third channel is distribution to library and academic institutions. CreateSpace restricts access to this option only to those who have elected to use a CreateSpace-assigned ISBN. I don't believe it is worth taking the CreateSpace ISBN to have this channel available. There are three other ways to get access to library distribution. First, if you register your copyright (detailed in *Chapter 14*), your book is added to the *Books in Print* publication and data feeds that are distributed from the Copyright Office to libraries and bookstores across the United States. Second, most libraries order books either from Baker & Taylor or Ingram. Under the Expanded Distribution channel you are already distributed by Ingram. Third, if you are a publisher with at least ten books you can work directly with Baker & Taylor or Ingram to enhance sales options to libraries. (Note: This costs money, usually paid through an annual contract for services.) There are also other options for free and paid services available.

Once your distribution channels have been selected, the final step is to determine the price you wish to set for your book.

Pricing Trade Paperback Books

In CreateSpace, the **Pricing** screen is presented with the cost of your book already calculated based on the number of pages you uploaded and the information you provided earlier about paper type and trim size. Beneath each distribution channel, a minimum price is also stated. This is the price CreateSpace indicates is required in order to participate in that channel. That minimum price is based on your cost for the book, plus the discount offered to the vendor.

For example, the discount at CreateSpace Direct is only 20%, so the minimum price for any book distributed by CreateSpace is only 20% above your cost of the book. If your book cost is $4.00, that means your book most be priced above $4.80. The minimum list price is displayed next to each channel.

On the other hand, the discount to Amazon is 40%. This means the price must be higher to distribute there. Finally, the discount to Expanded Distribution is 60%.

Authors often mistakenly believe this means their local bookseller receives a 60% discount on books. That is not the case. The 60% discount is distributed so that CreateSpace keeps their 20%. That means a 40% discount is offered to wholesalers Ingram and Baker & Taylor. (The same percentage Amazon is taking) The wholesalers then take 15% to manage their distribution process. That means the discount passed to the local bookseller is now only 25%. Is it any wonder they don't regularly stock their shelves with self-published or small publishers' POD books?

List Price	Channel	Royalty
$ 14.00 USD* [Calculate]	Amazon.com	$4.87
Minimum list price for this title is $8.83 What's this?	CreateSpace eStore	$7.67
	Expanded Distribution	$2.07
☐ Yes, suggest a GBP price based on U.S. price What's this?		
£ 9.20 GBP** [Calculate]	Amazon Europe For books printed in Great Britain	£2.58
Minimum list price for this title is £4.90		
☐ Yes, suggest a EUR price based on U.S. price What's this?		
€ 10.75 EUR** [Calculate]	Amazon Europe For books printed in continental Europe	€3.17
Minimum list price for this title is €5.47		

What CreateSpace lists as **Royalty** is the money you will receive in that market for each book you sell. In the illustration above, for one of my books, you can see that with a list price of $14.00 I will make the most money from the CreateSpace eStore at $7.67 and the least money from Expanded Distribution at $2.07.

Realistically, I will never make the $7.67 per book because *no one* buys from the CreateSpace estore except me. Readers don't buy from the store, even when I provide the link. Booksellers don't buy from the store because their discount is only 20%.

So what about purchases at the Amazon stores? In my personal experience, very few people buy print books from the Amazon stores. In 2012, with four titles available I sold a total of 17 print books at Amazon stores. So that $4.87 cent per book and its equivalents in the U.K. and Europe only materialized for 17 print books. In expanded distribution, at the $2.07 per book royalty I sold another 148 print books. Though still not a lot of money, it means of the royalty amounts I'm most likely to sell books in expanded distribution. That is the pricing determinant for my books. You cannot set a different list price for each distribution type. You must select one list price.

For me, 70% of my print sales come from my direct relationships with bookstores, which I will discuss at the end of this chapter. Those relationships and discounts are outside of CreateSpace and their distribution partners.

Looking at the choice I made above, many authors have asked why I chose to make over $2.00 per book in expanded distribution? Am I just greedy? Shouldn't I price the book as low as possible in order to get more readers? I could have priced it at $11.99 and made six cents per copy. If the price was decreased by $2.00, would it have made a difference? The answer is no.

Unfortunately, POD book pricing from Ingram and Baker & Taylor at the 25% discount to bookstores is insufficient for them to make a profit. Most bookstores' overhead (employee pay, building rent and maintenance, etc.) is about 25% if the store is running lean. That means once a store pays for shipping, it loses on the sale. The only way a store doesn't pay for shipping is to order a minimum of 15 copies of a book. Unless your book has already proven to be popular that is unlikely to happen. This is why local booksellers don't stock self-published POD books and why they don't order your book through their normal channels. Some stores will order it for a customer who makes a request. Others will not, unless it is priced high enough that after shipping there is at least a 10% margin.

Selling direct to bookstores

As I said earlier, 70% of my print sales come from my relationships with bookstores. Because of that I definitely believe it is worthwhile to undertake direct print distribution. This means I purchase books from CreateSpace at my cost and then deliver them to booksellers based on their orders. I do this in two ways. For local bookstores, I keep an inventory of my books at my house. I then deliver them in batches of four or five as their stock depletes and they order more. For bookstores that are not local, I again purchase the books from CreateSpace at my cost. Then I drop ship them to the bookseller. Depending on volume, the bookseller may pay for shipping.

This scenario requires two elements: a bookseller discount of at least 40%; and a relationship built on proof that your books can sell and that you can be counted on to deliver on time. The discount is the minimum I've found that is acceptable to booksellers and allows them to make a profit. The relationships are built one store at a time. Once you have five or six stores working with you, it expands more quickly. Booksellers belong to organizations. They talk among themselves about authors they like, and authors they don't. If you've been a part of helping a bookstore succeed it will get passed to others and then those stores will contact you.

Working one-on-one with booksellers also means we can plan special events together. I can partner with them on sales and promotion. The more I do to help them, the more they do to help me. It is a win-win scenario.

There is a downside to this arrangement. The more stores you supply, the more time consuming order fulfillment, event planning, and promotion becomes. Also, this is not something you can do when you feel like it. Nor is it something you can put off because you are on deadline to get the next book out and will be hiding in your writing cave for a month. Booksellers expect to receive a book within three days of ordering. This means you need to be on top of orders and fulfillment every day, not once a week or once a month.

By this time, it would be natural to wonder why bother with print books at all. For me there are several reasons.

1. Some readers prefer print and being able to satisfy them is important to me.
2. Many reviewers, bloggers, librarians, and bookstores take you more seriously if you have a print edition available.
3. When the print book is listed on Amazon, the cost of the ebook next to it looks like a great bargain. My $4.95 ebook is a good deal next to the $14.00 print book.
4. If you enjoy book signings, you need a book to sign.

5. If a book takes off, your print need will go up. If you reach bestseller status, both booksellers and librarians will be purchasing books in high enough numbers to get free shipping and realize some profit—even on POD.

Finally, I admit I love having a print book to hold in my hand. Though I read ebooks almost exclusively, I do pay for print books on occasion. What is more special than your own book?

One final comment on pricing. It is important to first erase the comparison of trade paperback to mass market. They are not the same product nor are the printing costs the same. Mass market is printed in lots beginning at about 10,000 units. That is how the price is kept low. Trade Paperback for most independent writers is printed on demand, one at a time.

Instead compare your price to book to New York trade paperback books. The list price for most trade paperbacks falls between $13.95 and $17.95. Do not look at the sale price on Amazon. Compare the list prices. Should you charge the same price as a bestseller? Probably not; you don't have the following. Aim for a couple dollars under trade paperback book pricing in your genre. Charge enough to make at least $2.00 per book.

Pricing low is making a statement about how you value your work. You are saying that your book is not as good as those from New York. If you believe that, then your book is not ready to be sold. If you know your book is ready and it is comparable to the average traditionally published book, then don't price low out of fear. Price based on value—a comparable value to other trade paperback books in your genre.

Finally, determine what your expectations are for your print book. If all you want is something to show your family and friends, and perhaps take to a bookstore signing. Then don't do expanded distribution at all. This means your print book will only be available through Amazon. However, you can still purchase your own books through CreateSpace and take them to book signings on a consignment basis. For many authors this is enough.

Personally, I like options for worldwide distribution. I don't like limiting my print distribution to one vendor. I also adore bookstores and want to support them as much as possible. But those are my choices. Do what is right for you, your goals and values, and your economic philosophy.

CHAPTER 16

Ebook Distribution

Unlike print books where the majority of POD printing is handled by only two vendors, ebooks have a plethora of distribution options. In fact, it seems that a new vendor pops up weekly.

This chapter discusses the variety of distribution channels available to the self-published author. I will illustrate how to add accounts and upload your work at the following large distributors, and discuss the options each offers.

- Amazon
- Barnes & Noble
- Kobo
- Apple

In addition to these large distributors, there are hundreds of other possibilities. Some are genre specific such as ARe (All Romance ebooks), while others are simply e-commerce portals that purport to offer better discoverability than the large distribution options. I will also cover options that are not available for direct upload but can be accessed through aggregators—a type of middleman distributor that feeds products to larger companies (e.g., Amazon, Apple, Kobo, Sony, etc.).

In my opinion, the only reason to use a middleman for distribution is if that entity has access to markets you do not. For example, Sony only allows larger publishers to upload direct. In order to upload directly to Sony you must have a minimum of 110 titles. It is unlikely that most self-publishing authors will meet that criterion. In order to reach Sony's market, you would need to use a middleman distributor.

Other distributors also have minimums or other access restrictions. For example, Overdrive (the leading library distributor for lending ebooks) requires a minimum of five titles before you can upload direct. Apple requires that all titles be uploaded from an Apple computer. If you don't have one, you either have to find a friend who will do it for you or go through a middleman or other service to have access.

Some authors believe the percentage a middleman takes (ranging from 5-25% depending on the company) is worth it. These authors don't want to take the time to upload to each distributor or to monitor sales at each distributor. They prefer to have a person or company handle it centrally and report combined sales. Personally, I prefer the control I have over distribution channels. Things tend to be processed more quickly from direct loads than from a middleman company, and I can track where I've made changes and where I haven't. I don't like giving up another percentage to yet another company.

You can determine what works best for you and what you are willing to pay for convenience. If you do decide to use a middleman, make sure you know the contract terms, understand the payment schedules, and have a complete detailing of all fees and percentages the company takes from your sales.

Distribution Partners Pros and Cons

Each vendor offers different options for distributing your ebook. It is important to understand these differences, their markets, and to make informed choices. Only one vendor, Amazon, provides certain options that require the author to only use Amazon for distribution.

Finding good statistics on the market share for each of these distribution vendors is difficult. That is, in part, because it changes all the time. The appearance of a new company in the market also changes the dynamics of sales. Some newer players, like Kobo, are growing by more than 100% a year right now while others are falling faster than ever , like Barnes and Noble. However, that doesn't mean you should write off any companies quite yet. New leadership, new vision, and new direction can turn them around.

Also, ebook market share statistics are reported in different ways. For example, some surveys rate ebook market share by the number of devices sold (e.g., ereaders, tablets, phones) by a vendor. In this scenario, Apple wins every time because it has sold the largest number of devices worldwide. But that doesn't necessarily mean Apple is selling the greatest number of ebooks. Other surveys rate market share by the number of titles downloaded from a company's e-store. That makes sense, except that many companies do not offer this information in formal reporting. For example, though Amazon provides annual public reporting of its profits and losses, it does not break out ebooks as a line item to be evaluated. is one of those companies. This means that those statistics are gathered from a limited number of resources (e.g., Commercial Publishers and Bowker), and that self-published titles that do not use an ISBN are not counted anywhere. Other statistics are gathered from aggregators like Smashwords. This provides insight into a certain number of self-published titles, but the revenue numbers are skewed to those formats distributed via Smashwords. For example, most authors do not distribute to Amazon via Smashwords. Others only use Smashwords to distribute to Apple.

Ebook companies keep their numbers very close and report them only in press releases that interpret the data in their favor. An organization like Bowker can only report on the ebooks which have an ISBN. The Wall Street Journal reports on apps used to download books. Publisher's Weekly can only report on those ebooks that are reported to data resources primarily in commercial publishing. Amazon does not report, which means that numbers related to Amazon may be skewed based on "best guesses."

In other words, take the table below only as a very broad brush stroke of trends. Do not take the actual numbers themselves as fact. The "Others" category refers to both proprietary device collections as well as bookstores that have a large online presence for ebook sales. These are found primarily in Europe, Asia, and South America. In those regions they often make up the highest percentage of ebook distribution.

The question for the five players listed in the table below is if any of them will partner with these large regional online retailers, and by doing so change their market share dramatically. There is already evidence that both Amazon and Kobo are doing that. The only other distributor doing this is Xin Xii http://xinxii.com a small German company that began partnering with German online bookstores. XinXii then expanded its network to Europe, particularly Germany, France, and Spain. Recently they added the UK and India as well. The extent to which these companies can build effective partnerships throughout the world will determine who, in the near term, garners the majority of the worldwide market in ebook sales.

Region	Amazon	Apple	B&N	Kobo	Google Books	Other
USA	51%	17%	13%	8%	5%	6%
Canada	25%	12%	--	52%	2%	9%
Australia	16%	22%	--	4%	15%	N/A
UK	44%	7%	6%	14%	11%	18%
Europe	29%	21%	--	12%	14%	24%
Asia	5%	27%	--	16%	12%	40%
South America	12%	16%	--	2%	41%	29%

In the table above, the Google Books downloads may represent an unusual number of free books as compared to the other four distributors. In the next sections, I will walk through the steps to upload your ebook to each of the four primary vendors in the chart above—Amazon, Apple, B&N, and Kobo. Certain requirements are common across all vendors. They all need metadata that describes the book. They all need regional pricing. You, as the author, must determine in which of the global markets your book should be sold. Each vendor offers different payments for books based on different rules. This may impact your pricing decisions. Finally, the vendors require you to upload your ebook file in a format that each of their different ereading devices can recognize and render effectively.

Uploading to Amazon

Amazon is the one distribution partner that bases pricing decisions and payment percentages on exclusivity in certain markets. It is also the only vendor with a proprietary ebook file type (MOBI, also known as Mobipocket). Self-published authors and small presses upload to Amazon through their Kindle Direct Publishing (KDP) site.

Go to: http://kdp.amazon.com

If you have purchased products at Amazon you can use the same account with KDP. However, you may wish to use a different account with KDP—one that reflects your business email and address, or simply one that recognizes you by your author pen name. Don't use an Amazon that is shared with your family.

To open a new account, click on the **Sign Up** button in the upper right portion of the screen, under "Don't have an Amazon account." Follow the instructions to provide your email address, selecting a password, etc. Once you have access to the KDP section, you will be presented with a screen indicating you have no titles currently available. Click on the **Add new title** button to proceed.

The next screen will begin the process for adding a book and uploading it to Amazon. The first option is whether you wish to have this book in the KDP Select plan. You can read the details in the screen shot below. In short, it means that you will market your book only with Amazon for a minimum period of 90 days.

1. Your book
i Not Started...

2. Rights & Pricing
i Not Started...

Introducing KDP Select

KDP Select is an optional program for you to reach even more readers and gives you the opportunity to earn more money. By making your book exclusive to Kindle, required for the 90-day enrollment period in KDP Select, the book is eligible for the following:

- The Kindle Owners' Lending Library in the US, UK, Germany, France and Japan
- Earn a share of the monthly global fund each time a Kindle reader borrows your book from the library
- Free promotion for up to 5 days , during each 90-day enrollment period
- 70% royalty for sales to customers in Japan, Brazil and India

Learn more

☐ **Enroll this book in KDP Select**
By checking this box, you are enrolling in KDP Select for 90 days. Books enrolled in KDP Select must not be available in digital format on any other platform during their enrollment. If your book is found to be available elsewhere in digital format, it may not be eligible to remain in the program. See the KDP Select Terms and Conditions and KDP Select FAQs for more information.

1. Enter Your Book Details

Book name

New Title 1

Please enter the exact title only. Books submitted with extra words in this field will not be published. (Why?)

To clarify, this means you cannot sell this book anywhere else—not at B&N, Kobo, Apple, ARe, Diesel, etc. and not at your own ecommerce site or website. On your website you can list that it is available at Amazon and provide a link, but you cannot sell it independently anywhere except Amazon during this time.

I do not advocate enrolling in KDP Select. For me, the benefits do not outweigh the exclusivity requirement. I want my book to be in as many markets as possible. I also want both the ebook and print book to be available at booksellers. I have a strong commitment to supporting local booksellers.

That being said, to be fair, I will share the reasons some authors and some small commercial publishers do elect to enroll their books in KDP select. I've listed authors' reasons in rank order from the most often stated to the least.

1. Because Amazon has the largest market share in the United States, some authors wish to take advantage of that power immediately by making their book free for five days. The hope is that this will increase the books visibility online, generate reviews and buzz, and when the free period ends the book will continue to do well because of the buzz generated from the free downloads.

2. Because Amazon has the largest market share, some authors do not plan to offer their books in any other venue. The ebook will always be offered only through Amazon. These authors believe that 50% of the market is sufficient for their sales.

3. Some authors indicate that having the revenue stream from the Kindle lending option is critical for them.

4. Only KDP Select authors can receive the 70% payment (instead of 35%) in Amazon stores in Japan, Brazil, and India.

In speaking with authors who have chosen KDP select in the past year, most report that the ability to gain extensive visibility through a free book offering no longer works. This is due to changes in how free books and paid books are displayed. Numerous authors now report that where in the past they have been vaulted to top rankings by making books free, it now only works if the free offering is simultaneously paired with paid advertising during those days.

The ability to increase revenue in Japan, Brazil, and India might be a motivator if Amazon were the only ebook retailer in those countries. That is not the case and their market share is not overwhelming.

As with all things in self-publishing, each author must make her own decisions about this. If you are willing to offer your book exclusively to Amazon for three months, there is nothing wrong with trying KDP Select for yourself and testing my statements.

To put your book into KDP select, click in the box next to the box which says: **Enroll this book in KDP select.** If you do not wish to enroll, skip that box.

The first step in completing your book details is to enter your book title in the field labeled **Book name.** Unlike previous programs covered in this book, there is only a single line available for your title and subtitle. If your book has a subtitle, enter it here with a colon as illustrated below. A colon in databases for print books is read as a separator to indicate a subtitle. At the end of uploading your ebook, you will want to match it to your print book on Amazon. This will help to do that.

Do *not* add anything in the title field that is not a part of your title and that does not appear on your book cover and your title page. Amazon is very strict about this. In the past some marketers would attempt to add words such as "bestselling novel" or "award winning book" or similar descriptors in the title field. Other marketers attempted to add keywords in the title field in the hopes of gaming the search engine.

Amazon will compare your title to what is presented on the title page of your submitted book. If you added extra words in your title on this page, Amazon will refuse to make the book available in its store. Leave them for the book description and keyword section provided later.

*Tip: At any time during the data entry process, you can scroll to the bottom of the page and click on the **Save as Draft** button. This will save any data you've entered and allow you to come back to it at a later time or date.*

1. Enter Your Book Details

Book name

> DIY Publishing: A step-by-step guide to print and ebook formatting and distribution

Please enter the exact title only. Books submitted with extra words in this field will not be published. (Why?)

☐ This book is part of a series (What's this?)

Edition number (optional) (What's this?)

Publisher (optional) (What's this?)

> Windtree Press

Description (What's this?)

> platform for the self-published writer. However, until now, few have tackled the actual DIY steps to get your finished manuscript from your word processor, through formatting for print and various ebook reading devices, to being distributed by all the major vendors and bookstores. Lynch demystifies the technology in her easy-to-read

2740 characters left

If your book is part of a series be sure to click in the box next to **This book is part of a series.** When clicked, an additional box opens for you to enter the series name and the book number.

☑ This book is part of a series (What's this?)

Series title   Volume

Enter your series title exactly (example: The Forest People). The volume number refers to the book order in the series. If this is the first book in the series, the volume number is 1.

Completing the series information correctly is important to help readers see all of the books in a series together. Amazon will automatically display other books available in the series if this was checked and titled.

The **Edition number** uses the same definition as has been used elsewhere in this book for walk-throughs of metadata entry. This needs to match what you have entered when creating your file in Jutoh, purchasing your ISBN, and registering your copyright.

The **Publisher** is you or your company name. It is not Amazon. Amazon is a distributor of your book.

The **Description** is what readers will see when they are browsing for your book. As with the CreateSpace section, I advise that you use the short, marketing description here. Long descriptions don't display in their entirety and require readers to click an arrow to see the rest of it. You will have other opportunities to provide the longer back cover blurb type of description. This is also your opportunity to use more descriptive words for the book, such as "by bestselling author" or "award winning."

The next section is **Book Contributors**. This is where you indicate the author's name. Click on the **Add contributors** button. That will bring up an additional display window for your entry.

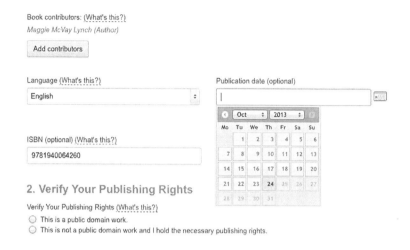

2. **Verify Your Publishing Rights**

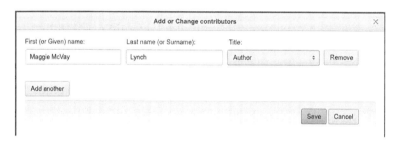

First enter the author's name as it appears on the book. If you use a middle name include that in the **First (or Given) name** field. Click on the arrows for the **Title** field to indicate the contributor's type. Select **Author**. If you have author contributors such as additional authors or an illustrator, click on the **Add another** button and go through the process again.

Once you have completed your contributors additions, click on the **Save** button to return to more information about your book. The next step is to identify the language and publication date. Notice that the language will default to English. Select the publication date from the calendar. As with CreateSpace data entry, you are not allowed to add a publication date that is in the future.

If you have purchased an ebook ISBN, enter it in the **ISBN** field. As discussed in *Chapter 13*, it is recommended that you have an ISBN in order to take advantage of certain international markets. However, it is not required to load your book to Amazon. If you do not have one, skip this field.

Step two is to **Verify Your Publishing Rights.** If you wish to make your book available to the public domain—meaning it is free for others to use in their own works—then click that radio button. Most authors should click the button next to **This is not a public domain work and I hold the necessary publishing rights.**

Step three is to **Target your book to your customers.** This is where you will identify the subject categories that pertain to your book. These subject categories are derived from the BISAC subject categories. Amazon allows you to select two subject categories. I recommend taking advantage of that option.

To select categories, click on the **Add categories** button. This will open a screen like that below.

Narrow your category selections by scrolling through options and selecting sub-categories. First click on the general **Filter**—All, Fiction, or Nonfiction. Depending on the filter, it will then bring up the subject headings available to that top-level heading. If there is a link and plus sign (+), it means the category has lower-level headings to select. If there is not a link, then that is the limit of the category.

Choose categories (up to two):

Filter | All | Fiction | Nonfiction

⊟ FICTION
☐ General
☐ Action & Adventure
⊞ African American
☐ Alternative History
☐ Amish & Mennonite
☐ Anthologies
☐ Asian American
☐ Biographical

Selected categories:

Choose a category

Save   Cancel

In the example Fiction / Anthologies is the only selection. You cannot filter lower to describe the type of anthology. However, Fiction / African American has a link which will then bring up a third level of headings for selection.

Once you have identified your category, click in the box next to the heading that best describes your book. Then click the **Save** button. Your category choice will be displayed. Again click the **Add Categories** button in order to add a second choice. Repeat the process of making a selection and clicking the **Save** button.

You may come back later and change categories following this same procedure. Because you are only allowed two categories, you must delete a previous choice before making a new selection.

The next step is to type in the keywords for your book. Amazon only allows you to choose seven keywords or phrases. Separate each with a comma. (e.g., self-publishing, formatting, ebook publishing, etc.)

Two things are important to know about how Amazon uses metadata. First, everything you've already entered before keywords is searchable: title, author, subtitle, series title, and the subject categories. So you do not need to waste any of your keywords on those items. Second, your top keyword should be a category that was not available to you in the drop down selection previously. For example, the first keyword for this book is "self-publishing." That is the most reflective of the purpose of this book, but it was not available from the BISAC categories.

This is particularly critical in young adult fiction and non-fiction. The BISAC category selections do not have a young adult option, so young adult fiction or non-fiction is properly placed in the juvenile category. However, no one searches for young adult books using the keyword "juvenile." In my YA fantasy series, I use the keywords "young adult" and "teen" to make sure that I am capturing those searches. The remaining keywords you select should follow the advice given in *Chapter 8, Keywords Metadata*.

Steps four and five are where you upload your cover image and your book file. In each case you first click on the **Browse** button to locate the file on your computer, then select it and click **Open** in your file manager. It will immediately display the file name. Click the **Upload** button to complete the process. The cover will then display in the rectangle. The name of the book file will be displayed in step five.

4. Upload or Create a Book Cover

Upload an existing cover, or design a high-quality cover with Cover Creator. (optional)

5. Upload Your Book File

Select a digital rights management (DRM) option: (What's this?)
○ Enable digital rights management
◉ Do not enable digital rights management

Book content file:

The cover image should be in JPG format. The minimum requirement is 1000 pixels on the long side. However, I recommend at least 2100 pixels in length, and preferably 2500 pixels. This is the new standard for HD tablet displays and is likely to be required in the future. So load the larger file now and don't worry about having to come back to all your books and reload the covers in larger sizes. The reason to upload such a large image is that Amazon provides several different sizes of that image throughout its system. It can be displayed as small as 150 pixels and as large 600 pixels depending on the page. In addition, the customer has the option to enlarge it and Amazon wants the image to look good even at large sizes.

Amazon will accept a variety of file formats for conversion to their proprietary MOBI file type:

- Microsoft Word (.doc and .docx)
- HTML (.zip, .htm and .html)

- ePub (.epub)
- Rich Text Format (.rtf)
- Plain Text (.txt)
- Adobe PDF (.pdf)

However, providing any of these file types will likely result in a conversion where some characters or formatting is jumbled. Of the ones mentioned above, PDF is the worst. The best way to control the look of the interior file is to upload a MOBI file. That is the format for all Kindle devices. If you used Jutoh or some other conversion engine to create your MOBI file it will be readily accepted by KDP and should upload without issues or errors.

Once the upload is complete, you should receive feedback in green type saying "Upload Successful." If there was a problem with the uploaded contents or the conversion process, an error message will be displayed. Troubleshoot the problem by going back through the instructions here. If you are still not successful, contact Amazon KDP support. They are very good about identifying the file and pinpointing where the problem lies.

Once the upload is a success, the next step is to preview your book in the online Kindle previewer. Though you may download a special previewer to your Kindle device. I recommend using the **Online Previewer**. It is kept up to date to reflect the latest devices Amazon offers for ereading.

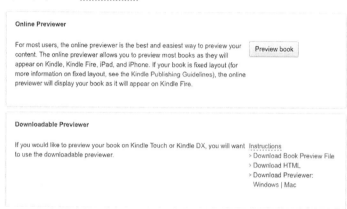

Click on the **Preview book** button and a simulation of a Kindle will display your book from the initial cover image through all of the contents. You can move through the preview by clicking the right and left arrows. Make sure that:

- the cover image is displaying on the first page
- the links in the table of contents work
- the content in a chapter accurately displays all texts, paragraphs, and headings.

The screen captures below show examples of how these elements may appear in the **Online Previewer**.

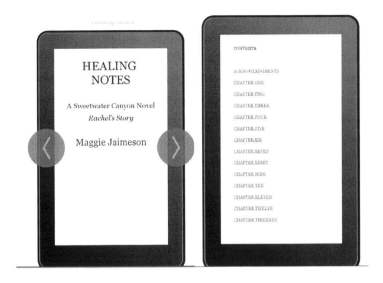

Once you are satisfied with the preview, move on to the **Verify Your Publishing Territories** section.

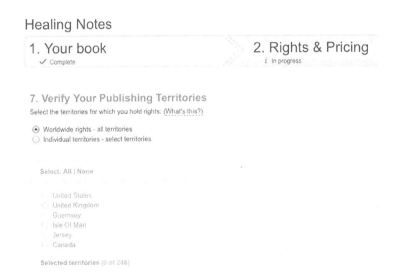

Amazon provides two options for identifying publishing territories. The first is the default, **Worldwide rights—all territories**. For most authors, this is the best one to select. It means that wherever Amazon distributes ebooks, yours will be included. When Amazon adds a new territory, your book will automatically be included there as well.

The alternative is to select **Individual territories** manually. Why would you select this? The most common reason is that you don't have worldwide rights for your work. This happens sometimes if your book was published previously by a commercial publisher and when you requested the rights back, only rights in North America were returned. Rights in other places in the world still belong to the publisher. Another reason you may wish to individually select territories is if you have granted foreign rights for your book to another publisher in a specific country. For example, after self-publishing a book in the United States, you get an offer from a publisher in Germany to translate the book into German. However, the contract also purchases the English language rights in Germany at the same time.

The next section is pricing. The payments related to your book (what Amazon calls "royalty rate") is linked to the price you set in the **Choose Your Royalty** section.

8. Choose Your Royalty

Please select a royalty option for your book. (What's this?)

○ 35% Royalty
◉ 70% Royalty

	List Price	Royalty Rate	Delivery Costs	Estimated Royalty
Amazon.com	$ 4.95 USD Price must be between $2.99 and $9.99.	35% (Why?)	n/a	$1.73
		70%	$0.08	$3.41
Amazon.in (What's this?)	☑ Set IN price automatically based on US price ₹302 ⚠ Your book must be enrolled in KDP Select in order to be eligible for 70% royalty for sales in India. Enroll now	35%	n/a	₹106
Amazon.co.uk	☑ Set UK price automatically based on US price £3.10	70%	£0.05	£2.14
Amazon.de	☑ Set DE price automatically based on US price €3.66	70%	€0.06	€2.52
Amazon.fr	☑ Set FR price automatically based on US price €3.66	70%	€0.06	€2.52

Always click the 70% **Royalty** option. However, selecting it does not guarantee you will be paid that percentage. Amazon attempts to convince authors to price their books in the range Amazon believes is most likely to make money. In the United States, to get the maximum royalty of 70% the book must be priced between $2.99 and $9.99. Anything else receives only a 35% payment. For other countries, Amazon provides the required minimum and maximum prices to also receive the maximum royalty. I recommend staying within the maximum royalty guidelines as much as possible.

As previously mentioned, Amazon is the only book distributor that requires exclusivity for some benefits. As a result of recent partnerships with other countries, Amazon now requires your book not only to meet certain pricing standards but also to be enrolled in KDP Select in order to get the 70% royalty. Currently, those countries are India, Japan, Brazil, and Mexico. All of these countries have been added in the last year. I would not be surprised if future additions also follow this same requirement.

Amazon will automatically convert the price from US dollars to the currency of each country. You may choose to accept that conversion or manually change it. If you keep the conversion suggestion, it is updated daily to reflect the current conversion rates from US dollars. If you manually set the rate, it does not update to the current currency fluctuations in the market. The reasons authors choose to manually set some prices is to reflect a market norm of rounded amounts (e.g., $5.00) or the 99 cent amount (e.g., $4.99).

Also be aware that Amazon deducts a "delivery charge" for each ebook sold at the 70% royalty level. The deduction is based on a calculation of the size of the book in megabytes. The typical book of about 60-70,000 words is assessed a delivery charge of about four cents. Amazon does not deduct a delivery charge on books that are sold at the 35% royalty rate.

The final decisions to make before publication is to determine if you wish to participate in the **Kindle MatchBook** program and **Kindle Lending** program.

9. Kindle MatchBook
☐ Enroll this book in the Kindle MatchBook program (Details)

10. Kindle Book Lending
✓ Allow lending for this book (Details)

☐ By clicking Save and Publish below, I confirm that I have all rights necessary to make the content I am uploading available for marketing, distribution and sale in each territory I have indicated above, and that I am in compliance with the KDP Terms and Conditions.

<< Back to Your Bookshelf   Save and Publish   Save as Draft

The **Kindle MatchBook** program allows you to offer your ebook for free, or at a reduced rate, whenever someone purchases the print edition of the same book from Amazon. Enrolling in this program automatically links the program to *every* print and ebook match you sell through Amazon. A number of authors have chosen to do this in order to allow readers more freedom in how they read the same book.

Personally, I have chosen not to participate in the MatchBook program for two reasons. First, I prefer to support local brick and mortar booksellers and provide them with a program that enhances their print book sales while allowing them an income from ebook sales. I sell significantly more print books through my bookseller relationships than through any online sales channels. I will discuss how this can be done in the Kobo and Direct Ebook Distribution sections of this chapter. Second, my sales of print books through Amazon is not sufficient for me to be believe that adding a free or reduced ebook to the sale will make a significant enough difference. Your experience may be different than mine. The choice is yours.

The **Kindle Book Lending** program is required for anyone who elects to receive the 70% royalty. It allows customers to lend a book they have purchased through the Kindle Store to their friends and family. Each book may be lent once for a duration of

14 days and will not be readable by the lender during the loan period. This is similar to what people do today where they read a paperback book and then give it to a friend to read. There is no additional royalty payment for being in the lending program. The only way to opt out of the lending program is to accept a 35% royalty rate.

The final step is to click on the box next to the rights verification statement. That statement reads:

"By clicking on the Save and Publish button, I confirm that I have all rights necessary to make the content I am uploading available for marketing, distribution, and sale in each country I have indicated above and that I am in compliance with the KDP Terms and Conditions."

Finally click the **Save and Publish** button.

It usually takes two to three hours before your book appears on the United States Amazon site. It can take up to 72 hours before it appears on all other Amazon country sites. Once it is on the site, you will receive an email saying "Congratulations! Your title has been published." That email will also provide links for you to go to Author Central and provide information about yourself for your fans.

It is highly recommended that you do follow the instructions for Author Central. At that location you can link to each of your books distributed through Amazon, link to a blog or other social media, and provide more information about yourself and how readers might contact you.

As your book is loaded on other country sites, you will get a similar email from each of those sites as well. Author Central is not linked through all Amazon sites. You must go to each separate country site and complete the information again.

At any time that you wish to make changes to the metadata for your book, the pricing, or a new upload, it takes your book off sale in the Amazon store until it has gone through processing again. This processing can take 24 to 48 hours, though it is usually only two to three hours. If your book is still not available after two days, contact Amazon support for assistance.

Barnes and Noble

Barnes and Noble direct ebook loads are done through Nook Press. The software at Nook Press specifically provides self-publishing authors and small presses access to Barnes and Noble distribution. Though B&N has had problems in the last year or two with determining their direction, I would not count them out of the game. In fact, some authors report B&N revenues as being close to or surpassing their Amazon revenues. For non-fiction, it is important that you work with Barnes and Noble. They are the largest distributor to academic institutions in the United States.

To begin the process of working with Nook Press go to: Http://nookpress.com

Click on the yellow **Get Started Now** button in the middle of the screen in order to create an account. Follow the instructions to enter your name, email, password, etc. This is a similar process at every distributor. You will be asked for your banking information at the end of the process.

Once your account is created, an email will be sent requiring your confirmation and providing login instructions. After your login you may begin the direct load process. Unlike all other vendors, Nook Press begins asks you to first load your manuscript before completing metadata for your book.

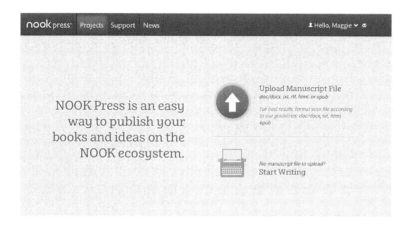

You do not have to load an EPUB file. You can load a Microsoft Word file (.doc or .docx), a text file (.txt) or an html file (.html or .htm) and it will convert that file to EPUB format. However, I strongly recommend you create your own EPUB file. The conversion engine will likely render your ebook in a way that is unexpected depending on the file type you load, how you used style sheets, and what type of linking you did. Whether you use Jutoh or some other means for creating an EPUB file outside of Nook Press, I recommend you do so. You will have significantly more control over the look of your ebook than allowing the Nook Press conversion engine to do it for you.

If the file upload is accepted, you will get an immediate confirmation. If there are problems with the file, you will receive an error message.

In the illustration above you may have noticed that Nook Press provides an option to write your manuscript within the

Nook Press system. In addition, the platform allows authors to share their developing content with a select group of peers, get feedback, and then publish their book as an EPUB at Barnes and Noble.

I *do not* recommend doing this. The conversion from your online written work to EPUB is even worse than the conversion from a Word Document. The resulting file does not look at all professional. If you have a desire to write in an environment where you are sharing your work, then I suggest joining a critique group. Personally, I don't share my work in progress with anyone except my two critique partners, my editor, and my beta readers.

Nook Press thinks of books as *projects*. You are asked to give your project a name. Then click on the **Create My Project** button to begin entering all the information about your book.

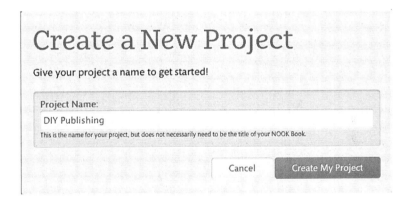

Though you don't have to use your book title, it makes sense to me that you would. It makes it easy to find and make changes later. Once a project is created, you may at any time in the data entry and uploading process click on the **Save** button at the top of the screen and exit. When you return later you may make changes and continue with the project.

The next step is to upload your cover. As with Amazon KDP, you want to upload a JPG file that is a good size. Nook recommends a minimum of 1400 pixels on the long side. I suggest you strive for the same 2100-2500 pixel size discussed earlier.

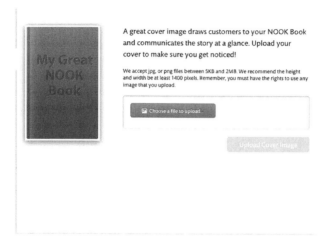

Click on the **Choose a file to upload** button. Browse for your cover file on your computer and select **Open**. Next you will be asked if you wish to add this cover image to your manuscript.

Click on **Yes**. This will automatically make your cover display once a customer downloads the book to her Nook device. You will see a screen with your cover displayed in place of the sample blue book.

A great cover image draws customers to your NOOK Book and communicates the story at a glance. Upload your cover to make sure you get noticed!

We accept jpg, or png files between 5KB and 2MB. We recommend the height and width be at least 1400 pixels. Remember, you must have the rights to use any image that you upload.

Your cover image has been successfully uploaded!

Replace Cover Image   Crop Original Image

If the cover does not look right to you, you have an option to **Replace Cover Image**. This will allow you to select a different file from your computer. Alternatively, you may choose to **Crop Original Image**. Authors will choose this if their original cover image doesn't meet the length to width aspect ratio expected. Cropping allows you to determine how to make it display optimally without having to redo your cover. Most distributors expect book covers to be created with a 1.5 aspect ratio. Refer back to *Chapter 11, Cover Design* where this was discussed.

Next you will describe your book's contents and subject categories. This data is very similar to what you put into Amazon KDP. When you place the cursor inside the first field, **Title,** Nook Press will display the fields associated with that information. Below is a screen capture of how the data was entered for this book.

As in many title fields, a subtitle is not presented separately. If you have a subtitle, separate it from the main title with a colon. For example: *DIY Publishing: A step-by-step guide for print and ebook formatting and distribution*

The **Publisher** is either you or your company name. It is *not* Nook Press or Barnes and Noble.

Unlike Amazon KDP, you may select a **Publication Date** in the future on Nook Press.

The **Contributors** field works the same as everywhere else. First enter your author name, then select the role from the drop down box as **Author**. If there are additional authors or other contributors to enter click on the **Add Another Contributor** link and define the role for that contributor.

Scroll further down the page to reveal the book description and author bio sections.

On Nook Press you are allocated up to 5,000 characters which is approximately 500 words. However, I recommend you use the short, marketing description of your book and limit it to approximately 100 words.

The **About the Author(s)** section is where the author bio is placed. Again, the short one is recommended. If there are multiple authors, such as with an anthology, be sure to include a brief bio for each author. The total character count for the author section is 2500, approximately 250 words.

Finally, you have the opportunity to enter your ebook specific ISBN. If you have purchased your own ISBN through Bowker (or are using one from a publisher) you may use that same ebook ISBN here. Select the **Yes** button to see new window to enter the ISBN-13 number for your ebook. Enter the ISBN without hyphens.

The next section is to **Add Categories**. These are the BISAC categories. As with Amazon, you click on the arrow to see the major headers available. Click on the header that best applies to your book and additional subcategories may be revealed. Select the one that fits.

Barnes and Noble allows for the largest number of category selections of any vendor. You may select up to five. Use as many as make sense to best describe the book and how users might search for it. You are not required to list five different categories.

Once you have selected the first category it will appear below the drop down box, as illustrated below. To select another category, go through the process again. First click on the down arrow and then make selections. Those subject headings will be added until you have reached the maximum of five categories.

The **Keywords for Search Engines** works similarly to what you've done before. However, instead of limiting the number of keywords or phrases, Nook Press limits the number of characters to 100, including spaces. Select keywords that are different from your category selections.

Finally, you are asked to identify the appropriate audience for your book and the language. Click on the drop down arrows to make the appropriate selections.

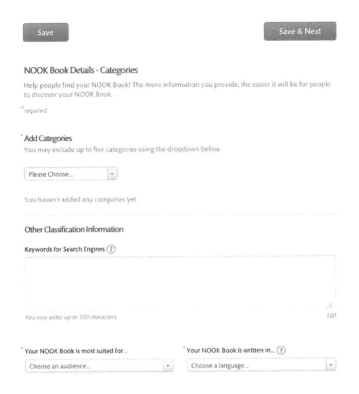

The next section contains rights and pricing. Barnes and Noble currently only distributes to the United States and the United Kingdom. Therefore, this section is significantly smaller than the other distributors discussed in this chapter.

Save

Save & Next

NOOK Book Details - Rights & Pricing

Select where you have the rights to make your NOOK Book available for sale and then set the list price
for each territory, or let us do the currency conversions for you!

required

* Sales Territory Rights ⑦

⦿ Worldwide Sales Rights

◯ United States Only

* List Price

Convert currencies based on my USD list price ☑

CURRENCY	LIST PRICE		EST. ROYALTY ⑦
United States		USD	
United Kingdom		GBP	

* DRM

Do you want DRM encryption for your NOOK book? ⑦
◯ Yes ◯ No

First, select if you want to distribute **Worldwide** or **United States Only**. It is possible Barnes and Noble will form relationships in other countries in the future. By selecting **Worldwide** you will automatically be distributed to those other countries when they become available.

By default the **List Price** is converted from United States dollars to pounds sterling for the United Kingdom. I suggest leaving it in this situation. Enter the list price in dollars and cents, without the dollar sign (e.g., 9.99). The royalty will automatically be calculated, and the equivalent price in the UK will also be calculated along with a royalty. If you prefer to change the automatic currency conversion, click on the check mark and enter the pricing yourself in each country.

The **DRM** section on this screen asks: Do you want DRM encryption for your NOOK book? DRM is digital rights management. This encryption restricts the buyer to downloading the book to only one device. So, if the buyer downloads to her Nook and then later decides she would rather read the book on her iPad, she is unable to move the file because it is encrypted.

Some publishers and individual authors like to use DRM because they believe it cuts down on piracy or theft. I disagree with that assessment. First, there are numerous ways to get around DRM. Instructions are easily found on the Internet. Second, ebook buyers tend to have multiple devices—smart phones, tablets, laptops, desktops, and ereaders. The device they choose to use may differ depending on their travel situation or simply wanting to change positions.

I do not put DRM on any of my books. I prefer to trust my readers to use the book for their enjoyment only. I also participate in any lending programs allowed by the distributor. So, I already know the book may be lent. DRM would exclude this option.

The final screen before publishing is the **NOOK Book Details – Other Information** screen. This screen provides further identifying information that helps Barnes and Noble create connections between this book and any other books you may upload in the future.

The first question is: Is this Nook Book public domain? For most authors the answer is **No**. Unless you are putting it up for free and allowing others to use all or part of it, you do not wish it to be in the public domain.

The second question: Is this Nook Book a part of a series? Similar to Amazon KDP and other places you've entered book data, this will allow Barnes and Noble to create a link between this book and others in the series when they are uploaded. Type the series name exactly as it appears on the title page. The series number is the relationship of the book in the order to be read.

The final question is: Is this Nook Book available in print? If you select **Yes**, another field will pop up to allow you to enter the **Number of Pages in Print**. Barnes and Noble uses this information to give readers a sense of the length of the book. However, it does not make an attempt to display the print book and ebook together like Amazon does. The number of pages would be the total page count in your PDF file sent to your POD distributor (i.e., CreateSpace or Lightning Source).

Save

Save & Next

NOOK Book Details – Other Information

*required

* Is this NOOK Book public domain? (?)
○ Yes ● No

* Is this NOOK Book a part of a series?
○ Yes ● No

* Is this NOOK Book available in print?
● Yes ○ No
* Number of Pages in Print:
364

When you click on the **Save & Next** button, you will have the option to **Publish**. The **Publish** button has a little shopping cart next to it. This does not mean you will be paying any fees to distribute your book. The shopping cart is a symbol to let you know you are making it available for sale on the Barnes and Noble site.

If you need to make changes to your Nook Press ebook, log back into the Nook Press website. It will display the status of all the books you have uploaded. If you only wish to change the details about the book (e.g., description, price, categories, etc.). Then click on the **View Details** link next to the book you wish to modify. Your book will remain on sale, but the changes you entered will take 24-48 hours to show up on both the United States and United Kingdom Barnes and Noble sales sites.

| | All In Progress On Sale Off Sale | All Projects My Projects Only | | | |

COVER	PROJECT NAME	MANUSCRIPT	NOOK BOOK DETAILS	LIST PRICE	PUBLISH ACTIONS
	Chameleon: The Awakening	Update Manuscript	View Details	$4.95	Take Off Sale
	ETERNITY	Update Manuscript	View Details	$5.50	Take Off Sale
	Healing Notes	Update Manuscript	View Details	$4.95	Take Off Sale
	Shifting Waters	Update Manuscript	View Details	$0.99	
	Undertones	Update Manuscript	View Details	$4.95	Take Off Sale
	Chameleon - The Choosing: Book 2 of the Forest People	Update Manuscript	View Details	$4.95	Take Off Sale
	DIY Publishing	Add Manuscript	Change Details	$9.99	

If you wish to update the book contents or change the cover, then click on the **Update Manuscript** link next to the book. Again, the book will remain on sale with the previous version. The update will take 48 to 72 hours to replace the files on both Barnes and Noble sites.

If your book is not updated within 72 hours, contact support for assistance.

Kobo

Kobo is picking up momentum in the United States, where it is thought to have about 8% of the market, and even more so around the world, where it is either the number one or number two ebook retailer in many countries, including Canada and Japan. Kobo now has 16 million readers, a quadrupling of readers from

2012 when it says its sales had already doubled. Choosing not to upload to Kobo would be a mistake.

Kobo provides access to its platform through Kobo Writing Life. Go to: http://www.kobo.com/writinglife

Click on the **Sign in to Writing Life** button. This takes you to a screen where you may log in if you already have an account. If you do not, click on the link that says *New? Sign up here* toward the top of the screen.

Sign in to Kobo with...

New? Sign up here

Email address

Password

Show password   *Forgot password?*

By continuing you confirm that you agree to the *Terms of Use* and *Privacy Policy*.

CANCEL   CONTINUE

Terms of Use | Kobo Privacy

This will bring up the account creation process where you may sign up with your email address and choose a password.

Sign up to Kobo with...

> Email address

> Password

> Confirm password

Show passwords

Must click here and agree to policies before you can continue.

I have read and agree to Kobo's *Terms of Use* and *Privacy Policy.*

CANCEL   CONTINUE

Terms of Use | Kobo Privacy

You must click in the box, illustrated with red arrow, and accept the Terms of Use and Privacy Policy. Note that these are the terms of use for every Kobo account—readers and authors. Click on the links to read about these documents. Once you have agreed to the terms, click the **Continue** button.

Next the BECOME A KOBO AUTHOR screen appears. This is where you will complete all of your contact information. The top half of the screen asks for the usual information. First and last name, publisher name, and email address are the required fields. In addition, you may provide a telephone number. Note that the option to receive updates, tips and information about Kobo Writing Life is automatically checked. I recommend keeping this checked. However, if you do not want to receive that information, click in the green box and you will be opted out.

BECOME A KOBO AUTHOR

CONTACT INFORMATION

First Name

Last Name

Publisher name

optional

Email address - one that we can reliably contact you at

Email updates

✓ *Get email updates, tips and information about Kobo Writing Life*

Telephone

Extension

optional

optional

Kobo publishing account ID

optional

If you previously had a publishing account with Kobo your account ID will help us link your old account with this new one.

There is a nice feature on this screen that may not apply to new authors with Kobo. However, it is something you may need in the future. The **Kobo publishing account ID** allows you to combine accounts at a later date. For example, if you established one account under your non-fiction writer name and another under a pseudonym for fiction, you could elect to combine the two accounts and manage all of your books and all of your sales data in one place. To my knowledge, Kobo is the only vendor that makes this so easy. All other vendors require you to request support assistance to combine accounts.

Next, scroll down to access the remaining fields in the CONTACT INFORMATION section. The bottom half of the screen asks for physical location information. Click on the arrow in the **Country** field to select the country in which you live. Enter your **Street address, City,** and **Postal Code.** The **Province** drop down box contains Canadian provinces and also U.S. states. If you live in other countries with provinces or states, they are not uniquely identified in this drop down box. Selecting the country name will be sufficient for users outside of Canada and the United States.

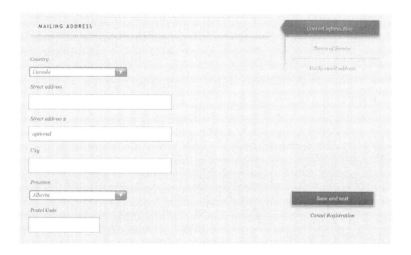

When all fields have been completed click on the **Save and next** button. This will take you to the **Terms of Service** screen. Included in this screen are the Terms of Use and Privacy Policies you accepted earlier. The primary purpose for this screen is to make you aware of the **Content Policy.** Most vendors simply have a link to the document and a check box. However, Kobo makes it obvious what they are asking you to agree to something important by featuring this large box with links to the actual documents. You must click in the check box that reads:

I have read, understand, and agree to the Terms of Service and I am authorized to bind the author/publisher to this agreement.

Must click here to accept the terms of service.

Once you accept the **Terms of Service**, click the **Save and next** button. This will generate an email to you that requires you to verify your email address before you may continue with your account.

After verifying your email, log back into Kobo via their instructions in the email. Now you are ready to upload your book.

Click on the **eBOOKS** link at the top of the screen. On the next screen click on the **Create New Ebook** button.

My Account ▼   English ▼   Kobobooks.com   Sign Out

DASHBOARD   eBOOKS   LEARNING CENTRE

Next you will see the screen where you enter all the descriptive information about your book. It's similar to other software you've used thus far and should look familiar.

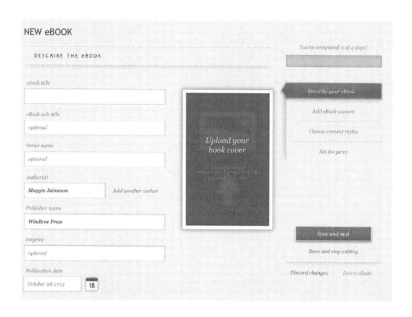

Notice that Kobo provides two separate lines for the main title, **eBook title**, and **eBook sub-title**. Whereas on Amazon you had to enter the title and subtitle together separated by a colon, at Kobo you enter them on separate lines.

Also on this screen is the **Series name** if you have one. Then type in the **Author(s) name**. To add additional authors click on the pink link *Add another author*. The **Publisher** is you or your company. Most self-published authors do not have an additional Imprint. A small press or publishing cooperative might have additional imprints. Finally, enter the **Publication date**. As with Nook Press, you may enter a **Publication date** in the future.

Click on the book sample, where it says Upload your book cover. The image requirements are similar to other vendors. You want to upload the image in JPG or PNG. Kobo recommends that the longest side be a minimum of 2100 pixels. Once the image is uploaded the cover will appear in that space.

Scroll down to complete the book description process.

Here you will enter the ISBN associated with your ebook, the eISBN. If you have a print book, also enter that ISBN under **Primary Print ISBN.**

Tip: It is very important to enter the print ISBN if you have a print book. Because Kobo partners with local booksellers, this helps identify books in both formats in order for the bookseller to assist customers in their purchase. In addition, there is a rumor that at some time in the future Kobo will offer a type of "match book option" similar to what Amazon is doing.

The language defaults to English, but you may select a different language if it applies to your book.

Unless you have made the book free and available for reuse and copying select **No** in answer to the question: Is this content part of the public domain?

Don't miss the pink link under **Categories,** located to the right of the eISBN field. This is where you select the BISAC categories that apply to your book. Like all other vendors, Kobo uses a drop down list with sub-categories below each arrow. It does not provide the entire BISAC list, so you must make your selections for best fit from what is provided. Kobo allows you to select up to three categories for your book.

As you select each one it will appear on the screen under **Your categories**. Once you've completed your selections, click on the **Confirm** button to return to the book description main screen.

The final field on the book description screen is to enter your book blurb or back cover copy. Kobo calls this the **Synopsis.**

Again, I recommended that you use the short, marketing blurb here. There is no limit to the number of characters on this screen.

Click **Save and next** to go to the ADD eBOOK CONTENT screen.

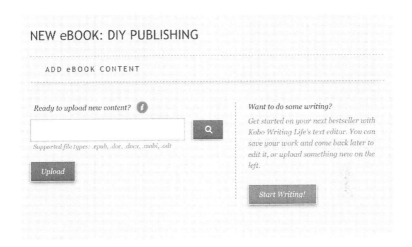

This is where you upload your file. Like other vendors, Kobo allows you to also upload a Microsoft Word (.doc or .docx) file, as well as a Kindle MOBI file or an Open Office ODT file. However, I still recommend that you upload the native Kobo ereader format, which is EPUB. This will provide you with the most control over the look of the content in the ereading environment.

Click on the **Upload** button to access the file on your computer. Once you have selected the correct file, click **Open** on your computer and the file will begin uploading. When the upload is complete, a confirmation of the upload will appear with a green checkmark box next to the word **Done!** It is at this point that you may download the EPUB file and preview it to make sure it is working the way you anticipated.

Kobo does not provide an online viewer immediately following this process. The download options assumes you either have a Kobo ereader or have already downloaded the Kobo app to your computer.

If you do not have a Kobo ereader, I recommend downloading the Kobo app for your desktop, laptop, tablet, phone, or other device to preview your Kobo ebooks. You can obtain that app at: http://www.kobo.com/apps

I use this app to preview my EPUB file prior to uploading to Kobo. If you upload an uncorrupted EPUB file, nothing will be changed in the upload process. However, if you uploaded a type of file that needed to be converted (e.g., Microsoft Word .doc file), then you will definitely want to preview the eBook using the Kobo app to ensure that the conversion engine did not add extraneous characters and that it divided the book correctly into chapters for linking.

Once you are satisfied with your upload, it is time to move to the next section, SET THE LICENSE AND GEOGRAPHIC RIGHTS.

NEW eBOOK: DIY PUBLISHING

SET THE LICENSE AND GEOGRAPHIC RIGHTS

Apply Digital Rights Management?

[X]

Geographic rights?

[✓] *Worldwide rights*
You own the rights in all territories.

The first question is: Apply Digital Rights Management? This is the DRM I discussed in the Barnes and Noble section of this chapter. Amazon applies DRM to all its ebooks. However, all other vendors give you the choice. As I stated previously, my recommendation is not to use DRM. To change the default selection click on the green box and it will change to a red box with an "X" as illustrated above.

The second question is: Geographic rights? As with other vendors, you can simply select **Worldwide rights**. That is the default selection on this screen, and what I recommend you choose unless there is a reason you do not have rights in a particular country or you know your book would have no market in that country.

As of this writing, Kobo has readers in 190 countries around the world and is adding new distribution points in these countries every month. By selecting Worldwide rights, your book will automatically be added to any new countries or booksellers in those countries where Kobo has formed a partnership. If you wish to individually select each country, click the box next to the checkmark and a listing of countries will be available for you to identify.

The final step prior to publishing your book on Kobo is to set the price. Similar to other distributors, Kobo allows you to set the price in the currency you have listed as your payments. It will then automatically calculate the price for other countries in the corresponding currency.

SET THE PRICE

Pricing is complicated!
When pricing your eBook, you need to take into account your opportunities for sales in other currencies, and
the royalty rates at different list price points. Find what you need to know in our user guide.

	CURRENCY	LIST PRICE	OVERRIDE PRICE		ESTIMATED ROYALTY	
Your currency	USD - US Dollar	4.95			70%	3.46
	AUD - Australian dollar	5.52	[x]		70%	3.86
	CAD - Canadian dollar	5.09	4.95 [✓]		70%	3.46
	EUR - Euro	3.72	[x]		70%	2,60
	GBP - British Pound	3.26	[x]		70%	1.90
	JPY - Japanese Yen	489	[x]		70%	342
	HKD - Hong Kong Dollar	38.40	[x]		70%	26.88
	NZD - New Zealand Dollar	6.22	[x]		70%	4.35

In this illustration, my book, *Healing Notes*, is listed at 4.95 in USD – US Dollar. All author currency pricing is automatically calculated. If you wish to manually change a price, as I did for Canadian dollars, click on the box next to the red box with an x. This will change it to a green box and open a field for you to enter the price you wish to charge.

Like other vendors, Kobo also has two royalty possibilities. One is 70%, the other is 45%. For any books priced below $1.99

the royalty drops to 45%. Currently, the upper limit price has been lifted. So, anything above $1.99 will get the 70% royalty. Check Kobo's website and FAQs for updates to that royalty scheme.

Now that everything is complete, you are ready to publish the book. Click on the **Save and next** button to proceed to the final step.

At the PUBLISH eBOOK screen double-check that the publication date is accurate, then click on the **Publish Book** button. This will put your book into the processing queue at Kobo. It typically takes 24 to 72 hours for your book to be available in the Kobo online book stores in the United States and Canada. Once processing is complete, it is another 24 hours until your book is available in other Kobo partner stores around the world. This includes your local bookseller who is affiliated with Kobo.

You can check your book status by logging in to your Kobo account. On the DASHBOARD screen, click on **eBooks**. You will see a screen with books that are currently for sale and books that are Processing. To make changes to a book, click on the book cover or title link.

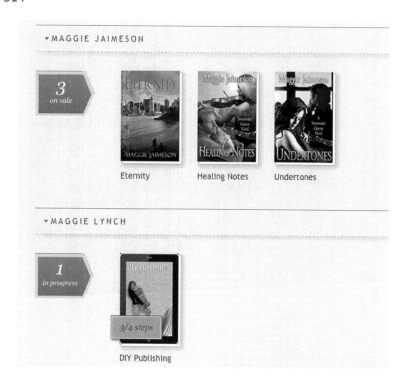

Clicking on the book you wish to review or change will take you back into the navigation structure I've covered in this section.

You may change any of the data you've entered about the book and it will not have to go through processing again. However, it will take between 24 and 48 hours to be distributed to all partners around the world. If you upload a new file (content or book cover) it will go through processing again. The previous version of your book will still be for sale. But the updated version will not be available until processing has ended—usually in 24 to 72 hours.

If your book has been stuck in processing beyond 72 hours, contact Kobo support for assistance.

Apple

Apple distribution is handled through their iTunes platform. Though you can sign up for an account via a PC, you are not allowed to physically upload files *except from an Apple device*. If you are going to use a friend or pay someone to upload your files to Apple, you will still want to have your own iTunes account in order to receive payment for your sales and manage your books.

If you already have an iTunes account (e.g., for music downloads) then you have an assigned Apple ID. If you do not have an iTunes account you will need to set one up and get an AppleID before you can sell books on Apple. My instructions assume you already have an iTunes account of some kind.

Go to: http://itunesconnect.apple.com/

Even if you already have an iTunes account for purchasing and downloading music or books, you will need to complete a separate application to distribute your content. Click on the **Get Started** link.

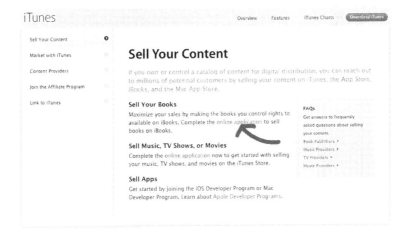

The screen above provides options for selling content. Click on the **online application** link associated with **Sell Your Books.**

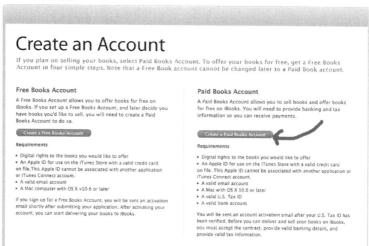

The above screen sometimes confuses people new to Apple iTunes content distribution. The choice is for a free books account or a paid books account. This does not mean that you pay a fee; it refers to whether the books you upload will be offered for free or will cost money. In the **Paid Books Account** you will be allowed to offer a book for free for short periods of time if you like. Click on the **Create Paid Books Account** button.

This will take you to the AppleID verification screen. Enter the AppleID you have already established with iTunes. You will be taken to screens to complete your bank information. It takes a day or two for Apple to verify your banking information. Once that verification process is complete, you will be provided a link to download the free iProducer application to your Apple desktop or laptop. It is then installed like all other Apple applications. You cannot download the iTunes Producer software without your being verified.

iTunes Producer is a software program that runs on your computer. It allows you to enter information about your book, attach your cover and EPUB file, determine pricing, and upload your content and cover. Instead of doing all this online as you have with other vendors, Apple requires you to do it within this application. The application then packages it and uploads it to the appropriate place for sale in iTunes and displays the book information on the iBookstore site. It does not convert files from other formats to EPUB. Your content must already be in EPUB format.

Do not confuse iTunes Producer with the Apple iBook software. That software is designed to create fixed-format, proprietary books that will run only on the iPad. iTunes Producer accepts EPUB files and will run on any Apple device.

Before opening the iTunes Producer application, there is a little preparation you should do that will help speed the process and avoid upload errors when it comes time to upload your EPUB file and JPG cover file. Make a copy of your EPUB content file and your JPG cover file. The filename for each file must be the ISBN number associated with your ebook. You cannot upload to Apple iTunes without an ISBN.

Example for content file: **9781940064260.epub**
Example for cover file: **9781940064260.jpg**

Following this file naming convention will help make file delivery to the iTunes site more successful.

To start entering your book information, open the iTunes Producer application. The first time you use the application you must initialize it by providing your iTunes Connect login information—AppleID and Password. The software will verify your iTunes Connect login information and then store your AppleID and password for later use when you upload your finalized package.

After initialization, each time you start iTunes Producer the application will automatically open to the package screen.

Click on the **Create New Package** button to start the book description process. During the creation process you work is saved each time you click on the **Next** button. When you come back select the **Open Package** options.

After clicking **Create New Package**, you will see a screen with the book icon selected as the default. If this is your first book upload or you are creating a new book, click **Next** to accept that you are creating a book package.

You will see a screen where you can enter the book details. This will require the same information as with other vendors.

The first field is the **ISBN** associated with the ebook. You may use the same ebook ISBN with each vendor if you purchased it yourself. Apple requires you to have an ISBN in order to upload to iTunes. The ISBN should be entered as a string of numbers, no dashes or spaces.

The **Book Type** has only two choices, Textbook or Book. Whether you are writing fiction or non-fiction, select **Book** unless you are actually preparing a textbook that would be distributed to academic institutions.

No default **Language** is selected. Click on the arrow to select the language of your book.

Note that both **Title** and **Subtitle** are available. The **Publisher** is you or your company. Similar to Barnes and Noble and Kobo, you can select a publication date in the future. The format for entering the **Publication Date** is yyyy-mm-dd. Example: 2013-10-31. Enter a **Series Name** if it is appropriate to your title and the **Number in Series**. Skip the Store Display Number. Enter the **Print Length**. If you do not have a print book, enter an estimate of the total page numbers based on your original manuscript file.

The **Pre-order samples allowed** box is checked by default. In order to market your book with a future publication date puts it on sale as a pre-order. This would allow the reader to sample the first 10% of the book in the same way she would if it were already available. If you do not want to allow sampling for pre-orders, click in the box to remove the checkmark.

The **Explicit Content** box must be checked for books geared to adults such as erotica, high violence, and some horror books. Be sure to check the content guidelines for Apple to ensure the book you are uploading is marked appropriately.

The **Book Description** box is where you put your book blurb. This should be the short, marketing oriented blurb. If the blurb is more than a single paragraph, you must use the HTML codes for paragraphing in order to get the spacing correct. Put a <p> at the beginning of the paragraph and a </p> at the end of the paragraph. See the example below.

<p>This book provides insights into formatting and distribution for the self-publishing author. The step-by-step ...</P>
<p>Lynch demystifies the technology while adding information regarding the state of publishing today and ... <p>

Click **Next** to move to the subject and category selection steps. Click on **Add Category** and you will see an option to select the type of **Category Scheme** to use. The default is BISAC as that is the system used throughout the United States. However, for other countries you may wish to select BIC2 (used in the UK) or CLIL (Content and Language Integrated Learning) schemas as is appropriate for the market you are targeting. Once a category scheme is defined, the typical list of headers to click is displayed. Click on the header that best matches your book and then select the subcategory that defines the header in detail.

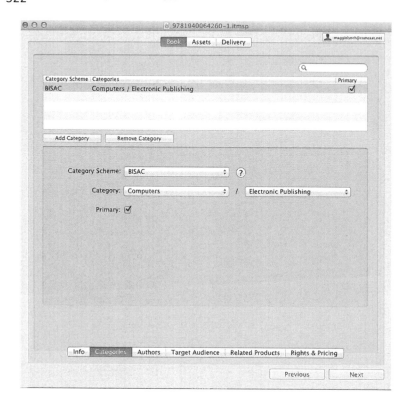

You may add up to three categories. By default, the first category you select becomes the primary category, the one you believe best defines your book. After selecting all of your categories, you may change the Primary category by clicking in the **Primary** box when that category is highlighted. Click **Next** to go to the **Author** section.

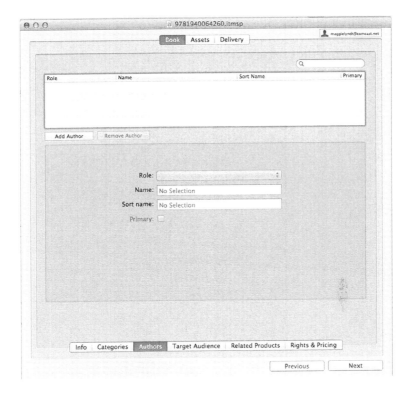

Click **Add Author**. Type in your author name. By default the role is selected as Author. The Sort name field lets you tell Apple to search for the name. I recommend typing the author's last name followed by a comma and then the first name. For example: Lynch, Maggie. If there is a middle name, then it would be associated with the first name. For example: Lynch, Maggie McVay.

Click **Next** to go to the **Target Audience** screen. This screen was designed primarily for textbook definition. It is not needed if the book is designed for adult readers. However, for juvenile fiction and non-fiction this screen allows you to select an age range that is most appropriate for the book. To add a target audience, click on the **Add Criteria** button.

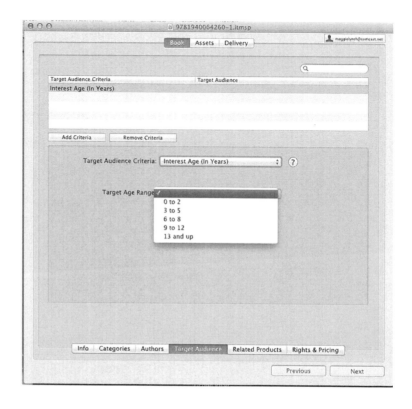

The default is **Interest Age (in Years)**. Other selections relate specifically to academic curriculum criteria. The drop down box allows you to select a specific age range for your book.

Click **Next** to continue to the **Related Products** section. This identifies other book formats that are related to the book you are uploading, such as a Print book or the same text in a different language. It does not refer to books that are related in a series.

If this applies, click on the **Add Related Product** button. The default selection is **Print Equivalent**. To make a different selection click on the down arrow.

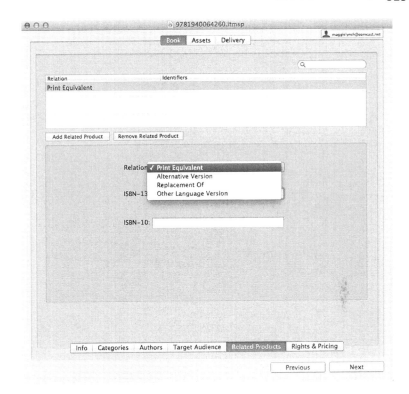

For any related book you select, you must provide its ISBN. I recommend always using the **ISBN-13** unless the book is older and only had an **ISBN-10** assigned. In this section you may add as many related products as apply. Once you're finished, click on **Next** to go to **Rights and Pricing**.

Pricing works very differently in the Apple iTunes environment. First click on **Add Territory**. I suggest beginning with your own country since you already understand the currency and likely have selected a price. In the **Territory** field click the arrow to select your country. In the illustration below I selected the United States.

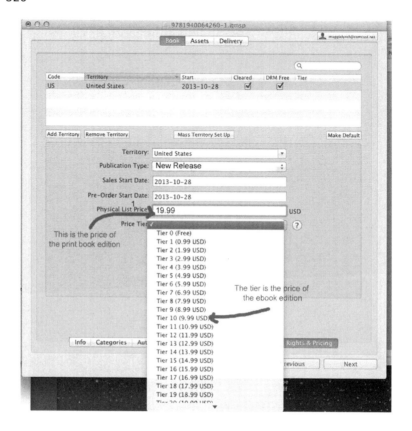

The **Publication Type** should be **New Release**. The Digital Only type refers only to books using enhanced features such as audio or video. This iTunes Producer software lets people upload music, so the digital only publication type also supports that.

You may elect to have a **Pre-Order Start Date** and a **Sales Start Date** if you are timing your release and trying to build initial buzz with sales. You must upload the finished book, however, to take advantage of pre-order dates.

The **Physical List Price** refers to the print edition of the publication. If you have both hardcover and paperback, then use the hardcover price. Most self-published authors have POD trade paperback. Enter that print price. If the book has never had or never will have a print edition, enter what the estimated retail price would be if there were a print edition. I suggest using the following approximate prices based on word count:

- $14.00 50,000 for 60,000 words
- $15.00 61,000 for 75,000 words
- $16.00 for 76,000 to 100,000 words
- $17.00 for books over 100,000 words

The suggested pricing equivalences follow typical trade paperback pricing for fiction. If the book is non-fiction, consider raising the equivalent pricing as non-fiction expectations are for higher prices at lower word counts due to the inclusion of tables, charts, research data, indexing, etc.

The actual price for the ebook you are uploading is selected by using **Price Tiers**. The tier serves as the upper limit for what may be charged in that country for the edition of the book you are uploading. Select the price tier that matches your book. This is the price without taxes added.

Unfortunately, you need to go through this process for each country and currency in which you wish to sell your book. There are 32 countries. You will want to have the currency converter open on your computer to determine the equivalents for each currency type. The software has a **Mass Territory Set Up** button, but it does not work.

Once all pricing for the territories is complete, click on **Next** to go to the upload screens for your EPUB and cover files. Click on the **Choose** button under **Publication**. This will open a window to your Finder (file manager). Locate the EPUB file and select it. Remember, the file name must be the ISBN with the .epub extension.

To offer readers a sample select the **Choose** button under the **Publication Sample** box. Most authors choose a sample that is approximately 10-20 pages. You want a sample size that is sufficient to show the writing quality and style, as well as interest the reader in purchasing the book. The sample file should also be in EPUB format. Title the file ISBN-sample. For example: 9781940064260-sample.epub This will help to keep the files straight in Finder (file manager), as well as in the iTunes Connect structure.

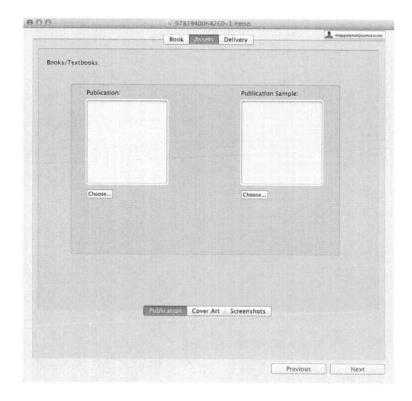

Click the **Next** button to upload your cover art. Cover art for Apple iTunes store follows guidelines that apply at other distributors. It should be in JPG format and the long side should be a minimum of 2100 pixels. The process for selecting the cover art is also the same as for the publication. Click on the **Choose** button and locate the cover art file in the file manager.

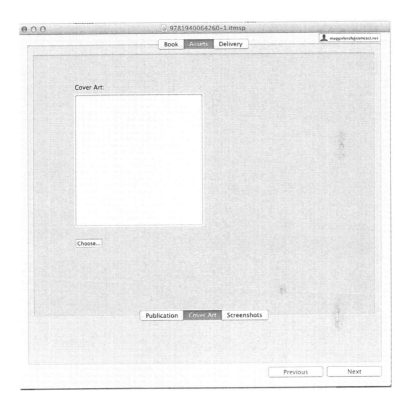

Once the cover file is selected and loaded, your cover will appear in the box. Click on the **Delivery** button at the top of the page to go to the final step. iTunes Producer will try to validate the two uploaded files and all the metadata you've entered. If everything is in the proper format, a message will appear saying: **Your package has validated correctly.**

Any problems or errors will appear on this screen. Typical problems are forgetting to fill in something on a prior screen (e.g., book description or publication date). More serious problems would be with the EPUB file or cover file. However, if you created your EPUB file in a good program like Jutoh, you should have no problem with the validation.

Once you get the message that your package has validated, click on the **Deliver** button on the bottom right of the screen.

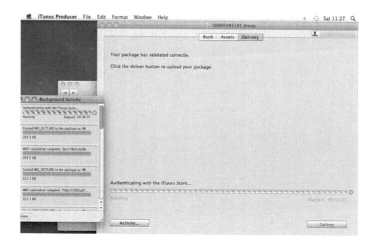

This will begin packaging the file to include all the metadata you have entered, your book content, and the cover file. It will upload the package to iTunes Connect via the Internet. Depending on the file size and your Internet speed this may take anywhere from 30 seconds to a few minutes.

If all goes well, the success screen will be displayed with a large checkmark in a green circle. A successful previous validation of the content and cover file ensure no problems. The only errors

I've encountered regularly is if the filename for my EPUB file or cover did not contain the ISBN as instructed.

Now that the files are at iTunes, the final step is to go to your iTunes account and verify they are in your account.

Log in at: : http://itunesconnect.apple.com/ and click on **Manage Your Books**.

This will display all the books that you currently have loaded on iTunes and their status. In the screen capture below, notice the green dot beneath each of the books displayed. The green dot indicates the books are active and for sale in the stores.

When you first upload a title there will be a red dot. The red dot indicates the title is still processing. The processing time varies from five days to about three weeks. Most of my titles uploaded to all stores within five to ten days.

Unfortunately, Apple does not notify you when the title is finally live in the iBookstore. This means you need to check back to see if it has a green dot yet. I suggest you check once a week.

If three weeks has passed and the title still has not gone live in the store, contact Apple support. Usually, after three weeks without proper processing, the best recourse is to delete the title from the store and upload it again.

Direct Ebook Distribution to Independent Booksellers

In addition to the Kobo partnership with booksellers around the world, there is another way to interest independent bookstores in selling your ebooks. That is through the use of download cards. The music industry has been using these cards for over ten years. Now, the same capabilities are being provided to authors.

A download card resembles a credit card. The front contains the book cover art. The back side contains a unique, one-time-use download code and instructions. If you order 250 cards, you receive 250 unique download codes. Companies that produce these cards provide the digital media hosting and a custom website landing page for the book and card. These companies do not take a percentage of the sale. The money is made in the upfront charge for the card manufacturing and fulfillment. Though prices vary from one company to another, they typically run between $1.50 and $3.00 per card depending on the number of cards ordered, their size, and the type of material used in the manufacturing (e.g., plastic, heavy card stock, etc.).

Download cards can be sold by bookstores with whatever specific discount you negotiate. I give a 30% discount of the ebook retail price. This is similar to the discount most distributors require (Amazon, Kobo, Barnes and Noble, etc.) to sell my ebooks at their online store. I am also experimenting in one bookstore with packaging a free download card if the customer purchases the print book. This is like a "match book" program that brick and mortar booksellers can use with their customers.

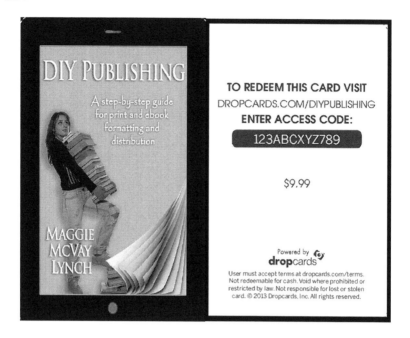

The illustration above shows the front and back of the download card I have for this book. (the access code is only a sample) These cards are sold through bookstores where I have a relationship. The size of the card is 2.125" x 3.375" and the codes expire in two years. Each vendor has different sizing options and policies regarding code expiration dates.

You may use these download cards in any way you like. You can give them away as prizes, sell them at signings where you are managing the purchases yourself, or sell them on your website. Use them in whatever way your creative marketing suggests.

Though there are many companies offering these cards, the three below are ones that have been recommended to me by people I trust.

Drop Cards http://www.dropcards.com

Greenerside Digital http://www.greenersidedigital.com/

Enthrill http://www.enthrill.com/endpaper/author-cards

When evaluating a potential download card provider, consider asking the following questions:

- How will they handle the different file types you want to distribute (PDF, EPUB, and MOBI)? Will customers have an option to select the file that they want, or will all three files be distributed with each download?

- Does each card have a unique one-time, secure download code? You do not want all the cards to have the same code.

- Does the system allow you to gather email addresses from customers? Can it be an opt-in to your mailing list.

- What type of reporting do they provide and how do you access it?

- Is there a time limit on how long a card is active? Also, if there is a charge to increase the time limit if needed? This is important if you buy a large number of cards, but may take a year or more to sell them all.

Of the three recommended companies above, turn around time for manufacturing and delivery of the download card varies from two to four weeks depending on the company. Drop Cards is able to do rush orders with a three to five day turn around, but you do pay Fed Ex special shipping fees for that.

CHAPTER 17

Marketing and Globalization

No book designed for self-published authors would be complete without an analysis of the current marketplace. Today, authors must think beyond a single distributor or country. It is important to be a part of the global book economy in order to realize the double- and triple-digit growth that is just now beginning outside the United States. I feel strongly that the key to success is to distribute internationally and offer as many formats as possible, including print, ebook, and audio book.

The United States and western Europe are no longer the sole centers of book sales. China's readership continues to grow and several of its largest publishing companies already have a role across east Asia. Today, both Kobo and Amazon are actively courting Chinese publishers, booksellers, and readers. This may turn into the most explosive market for book sales in the next few years. Brazil leads the way in South America, and India is a strong player among south Asian emerging economies. To remain relevant and profitable in this new publishing world order, Kobo, Amazon, and other distributors are expanding to reach readers in these new markets. Make yourself and your books a part of this growth.

While making every effort to widen your marketing focus, you should by no means overlook a valuable resource right in your own hometown—your local bookstores and their networks of regional and national organizations. It's easy to see that the more venues you have offering your books, the greater your sales will be. Even a small gain now can make a large difference over time. Networking with five or six local booksellers can pay off in benefits nationwide. A positive review from one of them may be shared with hundreds more. It will help you build a reputation as an author who is easy to work with and one who wants local booksellers to survive.

I know the U.S. market best. Therefore, my advice about markets and readership throughout this book has been tilted in that direction. However, it is important for us as American authors to realize that there are hundreds of millions of readers and potential customers beyond our shores. Kobo alone distributes to 190 countries! This trend is sure to continue into the future.

Let me conclude this book with three pieces of advice for the career writer:

1. *Pour yourself into your work.* You have to touch your readers with your energy and enthusiasm as well as your characters and your vision.

2. *Enlist the help of trusted collaborators.* Think team-publishing instead of self-publishing. No one can be an expert in all facets of creating a book. Remember, it's your name that appears on the cover. Don't be afraid to turn over certain tasks to others. It doesn't make the book any less yours.

3. *Be patient and keep writing.* Competition is fiercer than ever for readers and market share. In 2012, there were over 400,000 self-published titles. But ebooks are no longer the exclusive realm of self-publishers and small presses. Large companies are now well established in the ebook market and beginning to price their products competitively. But don't let that get you down or scare you away; success doesn't happen overnight. It builds over months and years. To make a living as a writer, you must produce books that can rise above the pack. One or two volumes is not enough. The more good books you publish, the more likely your work will be discovered and your sales will increase.

One thing is clear about the future: Change is not only inevitable, it will continue at an ever faster pace. The variety of options—from print books, ebooks, and audio books to formats that haven't even been invented yet—is transforming both the business of publishing and the pastime of reading. What this new world will look like remains unseen. However, I am confident that reader choice will be paramount. New platforms will evolve for readers to enjoy, share, and discuss content. Authors who can quickly adapt to changes as they come and respond with an abundance of options for readers will have the best chance of enjoying a long, satisfying, and successful career.

Want to stay up to date on changes in publishing?

Sign up for my mailing list http://eepurl.com/H1Up1 I will put out a newsletter twice a year with updates to the book, changes in the publishing landscape, and recommendations for any new formatting, distribution or marketing tools.

Consider Writing a Review

Word-of-mouth is crucial for any author to succeed. If you enjoyed the book, please consider leaving a review on Amazon, Barnes and Noble, Kobo or GoodReads. If you are a librarian and subscribe to LibraryThing or Shelfari, please also consider leaving a review there. Even if it's only a line or two, it would make all the difference and would be very much appreciated.

ABOUT THE AUTHOR

Dr. Maggie McVay Lynch is an acclaimed technology teacher and academic computing executive who spent over 30 years in education and computing. She spent eight years in executive management with two major software companies. Returning to graduate school later in life, she completed her doctorate degree in education, and then transferred her technology and teaching skills to Academia where she served in positions from Professor to Dean and eventually Chief Information Officer. She ended her career consulting for both large and small universities around the world.

Lynch previously authored four textbooks by publishers in London and New York. Also a fiction writer, she realized that far too many writers were choosing to self-publish by paying hundreds (and sometimes thousands) of dollars for technical assistance when they could learn to do it for under $50. This book is the result of helping other writers learn the technology.

Sneak Peak

SOME WRITERS DESERVE TO STARVE!

31 Brutal Truths About The Publishing Industry

~ 2013 REVISED AND UPDATED EDITION

BY JAMIE BRAZIL

INTRODUCTION:

"The process of finding someone, other than your mother, who will champion your book takes on a surreal feeling of a high school cafeteria. The popular kids hang out on one side of the room and the dweebs, the nerds, the geeks, the writers... you... cower on the other."
Some Writers Deserve To Starve, 2005

Ten years ago, working as a writing conference coordinator, I set out to record all the things I'd done right and wrong as I tried to get published. My manuscript, "Who Buys Lunch? Protocols for Writers" was represented by literary agent Angela Rinaldi, who sold it to Writer's Digest.

"Some Writers Deserve to Starve! 31 Brutal Truths about the Publishing Industry" was published in January of 2005. The Writer's Digest team rolled out the book, and in the process of promotion, I discovered I'm more of a writer than a teacher. I'm happier settled in at the keys vs. standing in front of a classroom.

Back then, e-publishing was still in its early stages. Nonfiction titles racked up big numbers, but the runaway successes of the self-published, and the independently published, like Amanda Hocking and E.L. James, hadn't yet happened. But the following five years radically changed the publishing industry. The Gold Rush years.

Yet here's the thing about digital gold rushes, they take a long time to peter out. Just when you think the rush is over, someone taps a new vein and suddenly there's a mad rush from one side of a mountain to the other. Or maybe even a different mountain range altogether.

Guess what?

We're still in the e-book gold rush.

Traditional publishers are in here, too. And while the millions of downloadable books published might eventually trickle to a few hundred thousand per year, no one actually knows when, or if, that will happen. The industry has changed. A lot. Which is why, ten years after I wrote the original manuscript, I decided to update and revise it.

Also, a conversation with my smartphone guru inspired me. By day he sells mobile devices and teaches technology-impaired people like myself how to use them. By night he writes high-concept thrillers. As it turned out, he was stuck in the purgatory between finished first novel and doing something with it.

Many writers get stuck in this place. They don't know what to do next.

My smartphone guru wanted to get his thriller to "those guys in New York."

"Literary agents?" I asked.

Yes, them! But he didn't know how to present his book. Even though he'd already posted his chapters online for critique, plus he actively participated in several groups devoted to the real-life concept he'd used as his book's premise, nothing was happening. Since he's young, well-spoken, and good-looking, I figured any enterprising agent would swoop upon him and sell him, lock, stock, and novel, to the highest bidder!

That didn't happen.

He still had some work to do, like write his first-ever synopsis, and get up to speed with what was going on in the publishing industry so he could decide his best course of action. The traditional route? The self-pubbed road? Or joining a co-op with other like-minded authors? Whichever trail he chose, he needed to stock up on things like a great pitch, knowledge, protocols, realistic expectations, and confidence BEFORE embarking on his very own gold rush adventure.

All that information is in here, revealed in the following pages. By reading this book and honing your skills, I hope you will become a savvy author – no matter which route you take to publication.

Because unlike ten years ago, **you will be published**.

Because we're not in the high school cafeteria anymore.

If you've written a book and you're considering making it available to the public, whether you know it or not, you are already part of the digital-age publishing gold rush.

Here is an Excerpt

Once upon a time, like the year 2000...

I WAS A WRITING CONFERENCE JUNKIE. You know the type. Heart pounding, manuscript clutched to my chest, I lined up firing-squad-style with two dozen other hopefuls and waited for my ten-minute consult with a publishing professional. I longed to hear those magic words, "Send me the first fifty pages." It was a validation of my self-worth. A reward for the long hours I'd logged on the chair, facing my monitor, pecking away at the keys. More than anything else in the world, I was determined to see my name in print on the cover of a book. I was going to be a world-renowned author. My *New York Times* bestseller was just an agent away. Surely somebody would recognize my talent, spelling errors and all.

That was quite the little fantasy I had playing between my ears. I did get published... eventually. But getting from dreamland to reality, and actually seeing my name in print, was an adventure in discovering the customs of a foreign land (publishing). I learned to keep my networking radar on at all times (you never know who you'll meet). And, most of all, face the fact that my daydream was nothing more than a business (that's right, dollars and cents, profit and loss).

Through my experiences I met thousands of writers just like me, all longing for their break. I also found out there are some core truths – truths that writers must learn and accept if they want to become part of this industry.

These truths apply to everyone, yet many writers who strive to make an impression aren't aware of the social hierarchies and cutthroat practices that have existed for decades. I wasn't. Not in the beginning. Oblivious to tell-tale signs, I was marked as a wannabe. Now that I know better, my chances for success have improved.

And so will yours.

Remember, this isn't a book on how to write, or why you should write. This isn't a book about how to market your book or brand yourself as an author. This is the book that will teach you how to gain acceptance as a professional among your peers.

TRUTH 1

SOME STARVING ARTISTS DESERVE TO STARVE

"I'm all in favor of keeping dangerous weapons out of the hands of fools. Let's start with typewriters." Frank Lloyd Wright

A novel, a memoir, a short story - whatever you've written - is a magnificent achievement. But finding a professional who will read your work may seem like a battle. Good. It is a battle. And a lot depends on the type of firepower you're packing. As a writer, your No. 1 job is to have the most dynamic book, article, poetry collection, whatever, out there. A professional masterpiece is essential, and anything less than that should not be sent into the fray.

A bit drastic? You bet. I'm a veteran now, but I too was once a novice...

Years ago, my local library announced a series of evening forums. I was writing my first novel and immediately perked to a session headed by Carolyn Swayze, a literary agent who represented William Kinsella (Shoeless Joe, which became Field of Dreams) and other famous writers. My heart soared. In my humblest opinion, my manuscript was simply magnificent. If I could just find a way to talk to Ms. Swayze privately, tell her my story, I was positive she would want to see the book. I was so convinced of this that I brought all 487 single-spaced, red-inked, coffee-stained pages along with me. There might have been a few misspelled words, run-on sentences, and maybe twenty or thirty thousand extra adverbs, but who needed accuracy when the work was my magnum opus? Surely she would see my Zen brilliance through my occasional spelling errors.

The big night arrived. I secured a front row seat and was promptly confronted by the motor-mouthed woman next to me. She was a self-professed "starving artist" with sparkling writing credentials (far more than I had), big dreams (bigger dreams than mine), and a PLAN (I hadn't planned anything other than being "discovered" by Carolyn that evening). She also had problems. Fifty thousand of them to be precise. Every one of them owed to a credit card company.

She shared her strategy with me: Cash in on one of those cheesy romance novels. After all, they paid at least $50,000 - even for a first book. After paying off her creditors, she would take the money left over and go on a tropical vacation. It would be there on a sandy beach, with the waves crashing in the background, that she would begin her life's work, seize upon her true artistic self and craft deep, meaningful literary prose that would leave the world speechless.

And then Carolyn took her place at the front of the room. Over the next two hours, to the detriment of motormouth's – and my own - fantasies, Carolyn squelched our misguided notions. She hammered on about how to break into the publishing industry. Who, how, when. Every five minutes she would launch into another "crackpot writer" story. Things NOT to do. Each time I heard the phrase "crackpot writer," my dream had another hole punched in it. Just because I was writing a novel, did that automatically qualify me as one of them, a "crackpot writer"?

Carolyn was very clear that she wasn't going to embrace spelling-challenged manuscripts or notions of big advances for unpublished writers of bodice rippers. That night, in the library's basement lecture hall, I lost my writing virginity and realized I was a "crackpot writer." So was the lady next to me.

THE REALITY TEST

Answer the statements below with "true" or "false."

1. All writers make a ton of money.
2. All writers become respected.
3. All writers have lovely homes, beautiful spouses, servants, and they throw Algonquin Round Table-esque cocktail parties where the literati bandy about bon mots.
4. Writing is easy.
5. Professionalism, content, talent, craft, and spelling are things a good editor can fix.

If you answered "true" to any of the above, go immediately to your nearest community college and enroll in a program that has a proven vocation.

TRUTH 2

PUTTING WORDS ON A PAGE DOES NOT OBLIGATE ANYONE TO READ THEM

"Thank you for sending me a copy of your book – I'll waste no time reading it." Moses Hadas

Unfortunately, this day and age has produced a sense of entitlement among creative types, including writers. To live in a first-world country is to be born with the inalienable right to reap huge rewards for a minimal amount of effort. As we become adults, many of us get sucked into those you-can-do-it cheerleading infomercials and then, somewhere along the way, decide that just because we've found the courage to show up at the page and jot down a few words, we will be lauded by readers and critics alike.

It takes more than that. It takes dedication, commitment to craft, and in some rash cases, tens of thousands of dollars in credit card debt. Is that enough? I wish.

The old adage says that if you stay in the game long enough, the number of rivals will thin and you will eventually become victorious by default. They didn't have an e-publishing gold rush back then. Still, who wants to be over a hundred years old when they sell their first novel or see their first credit roll across a screen?

There are better ways to succeed.

First and foremost, become a great writer. Practice. As follows in this book, learn your product and how to introduce it to readers. That's all practical stuff that will help you when the time comes.

So how do you separate yourself from the millions of people out there who call themselves "writers"? There are enough of them out there to populate their own student-loan-impoverished country. How the heck are you planning to leapfrog your way over every other hack with a laptop and an author page?

There are no shortcuts, but some people start off with an edge.

Reasons Why Publishing Professionals and Readers Will Consider Your Book:

1. You're already a public figure.
2. People like you.
3. You're connected. (Your uncle owns a film studio or your BFF is a literary agent.)
4. You have a platform. (Prominent diet doctor, spiritual leader, charity organizer.)
5. Your subject matter is a hot topic.
6. Your self-published sales numbers are astronomical.

Reasons Why Publishing Professionals and Readers Will Run Screaming Away From You, Your Book, and Your Social Media Presence:

1. Life's too short to endure your constant whining. Loudly and often, you complain about money, health, poor book sales and anything else you don't like – nobody likes constant negativity.
2. You're a pest. You are always asking for favors, telling people to LIKE you, etc. and NEVER giving anything in return because you're just too busy.
3. Plagiarism.
4. You don't engage. Readers - whether they're agents, editors, blog followers, fans or family – want to know they are important to you.

These reasons are mostly common sense. You need to know how to play the game, and how to play smart. And a warning: Entitlement comes from things acquired too easily. I'm not saying you should suffer for decades. We'll try to skip that. But what you work for, you appreciate more. So earn your success. Make something you can be proud of.

TRUTH 3

WE ALL HAVE TO START SOMEWHERE

"Evolution is not a force but a process." John Morley

Like the start of the universe, things have to come together just right. Books and screenplays do not spontaneously appear. They combust occasionally, but rarely do they form out of nothing. The process of wrestling your writing into existence often requires some of the following: The Idea, Life Experience, and/or Research. These fill the sea with story plankton. When it's ready to evolve and walk on land, it might morph into the Proposal, the Synopsis, the Partial Manuscript, or - the highest level on our evolutionary scale - the Completed Manuscript.

Sounds very academic, doesn't it? Luckily, it's much easier than calculus equations or gene splicing. We'll just take a peek at how a written product develops and what you can do with it along the way.

The Idea

The beginning of creative life. This is the point where lightning strikes the nucleic acids in your brain and something starts to move. You cannot copyright an idea. An idea is just that, an idea. Nothing is written down. This doesn't mean that your idea can't be sold for money, but be wary.

The great thing about ideas is that they're meant to be developed. They are seeds. If you are careful, they can be shared. Meeting others who are struggling between fantasy and the printed page is a good way to bounce storylines around and decide whether or not this seed of yours should be given life or burned. The downside is the chance someone will steal your idea, write the book before you can say "U.S. Copyright Office," and sell it to Hollywood.

Years later, you might meander into a theater and see your seed fully grown on the silver screen. The thief will walk the red carpet and collect an Oscar for the dazzling concept that you had first. And it gets worse. The Nobel Peace Prize for literature will be awarded to that no-good writer you blabbed your thoughts to over lunch.

Paranoia runs deep among creative types. Fortunately, there is only a very slim possibility that the above scenario will happen. Even if your idea gets pilfered, it was just an idea. I'd recommend that if cerebral lightning strikes, hustle to a keyboard, pronto.

Life Experience

You've just come from the cruise ship experience of a lifetime. The massive, fourteen-floor Contessa Guadelupe hit an iceberg. In the Caribbean. The boat sank. And you, thanks to your obsession with sunblock, emptied out your three-hundred bottles of lotion, tied them together with your pantyhose raft-style, and paddled through shark-infested waters to the safety of Cuba, where you had an affair with one of the Castros. God almighty, if the TV networks haven't already found you, an agent surely will. While you may not be the First Lady or Dianne Fossey, many life experiences are highly marketable to both the book and movie industries.

Life experience can also work on a smaller scale. Maybe your relationships with family, friends, and co-workers have given you great insight into the minds and actions of others. Divorces, deaths and bankruptcies are all fodder for drama. Many teachers advise us to write what we know. This could seriously impair our science-fiction contingent, though using what you know to bring emotional reality to your work, no matter what genre, can also bring success.

Research

Literary agent Robert Shepard recalled his experience with author Stephen Fatsis, who wrote the bestseller *Word Freak*. "One of the keys to doing research is to know when to come up for air. It's imperative that an author do as much research as the book needs in order to be accurate and thorough, but not so much that the book is merely cluttered with facts - research for the sake of research alone. Stefan had the luxury of doing a special kind of research involving total immersion in the subject. *Word Freak* is so vivid because he actually lived the experience he recounted, playing Scrabble tournaments and even sharing hotel rooms with some of the leading players. So the 'research' he did as an author not only rounds out the reader's understanding of the subject and the setting but also moves the narrative forward."

What a fantastic combination of life experience and research. No matter what you write, it's always good to have a thorough understanding of your subject, time period, and character. Many books that involve extensive research, such as *Seabiscuit*, have later sold to Hollywood.

Now, let's go up onto dry land and paper...

The Proposal

Sound romantic? Trust me, it's not. Prince Charming is not about to ride down from his Hollywood castle, get down on bended knee and offer you a three-picture, multimillion-dollar deal. Nor will the proposal make an honest writer of you. The proposal is generally used for nonfiction books and documentaries. The point of the proposal is to find out if targeted entities feel the project is worth developing.

It makes sense. Before any serious writing time and funds are committed, it's wise to see if there is a market for *Steam-Powered Street Clocks of America* or *Fetch: A Dog Trainer's Secrets to Successful Non-Canine Relationships*. Many proposals have been sold on the strength of the outline and a couple chapters. Ditto for documentaries. Some proposals are viable. Some couldn't get airtime on Pluto.

An excellent resource for those wondering if they have what it takes is *Nonfiction Book Proposals Anybody Can Write* by Elizabeth Lyon - a book she sold on the strength of a proposal.

For more books of the heart in fiction and non-fiction
please visit Windtree Press
http://windtreepress.com

Windtree
Press

Made in the USA
San Bernardino, CA
17 February 2014